THE ORDEAL OF ROBERT FROST

MARK RICHARDSON

The Ordeal of Robert Frost

The Poet and His Poetics

UNIVERSITY OF ILLINOIS PRESS
URBANA AND CHICAGO

Publication of this book was supported by a grant from the David L. Kalstone Memorial Fund, Rutgers University.

Manufactured in the United States of America

C 5 4 3 2 1

This book is printed on acid-free paper.

Library of Congress Cataloging-in-Publication Data
Richardson, Mark, 1963–
The ordeal of Robert Frost : the poet and his poetics / Mark Richardson
p. cm.
Includes bibliographical references and index.
ISBN 0-252-02338-2 (alk. paper)
1. Frost, Robert, 1874–1963—Style. 2. Frost, Robert, 1874–1963—Aesthetics. 3. Frost, Robert, 1874–1963—Political and social views. 4. Literature and society—United States—History—20th century. 5. Individualism in literature. 6. Poetry—Authorship. 7. Poetics. I. Title.
PS3511.R94Z9153 1997
811'.52—dc21
96-51279
CIP

For my family and friends and

Teruyo

When Nietzsche had worked out his theory of Greek tragedy and of Greek life, he set out, at once, to apply it to modern civilization, to see if it could explain certain ideas of the present as satisfactorily as it had explained one great idea of the past. He found that it could: that men were still torn between the apollonian impulse to conform and moralize and the dionysian impulse to exploit and explore. He found that all mankind might be divided into two classes: the apollonians who stood for permanence and the dionysians who stood for change. It was the aim of the former to live in strict obedience to certain invariable rules, which found expression as religion, law and morality. It was the aim of the latter to live under the most favorable conditions possible; to adapt themselves to changing circumstances, and to avoid the snares of artificial, permanent rules.

—H. L. Mencken, *The Philosophy of Friedrich Nietzsche*

Everything has not only formity but conformity.

—Robert Frost, 1934 letter

Contents

Acknowledgments

I OWE MUCH TO A NUMBER of friends for talking to me about this study (and related things), chief among them Mark Scott, Joe Thomas, and Rebecca Reynolds. I thank also Daneen Wardrop, Jil Larson, Peter Walker, Pat Gill, and Allen Carey-Webb, who read portions of the work while I was consolidating it in my mind and on paper. I am very much indebted to Shirley Clay Scott over these last four years for her generosity to me. Teruyo Shimizu helped me with the index; I am very grateful. Richard Poirier, Thomas Edwards, and Thomas Tanselle directed the dissertation from which this study derives; their advice continues to temper my work. I thank Gila Bercovitch and everyone at the Library of America for the education I got while working there for six years. I thank David Cowart for encouraging me at just about the right time. And I thank Dick Poirier again for what he taught me about American literature.

 Grateful acknowledgment is due to the repositories of the documents: Philip Cronenwett and the Dartmouth College Library; John Lancaster and the Amherst College Library; and the Alderman Library, University of Virginia. Gratitude is due also to Janet Thompson for permission to quote from Lawrance Thompson's "Notes on Conversations with Robert Frost."

Quotations from the works of Ezra Pound are copyright 1926 by Ezra Pound. Used by permission of New Directions Publishing Corporation.

Several sections of this book were published in earlier versions as "Robert Frost and the Motives for Poetry," *Essays in Literature* 20 (Fall 1993): 273–91, "Parables of Vocation: Frost and Pound in the Villages of (Gingrich's?) America," *Essays in Literature* 23 (Spring 1996): 99–123, and "Believing in Robert Frost," *Texas Studies in Literature and Language* 37.4 (1995): 445–74. I am grateful to these journals for permission to reprint this material here. Work on this project was underwritten in part by the Faculty Research and Creative Activities Support Grant program at Western Michigan University.

THE ORDEAL OF ROBERT FROST

Introduction

I BORROW THE "ORDEAL" OF my title from Van Wyck Brooks's study *The Ordeal of Mark Twain* (1920), a book that Robert Frost's own writings brought to my attention. Frost alludes to it in a crucial passage in his introduction to Edwin Arlington Robinson's last book of poetry, *King Jasper* (1935):

> The style is the man. Rather say the style is the way the man takes himself; and to be at all charming or even bearable, the way is almost rigidly prescribed. If it is with outer seriousness, it must be with inner humor. If it is with outer humor, it must be with inner seriousness. Neither one alone without the other under it will do. . . . One ordeal of Mark Twain was the constant fear that his occluded seriousness would be overlooked. That betrayed him into his two or three books of out-and-out seriousness. (*Collected Poems* 746; hereafter abbreviated *CPPP*)

These are modest claims, to be sure. But they are unusual claims, it seems to me, for a modernist poet to make. *Is* style a question of "bearability" and "charm"? *Whom* should the writer endeavor to charm? Why should a poet be concerned with the "prescriptions," "rigid" or not, of her audience? From what social criteria do these standards of charm and bearability derive? And why does consideration of these matters lead Frost to *The Ordeal of Mark Twain,* Brooks's iconoclastic study of a writer who had, like Frost himself, become a veritable institution—a wholly owned subsidiary of official American culture? The direct acknowledgment of audience in Frost's remarks on style—his acknowledgment of those agents of "prescription"—alerts us to the intersection in his work of social and aesthetic concerns, an intersection that also forms a major theme in Brooks's study. And although Frost is not often read as a theorist of such matters, he deserves to be. My study is intended to make a start in that direction. I examine certain characteristic themes and imagery in Frost's work in light of the social and personal difficulties out of which they seem to have developed. My argument is that Frost's style and also his comments about style and poetics are conditioned by a specifically social ordeal associated, in America, with the poetic vocation itself. After all, Frost might as well be writing about himself when he speaks of Twain's "constant fear that his occluded seriousness would be overlooked." It is at once a matter of Frost's particular location in the culture and of the location in American culture of poetry more generally, as we shall see in chapter 1. That is the social ordeal of which I speak, following Frost's lead in his remarks on Mark Twain.

But in speaking of Frost's "ordeal" I have in mind also certain key metaphors and patterns that recur throughout his writings on poetics (and also in his poetry), as in the following passage from the 1946 essay "The Constant Symbol": "Every poem is an epitome of the great predicament; a figure of the will braving alien entanglements" (*CPPP* 786). This too is the essential ordeal of Frost, as of any poet, and every poem "written regular," as he says, "constantly" symbolizes it: hence the variety and frequency, in his work, of figures embodying this ordeal. Later in "The Constant Symbol" Frost gives the idea yet another turn. The "individual will" of his "epitome" becomes instead what he calls "*self*-discipline"—or the discipline "from within," as he also puts it—while "alien entanglements" become what he terms "the harsher discipline from without." Every poem marks the convergence, the working-upon-one-another, of these two "disciplines," and they are, as his suggestive terminology often indicates, equally social, aesthetic, and linguistic in nature. Their convergence is the "constant symbol" of the poet's struggle to socialize his art in an audience and in the literary marketplace and yet preserve its singular integrity and temper. It is the symbol also of the poet's will engaged in working through the entanglements of particular poetic forms (the sonnet, the quatrain, blank verse, and so forth) and of the more general, systematic "forms" of language itself (grammar, syntax, vocabulary) as he struggles to realize, and in part simply to discover, what he is trying to say. "The Constant Symbol" has been widely read, and yet in my view neither widely nor seriously enough. It belongs among the major documents in twentieth-century American poetics and my aim, especially in chapters 2 and 3, is chiefly to follow out the extraordinarily far-ranging arguments of that essay.

"The Constant Symbol" also alerts us to a seldom-noticed circumstance: the complementary relationship in America between modernist poetics and cultural criticism. In speaking of cultural criticism I have in mind such books as Van Wyck Brook's *America's Coming of Age* (1915), *Letters and Leadership* (1916), and *The Ordeal of Mark Twain;* H. L. Mencken's *A Book of Prefaces* (1917), his several series of *Prejudices* (1919–27), and also his *Notes on Democracy* (1926); the iconoclastic collection *Civilization in the United States* (1922), edited by Harold Stearns, with various contributions by Mencken, Brooks, Lewis Mumford, and others; Randolph Bourne's essays from the 1910s; Ezra Pound's long essay "Patria Mia" (1912), which ranges from aesthetics to culture to politics; Malcolm Cowley's *Exile's Return* (second edition, 1951) and *The Dream of the Golden Mountains* (1981), memoirs of the 1920s and 1930s that incidentally contain shrewd criticism of American cultural politics and aesthetics; and Dwight Macdonald's *Against the American Grain* (1962). These works are seldom mentioned in histories of modern American poetry and almost never mentioned in studies devoted particularly to Frost's work. My purpose in bringing them in is to help us understand one possible alternative narrative of modern poetry, as described, for example, in Cary Nelson's *Repression and Recovery* (1989): namely, the "narrative of the interplay between formal innovation and social criticism" (7). Pound and Frost, I argue, certainly believed that debates about aesthetics and poetic form had important social and political resonance—indeed that they inevitably had such resonance.

Standing at the head of the tradition of cultural criticism with which I am concerned—at least in certain respects—is the work of Mencken. I follow out a kind of ongoing, indirect conversation that took place among Frost, Mencken, Brooks, and other writers strongly influenced by Mencken. In the passage quoted in the epigraph to this study, from *The Philosophy of Friedrich Nietzsche* (1908), Mencken writes: Nietzsche "found that all mankind might be divided into two classes: the appolonians who stood for permanence and the dionysians who stood for change" (72). Frost's answer to this is actually quite simple: There are not two *classes* of people but two *dispositions* within each man and woman. Instead of arrogating to one class of people tendencies toward "change" and to another class tendencies toward "permanence," Frost situates both tendencies in the individual personality: we all find ourselves, he would say, adopting at one moment strategies of intransigence and at another moment strategies of conformity. This idea is everywhere expressed in his poetry and prose; and complementing it is Frost's decision not to weight the values attached to these two tendencies—rebellion and conformity—as one-sidedly in favor of Dionysus as Mencken had. On the whole, Frost would say, neither change and rebellion nor permanence and conservation is to be valued absolutely. This is in marked contrast to Mencken, who, together with the cultural and literary critics that soon followed his lead, ranged "creative spirits" exclusively among the "Dionysians." This led to a mythology of the artist as a cultural rebel, a mythology that was further refined by the bohemian character of the Greenwich Village intellectual scene in the 1910s and 1920s, as we learn from reading Malcolm Cowley's memoir of the period, *Exile's Return*. Brooks expresses the ideal perfectly in *The Ordeal of Mark Twain* when he speaks of "that extreme form of individuality, the creative spirit, whose whole tendency is skeptical, critical, realistic, disruptive!" (85). Frost's writings on poetics, I will argue, essentially constitute a "skeptical," "critical," "realistic," and "disruptive" response to this ideal.

In his early essays on American culture and literature, Brooks argued that Twain and other writers had acquiesced to certain middle-class standards of decorum and sensibility that badly damaged their art and even their personal integrity. He argued further that the proper role of the artist should always be culturally oppositional—intransigent and nonconformist. This was especially necessary in America, he thought, where the dominant culture of "business" and of market-driven capitalism promised to repress all important manifestations of cultural or political difference. Frost implicitly answers Brooks, in the introduction to *King Jasper* and elsewhere, with the argument that cultural acquiescence should instead be regarded as a fortunate reconciliation of an artist's sense of personal "difference" to larger social constraints and "correspondence" (the terms are Frost's). In contrast to Mencken and Brooks, he thought that poetry is in fact what best symbolizes this process of "correspondence," not what best resists it; that the role of the artist—and by extension of the intellectual—should remain as much conciliatory as oppositional; and that the artist should work to *establish* fellowship with the larger patterns of culture rather than work (Emerson-like) to escape the consequences of that fellowship. At times these convictions led Frost to cast radical individualism in a distinctly unappealing light; at times in fact he seems quite suspicious of it. He particularly distrusts an artist's personal "difference" when this seems to him to have been "anxiously" cultivated, as he puts it (somewhat vaguely) in the introduction to *King Jasper*.

This aspect of Frost has been too seldom noticed. Jay Parini writes in the *Columbia History of American Poetry* (1995): "Frost is the loner, the individualist, and his poetry is the poetry of survival" (262). And in *Robert Frost and a Poetics of Appetite* (1994), Katherine Kearns suggests that Frost's "near-phobic distaste for systems . . . exceeds even the most potent American individualism" (26). Kearns's point is not without merit and her study is among the best ever done of Frost's work. But remarks such as this do not allow us adequately to understand Frost's commitment to what he called "conformity" (*CPPP* 735), or what he meant when he said that "there is such a thing as being too willing to be different" (*CPPP* 741), or what he meant when he said that "the sensible and healthy" live somewhere in between "self-approval" and "the approval of society" (*CPPP* 779). I mean to take seriously remarks such as these. Potent American individualism notwithstanding, Frost sought and achieved a kind of "social approval" unprecedented for an American poet. His career presents one example of what it might mean for a poet to fit "into the nature of Americans," as Frost put it in 1939, or what it might mean for him simply to "conform," if we set aside all pejorative suggestions of that word (*CPPP* 780). Frost can be uncommonly complex, flirtatious, and deceptive. But he had not nearly so intrepid or intransigent a literary personality as Emerson, Dickinson, or Thoreau, as much as he may otherwise have in common with them. I present a portrait of Frost that helps us understand why. Approaching his writings on poetry and poetics as I do here, we see how they developed in response to a particularly *individualistic* reading of American culture, and to a particularly *individualistic* assessment of the function and place of the literary artist within that culture, that was advanced variously by Mencken, Brooks, Cowley, Pound, and others in the 1910s and after. I place Frost back into this context the better to understand his remarkable contemporaneity and his engagement in what today we might call "the culture wars."

Unwilling to accept the Nietzschean-Menckenian values from which Brooks's account of the creative artist is derived, then, Frost was unwilling as well to claim that the purpose of the artist, whatever else it may be, is *never* to "conform." And thus we have the background, in a kind of thumbnail sketch, of an important letter Frost wrote to his daughter Lesley Frost Francis in 1934. This letter, another touchstone in my study, clearly brings out Frost's sense of his place among his contemporaries, poets and cultural critics alike. He particularly refers to the poet and critic Herbert Read, author of *Form in Modern Poetry* (1932):

> I assume you'll find in Reed [Read] his [Pound's] latest descendant a full statement of the doctrine of Inner Form, that is to say the form the subject itself takes if left to itself without any considerations of outer form. Everything else is to have two compulsions, an inner and an outer, a spiritual and a social, an individual and a racial. I want to be good, but that is not enough the state says I have got to be good. Everything has not only formity but conformity. Everything but poetry according to the Pound-Eliot-Richards-Reed school of art. (*CPPP* 735)[1]

This letter broadens the reference of Frost's central "ordeal" and it is easy to see how it engages the larger arguments carried on by writers as diverse as Mencken, Brooks, Pound, and Read himself. The opposition of "spiritual" to "social" "compulsions," which Frost employs with due precision, corresponds, respectively, to Dionysian and Apollonian compulsions: the one responds entirely to an individualistic inner desire, the other entirely to outer forces of "conformity" and sociality. Or to speak once again in the terms Frost establishes in "The Constant Symbol": *Individual* will, whether of the poet or of the citizen trying to "be good," falls under the heading of what Frost calls "formity," while "conformity" names the "alien entanglements" that ensnare and deflect the will of the subject, or that enforce "goodness" upon him. In excepting poetry from this dialectic of "formity" and "conformity," the theorists of "Inner Form," as Frost styles them, helped maintain a mythology of the artist as an aesthetic and cultural rebel, a mythology of the artist as, above all else, a "non-conformist": the artist is answerable to individualistic "spiritual" imperatives, never to "social" ones. As I have suggested, this is the idea against which Frost is working, as when, for example, he urges on the artist the necessity of "charm" and "bearability." In his alternative poetics the relation of "formity" to "conformity" remains thoroughly dialectical: "Everything," he writes—even poets and poetry—"has not only formity but conformity." Art must accommodate equally Dionysian and Apollonian dispositions.

As the highly "socialized" vocabulary of the 1934 letter indicates, Frost's writings on poetics are as well suited to treating more general problems of motivation as they are to treating, simply, the processes of art. The featured terms in his poetics take their place in a constellation of corresponding figures in American cultural criticism and in philosophy more generally. We might, for example, bring into conjunction with Frost's writings on poetics the Emersonian dialectic of Power and Fate, or more simply of Freedom and Fate. In chapter 2 I draw what seems to me a useful (if limited) analogy between Freud's dialectic, in *Civilization and Its Discontents*, of Eros and Ananke (or Fate) and Frost's overarching imagery of inner desire and outer constraint. Like Freud, Frost is particularly interested in the role that this dialectic plays in the evolution of "organized society," as he puts it in an essay titled "The Future of Man" (*CPPP* 869). Among the various writers I consider, Kenneth Burke most systematically addresses this basic problem: his *A Grammar of Motives* (1945) is an extended, labyrinthine investigation of the relation between "intrinsic" and "extrinsic" motivation, the relation between what Frost calls motives of "formity" and "conformity," or of "originality" and "governance" (*CPPP* 869). The comparisons to Burke and Freud are important because they help us see how Frost handles, in his poetry and poetics, highly generalized questions about human motivation and about the relation of the individual to the larger social body. "Everything," he says in the 1934 letter to his daughter, has "two compulsions, an inner and an outer, a spiritual and a social."

Of course the 1934 letter is also concerned with smaller-scale questions about literary art and literary history, as Frost gives a brief, perceptive account of modern poetry as it developed out of the Imagist reforms of Pound and T. E. Hulme in the mid-1910s. Frost himself had been present at the nativity, so to speak, when he lived in England from 1912 to 1915. While there, he discussed poetics with Pound, Hulme, F. S. Flint, Yeats, and others. His encounters with these poets helped him define his own alternative project and it is in letters written while in England that he most clearly and thoroughly explains his much-discussed theory of "sentence sounds" and related thoughts about prosody. For this reason, the years in England remained important to Frost as the period in which he fully realized and distinguished his place among his contemporaries. England is where he first declared himself. And it is almost as if his return to America in 1915 came to symbolize in his mind an assertion of aesthetic independence from the American expatriate poets and British poets centered in London.

Part of the distinction that Frost drew between Pound and himself turned upon his willingness and Pound's unwillingness to "conform" to the sometimes dispiriting "disciplines" of the American literary marketplace in the 1910s. As regards the commerce of art and artists, Frost essentially agrees with Emerson, who writes in the essay "Wealth," originally collected in *The Conduct of Life:* "The artist has made his picture so true, that it disconcerts criticism. The statue is so beautiful, that it contracts no stain from the market, but makes the market a silent gallery for itself" (*Essays* 993). The idea here, as throughout Emerson's essay, is that the verdicts of the marketplace are moral and just—that (as Emerson later puts it) "a dollar is not value, but representative of value, and, at last, of moral values" (998). At times Frost seems to accept this idea. He certainly rejected, at least in his public remarks, Pound's contention that the market somehow "stained" the works with which it came in contact. Consider his November 1913 letter to John Bartlett:

> There is one qualifying fact always to bear in mind: there is a kind of success called "of esteem" and it butters no parsnips. It means success with the critical few who are supposed to know. But really to arrive where I can stand on my legs as a poet and nothing else I must get outside that circle to the general reader who buys books in their thousands. I may not be able to do that. I believe in doing it—dont you doubt me there. I want to be a poet for all sorts and kinds. I could never make a merit of being caviare to the crowd the way my quasi-friend Pound does. (*CPPP* 667–68)

The figure is quite familiar to American readers: "really to arrive" means to earn a living. And of course Frost argues from principle, not merely from expediency: "I *believe* in doing it—dont you doubt me there," he says, invoking a central tenet of the democratic civil religion.

There is something invidious in Frost's suggestion that Pound made a "merit" of writing for a coterie audience—a merit of being elusive in particularly ostentatious ways. (Frost, his complexities most often "occluded," made a merit of being elusive in *un*-ostentatious ways.) Pound's elitism reflects, for better and for worse, the idea that the literary vocation is essentially countercultural and Dionysian; he always read Mencken with delight. Pound rarely omits an opportunity to denounce any situation in which, to his way of thinking, "the beautiful" is "decreed in the market place," as he says in "Hugh Selwyn Mauberley" (*Personae* 187). But for Frost, conformity to the disciplines of a commercial literary marketplace involved by extension conformity to a particular American "morality" or way of thinking about the social function of art and artists to which Pound could never assent; I treat these differences between them in some detail in the later sections of chapter 1. In chapter 2, I place "The Constant Symbol" and the introduction to *King Jasper* clearly in the context of Frost's ongoing engagement with the poetics and cultural politics of what, somewhat derisively, he called the doctrine of Inner Form. Reading Frost alongside Mencken, Pound, Brooks, Herbert Read, and Malcolm Cowley brings out more sharply the polemical edge of his essays, enabling us better to understand the alternative poetics he was trying to establish. And here we find his poetics, as a theory, working to accommodate the specific vocational choices he had made. We see that his essays on poetics have an apologetic motive, as I believe most theoretical enterprises do.

Above I described Frost's central ordeal as "dialectical." The opposition of "formity" to "conformity" or of "individual will" to "alien entanglements" is dialectical in this sense, as I explain in chapter 3: as Frost handles them, these terms shift and exchange positions, merge in a unitary perspective that transcends the initial opposition, and finally diverge again as he acknowledges that any such unitary perspective can only be temporary and partial. And here I pursue another aspect of the metaphors central to Frost's poetics by viewing them in terms of the "dialectic of tragedy," to borrow Kenneth Burke's useful phrase—another kind of "ordeal." I use the term "tragedy" in a fairly conventional sense. The tragic hero (sometimes heroine) undergoes an ordeal that somehow follows from his own initial action or willfulness—from his *intrinsic* motives. At first this ordeal seems to him unjust, arbitrary, or alien: "I am a man more sinned against than sinning," Lear says in the midst of his suffering. But the tragic resolution involves the hero's recognition that his misfortunes are *not* in fact arbitrary but mark instead the inevitable unfolding or revelation of his own character. That is to say, character and fate, in the tragic resolution, are at last seen as complements, not opponents. A corresponding movement in Frost's poetics discloses that "formity" (inner discipline and motivation) and "conformity" (the "discipline from without") are actually two aspects of the same fact. In a word, Frost imagines in his poetics a final transcendence or reconciliation of his own central "ordeal."

This transcendence has important implications. In chapters 2 and 3 I show how Frost recognizes that poetic form and language *as such* have motives alien to the ostensibly "personal" motives of the writer. To the extent that these "alien" motives are efficient, all writing is "impersonal," and the poet a kind of collaborator in his own work rather than its sole "author." Frost handles this question with considerable subtlety, anticipating much that was later canonized in literary theory. He is more sophisticated than many later theorists of authority, who have at times gone too far in dismissing, or in attempting to discredit, the category of the "author." To put the matter very generally: Frost shows us that the aim of literary theory in this regard is to investigate, however skeptically, the *extent* of a writer's "authority," not to haggle out an ultimately false dilemma of whether "authority" is either total or totally absent.

This is of course a considerably challenging project, especially given that the close reading Frost valued discloses possibilities of meaning that almost immediately begin to raise questions about a writer's authority. Frost would have us ask: Did the poet reach the same conclusions about the poem that we have reached in reading it closely? *Could* the poet possibly have reached the same conclusions, and, if so, does it matter *when* he arrived at them? Before he wrote the poem? While he was writing it? Some time after he wrote it? The last question is particularly interesting. What could it mean to say that a poet discovers "his own" meaning in a poem after the fact, perhaps even years after the fact? Does he suppose his authority to have a continuity and integrity lying deep beneath his conscious intention? Does he accept a gift of meaning on a subsequent reading of his work and then assume authority for it? If he does, then writing and reading his own work is an exercise in self-revelation, not self-expression—an exercise that puts him in touch with a deeper integrity. In "The Figure a Poem Makes" Frost describes the course of "lucky events" that every poem runs (*CPPP* 777). But if writing is a kind of self-revelation, then the casualties and chances a poet suffers in writing are really neither "casual" events nor merely "lucky" ones. All of the motives of the poem, both the poet's "self-discipline" and the "harsher discipline from without," are potentially "intrinsic" motives, deeply seated in the poet's personality. Once again, fate and character merge.

So, Frost tentatively imagines in his poetics a transcendence of the oppositional ordeal of "formity" to "conformity" and the result, to adopt his own terminology, is actually a poetics of pure "formity," or Inner Form. Writing does not alienate the writer from his own intentions and desire but instead gives these things over to him in a renewed and somehow more "authentic" experience of integrity; writing lets the poet see what he was in fact up to already. Such is the claim that Frost tentatively makes. As in tragedy, "self-expenditure" leads in his poetics to a higher self-possession. Or as he puts it in yet another impeccably dialectical figure in "The Constant Symbol": "Strongly spent is synonymous with kept" (*CPPP* 786). Frost finally entertains this transcendence only as a kind of *unrealizable* ideal. But it nevertheless constitutes, for him, an enduring concern and promise of poetry.

The overall arrangement of this book is as follows. Chapter 1 chiefly examines the social, cultural, and biographical significances of Frost's "ordeal." Here I concentrate on his problem of vocation in an attempt to catalog, through close readings of a number of letters, poems, and essays, the characteristics of "the literary life" in America as Frost experienced it. My idea, as I have already suggested, is that Frost's writings on poetry arose in response to a strain of Nietzschean individualism best exemplified in the work of Mencken. Mencken, of course, had little but contempt for the general run of Middle Americans, whom he called the "booboisie." His philosophy is nonconformist and antidemocratic. By contrast, Frost tried to arrive at a critical vocabulary that could affirm the value of "conformity" and acknowledge the salutary qualities of a "fear of Man" that keeps each of us from becoming too egregious—from standing too far apart from the herd. He sought to fit "into the nature of Americans" (*CPPP* 780)—the same people of whom Mencken felt disposed to write: "The great body of Americans themselves, [are] predominantly more amusing than inspiring, and less admirable than obscene" (*My Life as Author and Editor* 171).

The rub is that as a poet and intellectual in America Frost naturally felt himself to be a culturally oppositional figure, as have many others. This was particularly true in the years before he published his first book of poetry at age thirty-nine. His sense of cultural dislocation had much to do with problems of gender because in those years poetry and the literary life—as is everywhere suggested in the writings I will be examining—were rigorously gendered feminine. In the "villages" of America in 1905 poetry simply presented no kind of life for a man to lead, as critics such as Frank Lentricchia have lately argued. So, especially in Frost's early letters and poems, we find two opposed things: a natural tendency to regard himself as a culturally dislocated figure, *and* an aspiration to be, as a poet, a *representatively* American man. (This is why I use the masculine pronoun in speaking of the poet as imagined by Frost: the exclusion is his.) These two tendencies toward extravagance (standing out) and toward conformity (standing in) animate much of what he wrote about poetry and poetics and enter into even apparently "ahistorical" questions about literary style. That is to say, considering these matters helps us see that his statements about poetry—even about abstract issues of form and technique—are in fact rooted in specific social and cultural ordeals. In light of this, the first chapter poses such questions as the following: What did becoming a poet mean to an American man in the early decades of the twentieth century? How did he socialize his art or establish a constituency? How, as an artist, did he become "charming" and "bearable" in a society that often seemed hostile to the very ideals his "un-utilitarian" vocation represented, to borrow Frost's epithet? To what extent was poetry and the writing of it gendered feminine? And what were the social and personal costs (if any) incurred by a man wishing, under these conditions, to develop a "charming" literary personality? In pursuing these questions I try to account for the bearing they have on the style of Frost's writing as well as on the arguments and "address" of his essays on poetics.[2]

I am interested as well in the contemporary cultural implications of these matters, and the last section of chapter 1 considers the current situation of the academic intellectual in America in light of what both Frost and Pound have to say about their own problems of vocation. Their feelings of dislocation with regard to "Middle American" culture correspond to similar feelings voiced by American intellectuals and academics generally; their vocational ordeals have much to teach us about our own, particularly given the highly politicized turn the so-called culture wars have taken in the early and mid-1990s. In this part of the chapter, I follow arguments about the profession of literature advanced in such publications as *Profession* and the *MLA Newsletter*; I also consider arguments made in Michael Bérubé's *Public Access* (1994), an engaging book about the situation of the academic intellectual, and in Andrew Ross's *No Respect: Intellectuals and Popular Culture* (1989).

Chapter 2 is more strictly concerned with Frost's relation to other poets and critics and somewhat less with his general experience of American culture. I consider his "ordeal" as the distinguishing feature of his poetics, the feature that sets him apart from his contemporaries while nevertheless keeping them engaged. I also briefly consider, here, Frost's contribution to what we might call, following Kenneth Burke, "poetics in particular"—that is to say, poetics considered apart from social and literary-historical questions. Frost has much to tell us about any poet's transactions with language and poetic form, regardless of when or where that poet happens to write. The third chapter, as I have pointed out, describes the aspiration that I find in Frost's poetics to transcend its own central and defining ordeal.

At times each of these chapters addresses questions of biographical and social significance, and at times each, to varying degrees, turns its attentions strictly to formal and linguistic matters. But my own view, and I think Frost would agree, is that these two categories of questions are really alike in kind. Frost often describes poetry as a means to manage or clarify specifically personal and social entanglements. And he remarks in the preface to the first book edition of his play *A Way Out:* "By whom, where and when is the question. By a dreamer of the better world out in a storm in autumn; by a lover under a window at night. It is the same with the essay. It may manage alone or it may take unto itself other essays for help, but it must make itself heard as by Stevenson on an island, or Lamb in London" (*CPPP* 713). I read Frost's essays just as he, apparently, read the essays of Charles Lamb and Robert Louis Stevenson: as written by a particular man in a particular place at a particular time and as having important linkages, manifested in both style and theme, to these biographical and social situations. Kenneth Burke makes the point well in *The Philosophy of Literary Form* (1967): "Critical and imaginative works are answers to questions posed by the situation in which they arose. They are not merely answers, they are *strategic* answers, *stylized* answers. . . . So I should propose an initial working distinction between 'strategies' and 'situations,' whereby we think of poetry (I here use the term to include any work of critical or imaginative cast) as the adopting of various strategies for the encompassing of situations" (1). I am convinced that Frost's essays on poetics were also essays in living his own life.

Some remarks about Frost's place in the larger framework of American literature are perhaps called for here. In *A World Elsewhere* (1966) Richard Poirier describes a "tension" to be found everywhere in American literature: "the tension of bringing into conjunction the environment of nakedness, where there is no encumbrance to the expression of the true inner self, and the environment of costume, of outer space occupied by society and its fabrications" (30). It is a conjunction often entered into with bitterness, and it has at times been bitterly described by many American writers—most notably, perhaps, by Emerson and Twain. But there is a way of describing the experience that approaches eulogy and this is, in a sense, what Frost is aiming toward. Burke speaks of how the writer socializes her art; Frost, of how the writer accommodates his "difference" to social "correspondence." Both refer to the accommodation of the "true inner self" that Poirier describes to spaces already occupied by society. There is nothing *necessarily* unsatisfactory about this accommodation, as Burke sees it, and here he has much in common with Frost.

Frost sometimes seems to be arguing, against the American intellectual grain, that socialization is in fact a positive, unqualified good for the writer. At the same time, in a complementary gesture, he suggests the potentially pathological tendencies of extreme individuality—of eccentricity and willfulness. Here he could not be farther from the Dickinson of poems like "The Soul Selects her own Society." In such poems, the Dickinsonian self assumes regal, even divine lineaments. Her ideal self is autocratic, omnipotent, elect, austerely cold, and sardonic. She is radically individualistic. I find not a trace of democratic—let alone *populist*—

sentiment in her poetry. She made a merit of being caviar to the crowd, to borrow Frost's remark about Pound. The claims of society in Dickinson's work almost inevitably stand arrayed *against* the liberties that the soul desires to take. She felt impressively that society was, as Emerson says in "Self-Reliance," everywhere "in conspiracy against the manhood of every one of its members" (*Essays* 261).[3] Dickinson's scorn for society and its obligations is thoroughly Nietzschean and often assumes the literary and vocational significance that later writers would give it. "Publication is the Auction / Of the Mind of Man," she says in contempt of the stains that the literary marketplace imparts. On another occasion Dickinson figures merely *common* folk as smug, indifferently loquacious frogs: "How public—like a Frog— / To tell your name—the livelong June— / To an admiring Bog!" Better to be "nobody"—aristocratically elusive and unavailable—under these circumstances. We have to hear the disgust and condescension that attaches to a word like "public" here. Betsy Erkkila is certainly correct in suggesting that "within the political order of Dickinson's verse, the multitude and the democratic masses are consistently demonized" (304). Notwithstanding the precious and probably arch humility of "This is my Letter to the World," Dickinson harbored little desire, as Frost did, to fit "into the nature of Americans"—those "sweet countrymen" of the bog—or to conduct her life and thought with as much regard for "approval from society" as for "self-approval," to adopt again the phrasing of a speech Frost delivered in 1939 (*CPPP* 779–80). In arguing the virtues of "conformity" and "governance," or of the artist's accession to social and traditional authorities, Frost often seems to have much more in common with T. S. Eliot than is usually supposed and much less in common with the radically libertarian—even antisocial and "aristocratic"—tradition in which Emerson, Dickinson, and Mencken write. It is in fact quite instructive to consider Frost in this light, as I do in chapters 2 and 3.

But one rightly shrinks at placing Frost alongside Eliot and over against Emerson.

> They reckon ill who leave me out,
> When me they fly I am the wings,
> I am the doubter and the doubt,
> And I the hymn the Brahmin sings.
>
> (Oxford Authors edition 538)

So Emerson himself writes in "Brahma," one of Frost's favorite poems. And Frost's apparent movement away from Emersonian dispositions in fact leads him to what I take to be a quintessentially Emersonian destination. Frost is extraordinarily devious and subtle in his efforts to preserve imaginatively the integrity of his "true inner self," even within rigid prescriptions as to how, in his poetry, it ought to unfold. Consequently, his writing is often considerably less available than it may seem at first glance, or even at second and third. But more ambitious than devious is how Frost imagines, in his poetics, that writing is the very means by which the "inner self" is realized, even though it requires in so many ways that the "inner self" be brought into conjunction with the forms, or rigid prescriptions, of language, convention, and audience—forms that can alienate the writer from the self. Frost's poetics, as I argue in chapter 3, imagines a final marriage of inner reality with outer reality, a marriage of personal and artistic power with what he calls "the harsher discipline from without" (*CPPP* 789).

It is as if in certain moods he viewed this marriage as a passage in which the poet's "socialization" comes at little or no cost. (At bottom his is a Protean, not a Procrustean, mythology.) Frost ultimately refuses to believe in the possibility of this reconciliation. But his poetics does hold it out as a kind of ideal. And this idealism, so to speak, betrays his affiliation to the Emersonian tradition of American writing described in *A World Elsewhere*, wherein we find continually "the struggle to create through language an environment in which the inner consciousness of the hero-poet can freely express itself, an environment in which he can sound publicly what he privately is" (35). And at this point, Frost's poetics becomes essentially modernistic in his sense of the term, despite the fact that his work is so often opposed, in his own letters and essays, to the work of other major modernist writers. In short, the doctrine of Inner Form, which for Frost represents all that his own achievements stand against, reappears in his poetics as a visionary final reconciliation of "formity" and "conformity," of inner and outer "discipline." There is a thoroughly characteristic daring in this, even an audacity. Frost outmaneuvers the poets of Inner Form, arriving at a poetics of uncommon philosophical suppleness and complexity.

Of signal importance, here, are his complicated engagements with Emerson. In a famous passage in "The Poet," Emerson writes: "For it is not metres, but a metre-making argument, that makes a poem,—a thought so passionate and alive, that, like the spirit of a plant or animal, it has an architecture of its own, and adorns nature with a new thing. The thought and the form are equal in the order of time, but in the order of genesis the thought is prior to the form" (*Essays* 450).

Emerson is describing what Frost calls the doctrine of Inner Form: "the form the subject takes," as Frost puts it, "if left to itself without any considerations of outer form." According to this view the "spiritual" argument of the poem must make its form, not the meter; for meter, like all "conformities," is rigidly prescribed and has a social and traditional origin rather than a personal one. Frost's efforts to distinguish himself from this doctrine, as when he affirms the positive value of "conformity" and the "harsher discipline from without," often have the subsidiary effect of distinguishing him, apparently, from Emerson. And yet as I hope to show, Frost arrives, albeit skeptically and with reservation, at a position very like the one Emerson assumes in "The Poet."

At last, the marriage of "formity" and "conformity" in Frost's poetics comprehends the "genetic" priority, to take up Emerson's metaphor, of thought to form, equal though the two terms may be in "the order of time." He writes in "The Constant Symbol": "Form in language is such a disjected lot of old broken pieces it seems almost as non-existent as the spirit till the two embrace in the sky. They are not to be thought of as encountering in rivalry but in creation. No judgement on either alone counts. We see what Whitman's extravagance may have meant when he said the body was the soul" (*CPPP* 790). The consummation of the idea presented here—that the body, or "form," may actually *be* the soul, or "spirit"—is arrived at indirectly via Whitman; this is evidence, perhaps, of Frost's skepticism and reserve. But however that may be, the twofold point is clear. "Spirit" and "body" are "equal in the order of time": locked in an "embrace," neither term is to be considered "alone." And yet, in the "order of genesis," body or outer form is essentially reduced to "soul." *Spirit* is the prior, motivating term; spirit in fact *brings out* the form. I am ultimately concerned, in chapter 3, with how Frost's own poetics skeptically plays about the margin of an organicist ideal of inner form, in which "body" and "soul" merge, in which spirit achieves a kind of "genetic" priority over form, and in which the poet outwardly realizes his inner desire without compromise.

If Frost's poetics finally declines to resolve its contradictory attitudes toward the doctrine of Inner Form, this is perhaps because he understood that resolution is itself temporary and false. A poem is a "momentary stay against confusion," he writes in "The Figure a Poem Makes" (*CPPP* 777). And as readers we would hardly be equal to his work if we sought in it a foolish consistency. In writing this study I have often been startled by the feeling that Frost had already been here before me, seen the limitations of my surmises, and went on out ahead.

"All I know with any conviction," he wrote to Louis Untermeyer in August 1918, "is that an idea has to be a little new to be at all true and if you say a thing three times it ceases to be so" (*Frost to Untermeyer* 75–76). It might well be a caveat to his readers, who always run the risk of arresting him where he has truly ceased to be, not where he is.

1 *The Ordeal of Robert Frost*

> It is a good lesson—though it may often be a hard one—for a man who has dreamed of literary fame, and of making for himself a rank among the world's dignitaries by such means, to step aside out of the narrow circle in which his claims are recognized, and to find how utterly devoid of significance, beyond that circle, is all that he achieves, and all he aims at.
>
> —Nathaniel Hawthorne, "The Custom-House"

> Then there was the man who after telling me for hours about his big bold business adventures asked me toward morning what I did with myself. I staved off the confession. I likened myself to him in adventurousness. I was a long-shot man too. I liked not to know beforehand what the day might bring forth. And so till he lost patience with me and cried "Shoot!" Well I write poetry. "Hell," he said unhappily "my wife writes that stuff."
>
> —Robert Frost, 1938 letter

IT IS TELLING THAT Frost should remember Mark Twain's literary and cultural "ordeal" when he describes a signal fact about his own literary style and sensibility in the introduction to Edwin Arlington Robinson's *King Jasper* (1935), quoted on the first page of this study. The allusion, as I have pointed out, is specifically to Van Wyck Brooks's influential 1922 study *The Ordeal of Mark Twain.* Noteworthy about

Frost's reference to the book is the idea it is somehow meant to support: that the main concern of a writer—for that is what Frost is most immediately talking about—is to be "charming" or at least "bearable." More precisely, Frost's idea is that in order to remain charming and bearable a writer must not "take himself" *as a writer* with unalloyed "seriousness" (the terms are his). Ezra Pound would surely have objected to this proposition. Why, he might have asked, should a writer be guarded or defensive—let alone *demure*—about her vocation? Why should she temper her more "serious" thoughts with humor? And what, specifically, is meant by "humor"? In a characteristic article of the 1910s, "The Constant Preaching to the Mob," Pound derides literary artists who condescend to explain, justify, or otherwise recommend their vocation—artists who make a noticeable effort to be *charming:*

> We read again for the one-thousand-one-hundred-and-eleventh time that poetry is made to entertain. As follows: "The beginnings of English poetry . . . made by a rude war-faring people for the entertainment of men-at-arms, or for men at monks' tables."
>
> Either such statements are made to curry favor with other people sitting at fat sterile tables, or they are made in ignorance which is charlatanry when it goes out to vend itself as sacred and impeccable knowledge.
>
> "The beginnings—for entertainment"—has the writer of this sentence read *The Sea Farer* in Anglo-Saxon? Will the author tell us for whose benefit these lines, which alone in the works of our forebears are fit to compare with Homer—for whose entertainment were they made? They were made for no man's entertainment, but because a man believing in silence found himself unable to withhold himself from speaking. (*Literary Essays* 64)

After briefly discussing *The Sea Farer* and *The Wanderer* Pound concludes: "Still it flatters the mob to tell them that their importance is so great that the solace of lonely men, and the lordliest of the arts, was created for their amusement." Here "the mob" apparently refers not so much to men-at-arms, a quaint designation in this connection, as to the broad, general readership that the literary marketplace had created, apart from which stand solitary, *un*selfinterested artists who work for no one's particular benefit—let alone to *entertain.* In the introduction to *King Jasper,* literary writing, as a vocation, is by no means presented as the "solace of lonely men," which in any event is a peculiarly modernist (and late Romantic) way of thinking about poets, Pound's medieval reference notwithstanding. For his part Frost comes very close to suggesting that writers *ought* to be entertaining and amusing: "To be at all charming or even bearable, the way is almost rigidly prescribed." He was averse neither to "flattering the mob" nor to performing to entertain it.

Part of the difference between Pound and Frost derives from a simple fact. Pound writes for a rather restricted audience that takes for granted the claims and demands of his art, whereas Frost almost never does. Frost explained in a 1913 letter to John Bartlett that he hoped to reach "the general reader who buys books in their thousands. . . . I want to be a poet for all sorts and kinds" (*CPPP* 667–68). This aspiration required him to hold together constituencies so various as to be in certain respects incompatible. To write compellingly for "all sorts and kinds" is admirable, but also uncommonly difficult. Compare Frost's sentiments to Pound's in the following 1919 letter to H. L. Mencken about Mencken's volume *Instigations:* "What is wrong with it, and with your work in general is that you have drifted into writing for your inferiors. . . . Inevitable I think where one is in contact with a public" (146). For Pound, there is something vaguely pestilential about the "public," a word he seems able to utter only with contempt (as Dickinson does in "I'm Nobody—Who are You?"). Throughout his career, Frost would resist the seductions of this sort of condescension. He managed to become an eminently "entertaining" after-dinner speaker—to take up Pound's reference to "fat sterile tables"—appealing just about equally to audiences academic and rotarian. In keeping with this, he never "symbolizes" the poetic vocation, either in his writing or in his public demeanor, as "the lordliest of the arts," to use Pound's noticeably aristocratic (not democratic) metaphor.

In this chapter I consider how Frost imagined the vocation of poetry. I argue that he remained fundamentally unsure of his constituency, and consequently also of the status of poetry and of the poet; this is what accounts for the great variety, and also the humor, indirection, and circumspection, of many of his accounts of the poet's vocation. Persistent insecurities bred in him a certain tentativeness that kept him from ever becoming dogmatic, defensive, or especially embattled about being a poet in America—at least not in his public statements. A question of overriding interest to Frost is whether or not poetry, as an art and as a vocation, can comfortably accommodate a writer's sense of his own temperamental, cultural, and political difference from the broader community in which he lives and works and yet still meaningfully establish correspondence with that broader community—even when it may be hostile to the potentially countercultural values he represents as a poet and intellectual. Frost's conclusion (contra Pound) is that poetry can in fact accomplish this—even in America.

But how does a poet "charm" a specifically American constituency, both in his art and in his public personae, as Frost implied all poets ought in fact endeavor to do? What, if anything, does an artist forfeit by becoming "bearable" or by accepting what Frost blithely called "the trial by market everything must come to" (*CPPP* 845)? What aspects of the artist's personality suffer "occlusion" under these conditions, and what embarrassments do they entail? How do anxieties about gender and work figure into these problems for the male literary artist in America? And who ultimately determines what *is* charming in a writer? That is to say, who is the agent of "prescription" in Frost's formula "the way is almost rigidly prescribed"? And on what *social* criteria does that prescription depend? Questions such as these set the coordinates of my inquiry in this chapter. The chapter concludes with a consideration of the place of the academic intellectual in American culture in light of what Frost and Pound have to say about their own problems of vocation. The question, I will suggest, is whether American academics can afford to hold "the mob" of "Middle America" in contempt, as Pound did, or whether, alternatively, academic intellectuals should follow Frost's example and endeavor to remain "charming" and "bearable" even in the company of Mencken's "booboisie."

The American Male Writer and the "Businessman"

It is useful, here, to review Van Wyck Brooks's arguments in *The Ordeal of Mark Twain.* I am interested particularly in the difficult relationship that existed between the literary artist and a figure whom, in a kind of cultural shorthand, Brooks and other writers called the American "businessman." As Brooks saw it, the rigid prescriptions according to which Twain managed his own notoriously charming literary personality were laid down by "businessmen" who subscribed to a system of values opposed to those of "creative artists." Brooks has in mind the men who worked in white-collar occupations associated with the capitalist market economy in America during the Gilded Age. Such men, as Brooks saw them, held competitiveness, aggression, and acquisitiveness at a very high premium, and these values constituted the criteria by which "work" was generally assessed. I am less interested in determining whether or not tensions actually did exist between literary artists and "businessmen" of this sort—though no doubt they did to an extent—than in describing the animosities that Brooks and other American male writers believed they were reacting against. The stories these writers told about their vocation resemble the ones Frost himself often told about his work as a poet.

Brooks and Frost essentially ask the following question. How does an artist socialize his art—how does he make it *bearable?* The real interest in any such effort has to do with the degree, conscious or unconscious, to which the artist's themes, structures, attitudes, and imagery are borrowed from the patterns of life of those he wants, or somehow feels he must have, for an audience. Together, these attitudes and structures of feeling constitute what John Dewey called the "occupational psychosis" of a given society—a particular way of seeing and experiencing the world that ultimately derives from the means of production in that society. In *Permanence and Change* (1935) Kenneth Burke points out that Dewey's concept of "occupational psychosis" corresponds "to the Marxian doctrine that a society's environment in the historical sense is synonymous with the society's methods of production" (38). With reference to a hypothetical hunting culture, for example, Burke offers the following explanation:

> In stressing certain patterns of thought serviceable to the tribal occupations, the psychosis will come to have a kind of creative character which, when turned into other channels of action or imagery, will shape them analogously to the patterns of work. . . . The artist deals largely with the occupational psychosis in its derivative aspects. He projects it into new realms of imagery. If a hunt psychosis leads to a prizing of the new, we may expect him to socialize his art by discovering all the possible devices by which he can suggest the experiencing of newness. (39)

In *The Ordeal of Mark Twain,* Brooks attempts to show how the "occupational psychosis" of American market capitalism is "channeled" into the imagery and rhetoric of literary writing. He embarks on an essentially Burkean analysis in arguing that Twain unconsciously sought to charm his audience of businessmen by playing on the correct themes and attitudes in his art and by "shaping" his representation of the literary vocation on the analogy of capitalist "patterns of work." Twain's humor, especially in *The Innocents Abroad,* "expressly made the American business man as good as Titian and a little better: it made him feel that art and history and all the great, elevated, admirable, painful discoveries of humankind were not worth wasting one's emotions over" (264). Burke might say that Twain stressed patterns that were "serviceable" to the businessman's interests. Or to put it yet another way: In

Brooks's account, the businessman did not have the inclination to pursue the "elevated" "discoveries of humankind"—meaning literary and other forms of "unprofitable" work—and Twain's art confirmed this basic prejudice. Twain fashioned a literary appeal, derived from humor, that to a great extent depended upon the humiliation of "literariness" itself. "The study of ideology," Terry Eagleton suggests, "is among other things an inquiry into the ways in which people come to invest in their own unhappiness" (xiii). In a way, this is exactly what Twain had done, according to Brooks. Something important in his personality—his sense of his own intransigent cultural and vocational "difference"—had been forced into "occlusion," as Frost puts it.

Twain's friend William Dean Howells acknowledges outright that the patterns of thought serviceable to a capitalist "occupational psychosis" were dominant in America in the field of letters. In a revealing essay titled "The Man of Letters as a Man of Business," he writes: "At present business is the only human solidarity; we are all bound together with that chain, whatever intentions and tastes and principles separate us." Howells's figure is ambivalent. "Human solidarity" is all well and good, but what if it is the solidarity of being "bound" by a "chain"? The metaphor is not especially appealing, suggesting, as it does, constraint and bondage rather than the affectionate attractions of community. And what of those separate "intentions and tastes and principles" that promise to undermine this solidarity? Howells does not undertake to clarify these differences. He leaves the reader to wonder how comfortably they are accommodated within the larger "solidarity" of business and to estimate the extent to which they suffer "occlusion." The artist, Howells writes later in the essay, must "have a low rank among practical people; and he will be regarded by the great mass of Americans as perhaps a little off, a little funny, a little soft! Perhaps not; and yet I would rather not have a consensus of public opinion on the question; I think I am more comfortable without it" (6). Unlike Brooks, Howells does not write out of chagrin. But an uneasiness is nonetheless evident when he concedes: "I feel quite sure that in writing of the Man of Letters as a Man of Business I shall attract far more readers than I shall in writing of him as an Artist. Besides, as an artist he has been done a great deal already; and a commercial state like ours has really more concern with him as a business man" (4). Howells apparently has in view how a commercial "occupational psychosis," as Burke would say, had been "turned into other channels of action"—namely, literary work—and had shaped them according to dominant patterns.

For his part, Van Wyck Brooks found it vexing that a "commercial" culture like ours should view literary artists chiefly as "men of business." The source of his vexation is clear: "commercial" institutions and mores, he argued, encouraged a divorce of "ideals" from practical life and of thought from action, thereby fostering a kind of cultural schizophrenia. This worked to the detriment of creative artists because it dis-integrated them, as the supposed curators of these ideals, from what were deemed the most vital patterns of life in capitalist America. The result was that American culture ceased to have a holistic character; its sensibility had been dissociated. Poetry, philosophy, idealism—everything associated with what Brooks vaguely calls "the creative spirit"—had been abstracted from the *real* business of American life and shunted into the sacrosanct realm of "High Culture." Poetry had been flattered into irrelevance.

Brooks's arguments are confirmed by E. Anthony Rotundo's findings in *American Manhood: Transformations in Masculinity from the Revolution to the Modern Era* (1993). In discussing the late nineteenth-century phenomenon of "Muscular Christianity," for example, Rotundo asks: "If physical strength was a source of character in a man, what were the specific virtues that it bred? One of them is evident in the call for a 'vigorous, robust, muscular Christianity . . . devoid of all the etcetera of creed.' This statement expresses a growing sense of opposition between action and thought." "Yankee businessmen," Rotundo goes on to explain, "had for years harbored a suspicion of educated men who 'thought too much.' But what was once a harbored suspicion became gleeful public scorn late in the century—and no one was more scornful than educated men themselves. As Charles Francis Adams said in 1883: 'I think we've had all we want of 'elegant scholars' and 'gentlemen of refined classical taste,' and now I want to see more University men trained to take up a hand in the rather rough game of American nineteenth-century life.'" From these remarks Rotundo draws the following conclusion, with which Brooks would ruefully have concurred: "A new concept of masculinity was emerging here. In this view, male rationality was not a capacity for deep, logical reflection but rather an absence of complex emotions—an absence which freed men to act boldly and decisively" (224–25). It is easy to see how these developments created problems of identity for male literary artists; Howells presents a fine example of this in the essay quoted above, as does also Mark Twain in Brooks's analysis. And as we shall see, Frost was himself very much affected by the same developments, whereby thought and action, ideals and utility, suffered a divorce.

In "The Culture of Industrialism," Brooks suggests that America had "cleared the decks for practical action by draining away all the irreconcilable elements of the American character into a transcendental upper sphere." The "old writers" of the nineteenth century had "shelved our spiritual life, conventionalizing it in a sphere above the sphere of action" (105–6). He writes to similar effect in his highly influential essay "America's Coming of Age" (1915): "In everything one finds this frank acceptance of twin values which are not expected to have anything in common: on the one hand, a quite unclouded, quite unhypocritical assumption of transcendent theory ('high ideals'), on the other a simultaneous acceptance of catchpenny realities" (3). Brooks believed that this "frank acceptance of twin values" masked a fundamental poverty in American society, for it amounted to an acquiescence in the idea that the merely practical energies a people collectively and individually devote to making a living should be utterly distinct from the satisfactions of what he vaguely calls the "spiritual life." It was a situation in which the *a-morality* of business endeavors could be not only protected but also cultivated—and even celebrated. This is why, according to Brooks, Twain's peculiarly *anti*-literary appeal met with such success in the culture of American "business."

Brooks had tapped into a deep vein of American cultural criticism, which begins with Emerson, a writer whom, in his early years, Brooks nevertheless disdained. His complaints essentially echo "The American Scholar." In America, Emerson suggests, proliferating divisions of labor had been terrifically unfortunate: "Man is . . . metamorphosed into a thing, into many things. The planter, who is Man sent out into the field to gather food, is seldom cheered by any idea of the true dignity of his ministry. He sees his bushel and his cart, and nothing beyond, and sinks into the farmer, instead of Man on the farm. The tradesman scarcely ever gives an ideal worth to his work, but is ridden by the routine of his craft, and the soul is subject to dollars" (*Essays* 54). Over against this mercenary state of psychological division Emerson essentially imagines a unity of "avocation and vocation," to borrow a phrase from Frost: a unity in which the plain business of men and women is dignified and directed by some sense of the higher "ministry" their labors might ideally perform. Robert Francis remembers Frost's own explanation of "Two Tramps in Mud Time," the poem from which I borrow the phrase just quoted: "Frost contrasted his idea in the last stanza: 'My object in living is to unite / My avocation and vocation / As my two eyes make one in sight—' with the popular American ideal of having one hour of drudgery with twenty-three hours of play. Frost wants his play and drudgery inextricably mixed" (71). And in a never-published lecture given in Boulder, Colorado, in 1935, Frost remarked, after reading "Two Tramps in Mud Time": "I have also called it, as a sub-title, 'A poem against hobbies.' That is, against having a divided life."

Here, Frost is closely allied to the so-called "literary radicals" of the 1910s. In his 1914 essay "In the Mind of the Worker," Randolph Bourne lamented that "the clerk dulled and depressed by the long day, the factory worker—his brain a-whirl with the roar of machines—must seek elation and the climax which the work should have given them, in the crude and exciting pleasures of the street and the dance and the show." In poems like "The Ax-Helve" and "A Blue Ribbon at Amesbury" Frost shares Bourne's and Brooks's ideals of artisanship and craftsmanship, as against the new techniques of mass production. The laboring men featured in these poems have not "sunk into the farmer," as Emerson puts it; they are not *alienated* wage laborers, bereft of the means to produce the goods they use and to sustain the life they lead independently. They maintain a sense of "ministry" in their vocations, a sense of what their labors may be said to symbolize in moral and even philosophical spheres. Beginning with "The Pasture," which he placed at the head of his collected editions, Frost's poems of labor acquire a polemical edge when read in light of the cultural criticism contemporary with their publication. His remarks about "Two Tramps in Mud Time" express regrets that Brooks would certainly have shared about the division of the "practical" life from the "spiritual" life in America. Frost is to this extent a critic of the culture of industrialism. And though he would never have put it quite this way, Frost essentially agrees with Brooks's remark in "America's Coming of Age": "Desiccated culture at one end and stark utility at the other have created a deadlock in the American mind, and all our life drifts chaotically between the two extremes" (7).

In "The Culture of Industrialism," Brooks went further to claim that "the creative impulses of men are always at war with their possessive impulses, and poetry, as we know, springs from brooding on just those aspects of experience that most retard the swift advance of the acquisitive mind" (104). *Poetry* here signifies much more than literary art; it is the very life of resistance to bourgeois culture. With Bourne and Lewis Mumford, Brooks contended that our chief cultural authorities, among them William James and John Dewey, had acquiesced in this American divorce of ideals from "practical" life—that they had essentially sold "poetry" out to capital. Bourne writes in "Twilight of Idols," first published in *The Seven Arts* in 1917, a magazine on whose editorial board Frost served:

> What is the matter with the [pragmatic] philosophy? One has a sense of having come to a sudden, short stop at the end of an intellectual era. In the crisis, this philosophy of intelligent control just does not measure up to our needs. What is the root of this inadequacy that is felt so keenly by our restless minds? Van Wyck Brooks has pointed out searchingly the lack of poetic vision in our pragmatist "awakeners." Is there something in these realistic attitudes that works actually against poetic vision, against concern for the quality of life as above machinery of life? (198)

The last sentence is more an indictment than a question. "Poetry" carries the same countercultural, anticapitalist force, here, that attaches to Brooks's use of the term. In essence, Bourne argues that this "lack of poetic vision" was probably not accidental, and that if "our pragmatist 'awakeners'" actually worked "*against*" a "concern for the quality of life"—which he seems to equate with "poetic vision"—then there was something intentional and necessary about it. In short, the industrial culture of the Gilded Age *required* a philosophy and an art that could relieve its subjects of the responsibility to refer the ends, development, and even the "progress" of American capitalism to prior ideals: this philosophy and this art helped protect the "a-morality" of capitalist endeavor, as I have already suggested. According to Brooks, that is why Twain's art, if it was to reach an audience of businessmen—or even remain "bearable" in its presence—had to "degrade as pretentious and absurd everything of a spiritual, aesthetic and intellectual nature the recognition of which, the participation in which, would retard the smooth and simple operation of the business man's mind. Mark Twain . . . enables the business man to laugh at art, at antiquity, chivalry, beauty, and return to his desk with an infinitely intensified conceit of his own worthiness and well-being" (259). In this unflattering account, Twain's art implicitly affirmed the separation of ideals from practical life, of theory from practice, thereby underpinning the most fundamental assumptions of the "occupational psychosis" of American capitalism. These developments achieved ultimate expression in Calvin Coolidge's famous tautology: "The business of America is business."[1]

The position occupied by the "man of letters" in America had been precarious long before Brooks emerged to lament the fact. He did not invent the problems he attempted to describe, though he did color them according to the needs of his broader polemic. In *Counter-Statement* (1931), his first book of criticism, Kenneth Burke points out that the criteria of value derived from the "rise of technology" in the nineteenth century had come entirely to be defined by the characteristics of utility and commodity: if a writer's "product" did not meet these criteria, his labors did not qualify as "work." One solution to this was the justification "art for art's sake." But as Burke explains, there is a problem with such justifications: "If the aesthetic had no *purpose* outside itself, the corollary seemed to be that the aesthetic had no *result* outside itself. Logically there was no cogency in such an argument, but psychologically there was a great deal. And the damage was perhaps increased through attempts to justify art by the postulating of a special 'art instinct' or 'aesthetic sense'" (63). The consequences are plain. If the professions could not accept art's claim to transcend utility, then any successful *literary* appeal to the professions as a possible constituency for literature would be obliged somehow to satisfy that basic skepticism. This obligation probably explains Brooks's argument—more partisan, of course, than Burke's—that Twain had to arrive at a style that degrades "everything of a spiritual, aesthetic, and intellectual nature." That is to say, he arrived at a style that ridiculed everything promising to *distinguish* the value of literature and the literary vocation, which to the "businessmen" of his day may have stood as a reproach to the remission of ideals in their own professions.

The Muscular Poetics of Frost and Pound

Vocational problems are almost inevitably also gender problems. Brooks and the literary radicals were reacting against what they perceived as a "feminization" of the arts. Literary style, they believed, had come entirely under the control of genteel critics, editors, and anthologists, who themselves acknowledged a readership comprised chiefly of women. H. L. Mencken writes in a 1911 review of a new book by Pound: "Nine-tenths of our living makers and singers it would seem are women, and fully two-thirds of these women are ladies," he says, adding with that last word a class dimension to the issue of gender that forms his main subject. "The result is a boudoir tinkle in the tumult of the lyre. Our poets are afraid of passion; the realities of life alarm them; the good red sun sends them scurrying" (*Smart Set Criticism* 76–77). "Passion" had by this time become the proper province of men. They were, it seems, best equipped to confront life's "realities" (the body, sexuality, the exhilarating struggles of living and dying). Their arena lay outdoors under the "good red sun," not in the boudoir—a chamber in reference to which, in any case, they would not mince words by adopting a French term. With a geniality almost entirely unavailable to Mencken and other male writers of his generation, William Dean Howells observes that "the man of letters must make up his mind that in the United States the fate of a book is in the hands of the women. It is women who have the most leisure, and they read the most books" (*Literature and Life* 21). Two assumptions underlie Howells's remark. The first is that it is a *man* of letters he chiefly addresses, who will have to refashion his work to make it eligible for a female audience. If there were no important difference between the male writer and the women he wished to reach, why would he have to "make up his mind," no doubt with a haggard sense of constriction, to take that difference into account? This is another example of how uneasy the "solidarity" of the male writer and his constituency had apparently become. Howells's second assumption, already a concession on his part, is that reading is "leisure." Almost by definition this makes reading a counterpoint to "work" and consequently irrelevant to the daily, "utilitarian" concerns of the American men who (so the logic goes) earn the money to buy their wives the books that will, in turn, support the altogether impertinent American writer. A "boudoir tinkle" indeed. Burke shrewdly observes in *Counter-Statement:* "In an age when 'work' was becoming one of society's basic catchwords, art could not very well be associated with play without some loss of prestige" (64). And yet Howells seems to take art's association with "play" for granted when he remarks: "It is women who have the most leisure, and they read the most books."

Howells's concerns reflect a general apprehension among men of his generation that American culture had become feminized. In Henry James's *The Bostonians,* Basil Ransom complains: "The whole generation is womanized; the masculine tone is passing out of the world; it's a feminine, a nervous, hysterical, chattering, canting age, an age of false delicacy and exaggerated solicitudes and coddled sensibilities" (qtd. in Rotundo 252). Anthony Rotundo characterizes the anxieties of such men in the following way: "They noted with concern that women now set the standards of appearance and decorum. Women established the sentimental tone of bourgeois Protestant religion, and their values and sensibilities played a major role in forming literary tastes. In private, women enforced sexual virtue. By carrying out their role as the guardians of 'civilized morality,' middle-class females affected men as agents of unreasoning restraint" (252). Remarks such as Basil Ransom's and Howells's suggest that *the feminine* had come to designate a kind of force field impinging upon the free movements of American men—even upon the free movements of their thoughts and feelings. It was as if conscience itself had been "feminized," as indeed in certain respects it apparently had. Of course, these symptoms of a new anxiety rigidly to codify gender roles reflect, as Rotundo points out, a specific set of social and historical developments. In the last decades of the nineteenth century, American women entered the work force in unprecedented numbers. The separate spheres of male and female endeavor—a prominent characteristic of the antebellum decades—had begun to merge, however inequitably, with the result that gender distinctions were reasserted all the more vigorously in the ideological sphere. These developments very much affected the poetry of the male American modernists, as we shall see presently.

Van Wyck Brooks, then, believed that a feminized cultural regime was comprehensively destructive. It desiccated poetry by establishing and maintaining a false decorum—the "boudoir tinkle" of which Mencken speaks. The consequence was that poetry became stigmatized as irrelevant, at least in the eyes of Brooks's "businessman." Within a patriarchal and capitalistic "occupational psychosis," literature and the literary vocation itself had come to signify "femininity" and "powerlessness" simply because, under such a regime, these two values coincide. This is partly why Hawthorne, who complained about the "scribbling women" of his own day (and also about their audience), writes in "The Custom-House": "It is a good lesson—though it may often be a hard one—for a man who has dreamed of literary fame, and of making for himself a rank among the world's dignitaries by such means, to step aside out of the narrow circle in which his claims are recognized, and to find how utterly devoid of significance, beyond that circle, is all that he achieves, and all he aims at" (141). Brooks was convinced that the blame for this condition of impotence lay precisely here: the "narrow circle" in which the claims of literature were acknowledged had become feminine—by marketplace association, but also by *nature,* since it was in the sphere of leisure rather than of work, competition, and money. He expresses this intersection of gender and diminished cultural power in "The Literary Life in America," his contribution to *Civilization in the United States* (1922): "Samson had lost his virility before the Philistines bound him; it was because he had lost his virility that the Philistines were able to bind him. The American writer who 'goes wrong' is in a similar case" (167). Genteel, bourgeois tastes—a peculiarly Victorian-American philistinism—had bound the American writer to a specifically feminine decorum. Brooks's phrase "the American writer" is of course only apparently neutral: the concern is unmistakably with *male* writers. And in the remaining pages of this section I will consider how, in their different ways, Frost and Pound managed by main strength to unbind the literary Samson from his philistine, feminine restraints.

At first it may strike readers as odd to think of Frost as deeply involved in these literary debates about vocation and gender. But traces of them are to be found everywhere in his work, both early and late. In fact, Frost developed something like a "muscular" poetics specifically in response to the vocational anxieties we have been examining. That is to say, he developed a way of describing the literary vocation, and more particularly the composition of poetry, that would reclaim them as respectable arenas of masculine endeavor. In this project he was hardly alone, and similar efforts may be discerned in Pound's writings and in the writings of American male modernist poets generally.

In May 1960, Frost testified before the Senate Subcommittee on Education of the Committee on Labor Public Welfare in favor of establishing a national academy of culture—the prototype of what would soon become the National Endowments for the Arts and for the Humanities: "Everybody comes down here to get declared equal to somebody else and I want poets declared equal to—what shall I say? Scientists? No, big business" (U.S. Senate 10). At least in certain moods, Frost shared Howells's apprehension that a "commercial state" like America was interested in poets only as men of business, when it was interested in them at all. But he was better accommodated to the American businessman than Howells had apparently ever been. Beginning with the 1916 poem "Christmas Trees," Frost insisted that poets must accept what he calls the "trial by market everything must come to"—that they must work from within (as Burke would say) the "occupational psychosis" of American capitalism (*CPPP* 845). He was suggesting—at least experimentally—that cultural and aesthetic prestige ought properly to be decided in the marketplace that governs most other aspects of life in America.

In a 1915 letter to Louis Untermeyer that I associate with "Christmas Trees," Frost declared that "a book ought to sell. Nothing is quite honest that is not commercial" (*Frost to Untermeyer* 8–9). The idea seems to be that elitism of Pound's romantically anticommercial sort was somehow "dishonest," that it was a way of deciding that the grapes of popular approval were sour if one could not get at them. When he was named Consultant in Poetry to the Library of Congress in 1958, Frost drafted a brief response accepting the position in which he sounds more or less the same theme: "I was not brought up to the distrust of politics that so many scholars and artists seem to suffer from. Neither was I to distrust of big business for that matter. Nor of small business either. Long before my luck changed I went on record as willing to accept the trial by market everything must come to" (*CPPP* 845). "Long before my luck changed": he lets us see that it was not, for him, a case of his ratifying the rules of the game only after he had won it; instead, he had entered into the enterprise in good faith all along. No sour grapes here. But why, it seems reasonable to ask, did it occur to Frost to make these explanations in accepting a position as Consultant in Poetry to the Library of Congress in 1958, by which time he had achieved a celebrity and popular prestige unprecedented for an American poet? How are his explanations at all relevant to the circumstances in which he offers them? And how are we to account for the vague air of apology and defensiveness that hangs about his remarks? The answer lies in the history of the embarrassed relationship between literary writing and work variously traced, as we have seen, by Howells, Van Wyck Brooks, and Kenneth Burke. In 1960 Frost appeared before the U.S. Senate to declare poetry equal to business, but in a sense he had been making the same declaration throughout his career.

Years earlier, in 1938, he wrote to the literary critic R. P. T. Coffin describing a significant encounter he had had with a man on a train: "Then there was the man who after telling me for hours about his big bold business adventures asked me toward morning what I did with myself. I staved off the confession. I likened myself to him in adventurousness. I was a long-shot man too. I liked not to know beforehand what the day might bring forth. And so till he lost patience with me and cried 'Shoot!' Well I write poetry. 'Hell,' he said unhappily 'my wife writes that stuff'" (465). This anecdote perfectly depicts the confusion of questions about gender and the profession of literary writing that troubled Brooks. There is a margin of discomfort and embarrassment here, as Frost—partly in a spirit of parody but partly not—forms his own vocation on the model of American business: "I likened myself to him in adventurousness. I was a long-shot man too," and so on. It is a playful example of how (as Burke explains) the "occupational psychosis" of a given society "will come to have a kind of creative character which, when turned into other channels of action . . . will shape them analogously to the patterns of work." In the letter to Coffin, Frost locates in himself the same kind of apologetic disposition when it comes to owning himself a writer that colors Howells's essay "The Man of Letters as a Man of Business." Frost writes in a spirit of comedy. But he preserved the incident in anecdotal form—the letter indicates that he used it in his lectures—and this suggests that it struck him as representative. He believed it summed up something important about his own literary life.

The letter to Coffin provides a small example of how Frost's characteristic aesthetic vocabulary of "work" and "deeds" is in part constituted by social anxieties associated with his vocation. Burke explains in *Counter-Statement* that "with the development of technology, 'usefulness' was coming into prominence as a test of values, so that art's slogan was necessarily phrased to take the criteria of usefulness into account" (63). He refers specifically to the slogan "art for art's sake," but the same thing may be said of others: "Perhaps Flaubert's constant talk of toil was prompted in part by a grudging awareness of the new criterion" (64). No doubt many of Frost's remarks about his vocation are similarly motivated. "Two Tramps in Mud Time," for example, comes immediately to mind: Frost's idea throughout that poem is to fuse the vocabularies of leisure and work, play and labor, and therefore implicitly to fuse the vocabularies typically used to define poetry in American culture with those used to describe more recognizably laborious vocations—just as he does in the letter to Coffin. In a sense, the poem attempts to take back the ground that Howells concedes, as we have seen, when he writes: "It is women who have the most leisure, and they read the most books."

Speaking of the American pragmatist tradition to which Frost belongs, Richard Poirier suggests in *Poetry and Pragmatism* (1992) that "in the philosophical writings, no less than the poetry . . . the correspondence between physical work and mental work, between manual labor and writing (which is no less an operation of the hands), is expressed with an eagerness that effectively blurs the social and cultural distinctions known to exist between these different kinds of activity" (81). The reasons for this eagerness are several and include the recognition that writing is, as Poirier puts it, "necessarily hard work. It is a wringing, a screwing, a turning of words" (80). He goes on to point out: "To the very degree that Emersonian pragmatists insist that writing is a form of work there seems to be an implicit acknowledgment that, if writing were to be otherwise perceived, it might alienate the writers themselves from the larger human community they hope to please and persuade" (81). I take it that he refers, with Burke, to an increasing awareness on the part of these pragmatist writers of "new criteria" for assessing the meaning of "work," and therefore for assessing the "place" the writer holds within the larger social body. When we add to Poirier's remarks a concern for gender, the full range of this problem becomes clear. Frost's 1938 letter to Coffin, for example, rather humorously follows from these new patterns of justification. He shows his own "grudging awareness" of the new criteria, his sense that he must "liken" his work as a poet to a more prestigious pattern of work if he is to "please" and "persuade." This is exactly the sort of thing that Van Wyck Brooks has in mind in his essay "The Literary Life":

> Howells . . . instinctively shared, in regard to the significance of his vocation, the feeling of our pragmatic philosophers, who have been obliged to justify the intellectual life by showing how useful it is—not to mention Mr. R.W. Chambers, who has remarked that writers "are not held in excessive esteem by really busy people, the general idea being—which is usually true—that literature is a godsend to those unfitted for real work." After this one can easily understand why our novelists take such pains to be mistaken for business men and succeed so admirably in their effort. (192)

The motives of justification outlined by Poirier, Burke, and Brooks color many of Frost's descriptions of the work of poetry, descriptions which show that he suffered through problems of vocational identity quite common among American men. Anthony Rotundo explains that "the gender meanings of different professions probably led to a self-selection in the kinds of young men who entered various lines of middle-class work, although the evidence here is not sufficient to confirm the point. At the very least, the link between gender and profession created identity problems for certain men—problems that cried out for a solution" (172). Rotundo further points out that in nineteenth-century America "male callings rested on power, pride, and public eminence, while female careers involved nurture and sentiment, an understanding of human feeling used to cultivate and ennoble the human spirit" (170). The terms of this opposition gendered the literary life feminine, as we have seen, and Frost arrived at an arresting solution to this problem of vocational identity.

In the same letter to R. P. T. Coffin quoted above, Frost writes: "A real artist delights in roughness for what he can do to it. He's the brute who can knock the corners off the marble block and drag the unbedded beauty out of bed. The statesman (politician) is no different except that he works in a protean mass of material that hardly holds the shape he gives it long enough for him to get credit for it. His material is the rolling mob" (*Selected Letters* 465). The imagery is athletic, masculine, and aggressively sexual. Indeed, the act of artistic creation is likened to sexual conquest: "He's the brute who can knock the corners off the marble block and drag the unbedded beauty out of bed." Frost specifically counteracts a genteel way of thinking about poetry that might be called, to follow his cue, Woodrow Wilsonian: "Meet with the fallacy of the foolish: having had a glimpse of finished art, they forever after pine for a life that shall be nothing but finished art. Why not a world safe for art as well as for democracy." As for Wilson and his world made "safe" for art: Frost prefers illiberal, rigorously male statesmen who delight in their own crude power to work the "rolling mob" and who, like "real" artists, never "pine" for safety. The "literary life" begins to look remarkably like the "strenuous life" of Theodore Roosevelt's passionately masculine ideal.

In Frost's letter, the phrase "*pine* for a life that shall be nothing but finished art" carries a slight suggestion of sentiment and femininity—qualities from which he is attempting to distinguish his own, more muscular line of work. In fact, Frost imaginatively realigns himself as a poet with the crude businessman described later in the same letter—the kind of man who presumably did not vote, the logic of the letter implies, for Woodrow Wilson. (He would have voted instead for Roosevelt, who denounced Wilson as a "white-handy Miss Nancy" when Wilson unmanfully delayed America's entry into World War I.) We must assume that Frost's businessman would assent to the masculine kind of art that Frost describes here, in the production of which the virile artist "drags the unbedded beauty out of bed." This is hardly what he has in mind when, according to Frost's attribution, he exclaims: "Hell. . . . My wife writes that stuff." Frost eventually comes right out and "likens" himself humorously to the "adventurous" capitalist. But reading for gender shows us that he has implicitly been doing the same thing all along. In moments like this he is engaged in what Poirier, in another connection, calls the "social repositioning" of literary work (*Poetry and Pragmatism* 84). Frost appropriates to poetry specifically masculine motives of virility and power not culturally associated with it, at least in America. He thereby solves the general problem of vocational identity that Anthony Rotundo discusses in *American Manhood.* In fact, Rotundo describes a related solution arrived at by men in the ministry (which was also gendered feminine) and in business and law (both gendered masculine). Such men, in their several ways, "merged the worldly with the godly, the 'male' with the 'female'" (172). Ministers modeled their vocation on metaphors of "Christian warfare" giving rise to the doctrine of "muscular Christianity," while businessmen and lawyers dedicated their vocational energies to altruistic or "godly" ends. They achieved a union of masculine "energy" and "action" with the supposedly feminine virtues of compassion and sentiment.

If gender troubles contributed to the development of a "muscular" Christianity, they no less contributed to what might be termed a "muscular poetics," in which the manly artist—dispensing with courtship, seduction, and panderers alike—simply drags the unbedded beauty out of bed. It is appropriate to regard these developments in light of a far-ranging tendency in late nineteenth and early twentieth-century American culture in which, as Rotundo explains, "men with artistic sensitivities often cultivated a manly veneer" (278). And this is perhaps the place to consider some more general aspects of masculinity as an issue in American male modernist poetry.

I begin with Ezra Pound's "Tenzone," which appears in the section of *Personae* titled "Poems of Lustra 1913–15." The poem very much belongs to the episode in American literary history that we have been examining:

> Will people accept them?
> (i.e. these songs).
> As a timorous wench from a centaur
> (or a centurion),
> Already they flee, howling in terror.
>
> Will they be touched with the verisimilitudes?
> Their virgin stupidity is untemptable.
> I beg you, my friendly critics,
> Do not set about to procure me an audience.
>
> I mate with my free kind upon the crags;
> the hidden recesses
> Have heard the echo of my heels,
> in the cool light,
> in the darkness.
>
> (83)

The title refers to a form of verbal exchange in Provençal poetry that often consisted of invective, and the satirical energies of Pound's poem certainly fit this description. Of course, the antecedents here are American as much as European: "Tenzone" is a kind of Whitmanesque "salut" concerned with the poet's "songs" and readership. These readers are gender neutral in the first line, which speaks only of "people." But in the third line, and then throughout, they are gendered feminine ("as a timorous wench . . . already they flee"). The relation of poet to reader is imagined, here, as a relation of virile man to prudish, "virgin" woman. One recalls H. L. Mencken's remarks, quoted above, about the situation of poetry in the 1910s: "Our poets are afraid of passion; the realities of life alarm them; the good red sun sends them scurrying."

Pound's satire is actually quite complex. In part, he is gunning for readers who misperceived his work, or so he thought, as belonging to the so-called Red Blood school of writing prominent in the first decades of the century. This becomes clear in "The Condolence," which follows "Tenzone" in *Personae:*

> O my fellow sufferers, songs of my youth,
> A lot of asses praise you because you are "virile,"
> We, you, I! We are "Red Bloods"!
> Imagine it, my fellow sufferers—
> Our maleness lifts us out of the ruck,
>   Who'd have foreseen it?
>
> (83)

He has in mind such views as Mencken expressed in a 1911 review of his work that eloquently speaks the language of gender: Pound "writes in the clangorous, passionate manner that he advocates—and it must be said for him in all honesty that his stanzas often attain to an arresting and amazing vigor. The pale thing we commonly call beauty is seldom in them. They are rough, uncouth, hairy, barbarous, wild" (*Smart Set Criticism* 77). He refers particularly to "The Ballad of the Goodly Fere" and "Sestina: Altaforte," but "Tenzone" is a good enough example of the type. In any event, examining "Tenzone" and "The Condolence" together we can see clearly the main targets of Pound's invective. On the one hand, there are prudish, "feminized" (though not necessarily female) readers of refined Victorian taste—readers who were shocked at the extravagant crudities of the "virile school" and who associated the ostensibly normal virility of Pound with it. On the other hand are readers who, rebelling against the canons of Victorian taste, had erred in the opposite direction by establishing a cult of virility that formed a sort of mirror image of the prudes and meaningfully existed only in relation to them. In "Tenzone" Pound adopts the Red Blood persona chiefly in order to parody it: he becomes a centaur, the half-man, half-horse of classical mythology; or he becomes a centurion, the Roman commander of one hundred men. He also assumes the role of sexual tempter, only to reject it as an exercise in futility because, it turns out, the "virgin stupidity" of his stiff-backed readers is "untemptable."

In this bawdy context the word "procure" takes on sexual connotations proper to its place in the language of prostitution: panderers "procure" women for customers. The unsurprising implication is that pandering to a literary marketplace such as the one imagined here would constitute a kind of literary prostitution—a solicitude (and solicitation) marked "feminine."

Pound means ultimately to chart a *via media* between the unsatisfactory alternatives of "prude" and "Red Blood." In so doing, he dislocates and then redefines the gender both of poetry and of poet. In poems such as "Tenzone," then, something relatively new in American writing occurs. With some notable exceptions, in the early decades of the nineteenth century "femininity" had been associated in the writing of American men with the body, with passion and sexuality, whereas "masculinity" had been associated with the mind, with reason and chastity. In the writing of Hawthorne and Emerson, for example, "civilization" typically signifies order, reason, the conquest of the passions and of nature, the subordination of "animal" instincts to "higher" faculties, and so on. It is discernibly a masculine ideal and is conferred and maintained by men. A claim is implicitly made in these writings that women, with their passionate sexuality and "uncivilized" disposition, threaten the precarious integrity of civilization. This is abundantly evident in Hawthorne's story "Young Goodman Brown" as well as in *The Scarlet Letter.* I think also of Emerson's subtly gendered arguments in "Wealth," published in *The Conduct of Life.* Associating unrestrained expenditure with what he calls "the riot of the senses," Emerson makes scornful reference to the effeminate men—he calls them "fops"—who indulge themselves in this way. One consequence of their indulgence, he argues, is that society in large towns becomes "babyish" and "ends in cosseting." If this were the only use to which wealth were put, Emerson suggests, the practice "would bring us to barricades, burned towns, and tomahawks, presently" (*Essays* 992–93). His arguments are complex and intricate but they derive, it may be said, from the idea that masculinity, properly understood, designates a disposition to control effeminate, childish, sensual, and potentially "savage" indulgences: ordinately "chaste" principles of masculinity are what stand between us and "tomahawks." (The same association of "femininity" with the "uncivilized" American Indian informs Hawthorne's portrait of Hester Prynne and her daughter Pearl.)

Later in the nineteenth century, with the advent of what Anthony Rotundo calls the cult of "passionate manhood," these coordinates shift, as the concept of "civilization" becomes associated with femininity rather than masculinity. Women now confer and maintain "civility," which refers more to the uncomfortable *restraint* of specifically masculine passions than to the necessary management and subordination of them in the name of reason. For the first time, "civilized" and "refined" become derisive terms in the mouths of American men. The full significance of this new way of thinking about civilization is felt in *Huckleberry Finn,* though earlier intimations of it are found in Irving, Cooper, Thoreau, and Whitman. Huck's uncomfortable feeling of restraint, when subordinated to the regime of women, is in fact perfectly representative of this mode of thought. As Rotundo points out, "civility" was at this point associated with the repression of "natural" masculine sexual instincts and with a "natural" and healthy male unruliness and aggression. Women, it was believed, established prudish and false decorums, leading men to watch what they said, what they ate, smoked, and drank, what they did—even what they *felt.*

We find evidence of these developments in Pound's *Lustra,* and in poems such as "Tenzone" and "Salutation the Second" the change in the gender of "civility" has a special bearing on the problem of the literary vocation. Pound's poet-speaker in "The Garden," for example, is implicitly the virile, fertile, passionate figure, whereas the woman he regards is "anemic"—cerebral and as disembodied as a skein of ethereal silk. She is the "end of breeding" in two senses: the tragic "culmination" of haute-bourgeois refinement and also the sexually barren "end" of the line.

> Like a skein of loose silk blown against a wall
> She walks by the railing of a path in Kensington Gardens,
> And she is dying piece-meal
> of a sort of emotional anaemia.
>
> And round about there is a rabble
> Of the filthy, sturdy, unkillable infants of the very poor.
> They shall inherit the earth.
>
> In her is the end of breeding.
> Her boredom is exquisite and excessive.
> She would like some one to speak to her,
> And is almost afraid that I
> will commit that indiscretion.
>
> (85)

The woman in "The Garden" and the masculine poet-speaker are meant to be representative. Pound suggests that the aristocracy itself, as realized in a woman who is the perfection or "end" of her class, had become dangerously "feminized." The cultivated upper classes are desiccated, barren, bereft of passion; they are all mind and no body—the "end of breeding" in the sense of "cessation." The *virgin* stupidity of the wenches in "Tenzone"—a kind of prudish, cultivated ignorance—has here become an intractable cultural *sterility,* which amounts to pretty much the same thing: in neither case are a fruitful consummation and "pregnancy" possible. It is a familiar male modernist idea about Anglo-European high culture. Pound's lady is cousin to the woman in Eliot's "Portrait of a Lady," as well as to the neurasthenic woman in the "Game of Chess" section of *The Waste Land.* (One recalls also the subjects of Pound's "Portrait d'une Femme" and "Ortus," elegant women who, he believes, notably lack a vital center.) By way of contrast to frigid (upper-class) women such as these, Pound acknowledges the "unkillable infants of the very poor." The argument seems to be that the working-class is in some sense all body, and an astonishingly fecund one at that. The lines savor a little of Pound's Menckenian, antidemocratic arrogance and may also engage the racist idea that immigrant workers threaten the integrity of Anglo-Saxon culture. In other poems Pound will celebrate a kind of pastoral peasantry, as for example in the Whitmanesque "Salutation." But in *Lustra,* the proletariat, the specifically urban and *industrial* poor, never seem to engage his sympathies.

In any event, Pound's reference to the "very poor" should not allow us to forget that the poet-speaker is himself placed well outside and beneath the social class of the exquisitely, excessively bored lady (her boredom has actually become her pastime—a kind of hobby). "The Garden" suggests a sort of Lady Chatterly affair in which a seduction—in this case only imagined—transgresses ordinarily well-policed class boundaries. (I am reminded also of section eleven of Whitman's "Song of Myself," in which a cloistered, effete lady gazes down on "twenty-eight" male bathers; there, as in "The Garden," unrequited sexual desire crosses boundaries of social class.) These sexual/cultural arguments are by no means specific to the literature of white male modernists. The same concerns animate Jean Toomer's *Cane* (1923), albeit with interesting complications. A good example is the section of the book titled "Box-Seat," in which Dan Moore (Toomer's hero in the story) proposes to seduce Muriel, his beloved, out of her repressive bourgeois cage: "Dan looks at her, directly. Her animalism still unconquered by zoo-restrictions and keeper-taboos, stirs him. . . . Muriel's lips become the flesh-notes of a futile, plaintive longing. Dan's impulse to direct her is its fresh life" (112). The story as a whole makes clear that Dan's emergent sexuality represents larger *cultural* imperatives of renewal and "fertility" that are directed against the prohibitions of white bourgeois gentility. In fact, Dan represents a chthonian sexuality that will "stir the root-life of a withered people" (104)—preeminently a male modernist theme.[2] The withered people of whom Toomer speaks are racially specific, but then again so are the people whom Pound's and Eliot's anemic ladies represent. At moments like this the differences among these writers seem less remarkable than the similarities; gender affiliation momentarily transcends racial division. As in Toomer's "Box-Seat," the seduction imagined in "The Garden" is in fact a *cultural* "insemination" figured as a sexual one. Pound-the-poet is "dancing the dance of the phallus," as he says in "Salutation the Second" (87). One can readily see why readers associated him with the Red Blood school, his impressive incredulity notwithstanding; the shoe fits pretty well. It is not for nothing that Mencken admiringly calls him a "rough, uncouth, hairy, barbarous, wild" poet. After all, in *Pavannes and Divagations* he crudely characterizes the genteel poetry of the later nineteenth century, and the literary scene in London, as a "great passive vulva" (204).

One way to understand what has happened to the logic of gender in poems like "The Garden" and "Tenzone" is to read them in light of Pound's antibourgeois, anti-Victorian disposition—a disposition he shared with other male writers of his generation, Anglo-American and African-American alike. He hated Victorian prudishness, which to his way of thinking sought to erase sexuality and the body from social and literary discourse. To his mind this was a feminine imperative, though as often as not enforced by men—for example by John St. Loe Strachey, editor of *The Spectator,* whom Pound satirized as the type of the "male prude." In Pound's view, this prudishness had led to a specifically *cultural* frigidity and sterility that virtually precluded all meaningful renewal. "The Garden" is only one among many in *Lustra* that socially reposition the vocation of poetry, placing it under the sign of a passionate masculinity (the "dance of the phallus"), while at the same time associating it with qualities of fertility and sexuality that had earlier in the nineteenth century been gendered feminine. Pound inverts gender values, as poetry and poet alike become the means for renewal and fertility in European culture. His work provides an excellent example of how, in Frank Lentricchia's words, "the lyric is culturally sanctioned in modernist polemic when what is culturally branded (and denigrated) as essentially feminine is not done away with but is married to the male principle" (*Modernist Quartet* 92).

Eliot presents an intriguing variation on these themes. In his case we encounter a peculiarly high-brow version of the masculine mythology of woman and a poetics of male impotence that forms the inverse image of the more muscular poetics of Frost and Pound. Eliot speaks of a "dissociated sensibility," a pathology in which the mind is cut off from the life of the passions and the body; we no longer "feel our thoughts" or "think our feelings." "The ordinary man's experience," he writes in "The Metaphysical Poets," is "chaotic, irregular, fragmentary. [He] falls in love, or reads Spinoza, and these two experiences have nothing to do with each other" (*Selected Essays* 64). Eliot famously opposed to this pathology the healthier, associated sensibility encountered in the work of Donne: there we find a passionate love poetry in which the discourse of courtship and sexuality is intimately bound up with the highly civilized discourses of philosophy, theology, and science—a poetry in which all of these varied experiences somehow have very much to do with each other and form an organic whole. In Donne's poetry, thinking is almost always erotic and eroticism is inevitably an occasion for thought. It is not customary to assign a specifically sexual significance to Eliot's concept of a "dissociated sensibility," but I propose that we take quite literally his reference to "falling in love" in the passage just quoted. To speak merely of a dissociation of "thought" from "feeling" seems much too abstract, particularly when we consider that the pathological dissociations that afflict the men and women in Eliot's poetry of the late 1910s and early 1920s have a specifically *psychosexual* etiology.

We should regard Eliot's ideas as a part of the general development that Anthony Rotundo describes in *American Manhood.* European civilization had (Eliot implicitly argues) repressed the passionate life of the body; it had become overrefined and overcivilized. In this connection, I would cite such poems as "The Love Song of J. Alfred Prufrock," "The Preludes," "La Figlia che Piange" and "Rhapsody on a Windy Night." In each of these, Eliot's male speakers are alienated from their sexuality, which for them inevitably dwells in the sordid, forbidden districts of the cities that most of these poems describe. When Eliot's male personae move, or imagine themselves moving, beyond their proper social and "neighborhood" boundaries, they are in fact transgressing a *moral* line as much as a geographical one: they are "slumming," as is plainly evident in "Rhapsody on a Windy Night." The women in these poems consequently take one of two shapes: either they are bland, frigid, and intimidating, as in "Prufrock," or they are lewd, uncultivated doxies, as in "Rhapsody" or certain of Eliot's "Sweeney" poems. Indeed the entire landscape into which the male protagonist wanders in "Rhapsody" is gendered feminine, under the sign of a lasciviously whispering Moon. This landscape, this *aura,* is (as the Lacanians like to say) the feminine, sexualized Other of the male speaker's unconscious. The nighttime journey out into forbidden districts of the city is therefore a journey into the forbidden, highly sexualized reaches of his own sensibility—reaches from which he has been "dissociated": his sexual geography is all screwed up. And his condition, we are to understand, is in some sense *representative* of his social class; in this regard, he is very much like the woman in Pound's "The Garden."

Here, we should also notice the Hawthornian qualities that persist in Eliot's essentially Puritan imagination: his male persona in "Rhapsody" is very much a "Young Goodman Brown" sort of figure, making his errand into a sexual wilderness. Of course, Eliot had also read Baudelaire, and, accordingly, the sexual wilderness of Hawthorne—which is also *literally* a forest—becomes in Eliot's writing specifically *urban.* But its French antecedents notwithstanding, the atmosphere of this "urban wilderness" is unmistakably Hawthornian and American. Eliot therefore presents an interesting case. He exhibits certain ideas about femininity that belong to an earlier era of male American writing: women are the uncivilized, sexual Other of civilized and chaste men, as in "Rhapsody." But he also exhibits attitudes characteristic of his own generation: women are overcivilized, frigid, intimidating opponents of male passion, as in "Prufrock." This apparent contradiction can be reconciled in the following way. Eliot effectively divides up the two roles that women play in his early poetry, assigning one role to the working class—which, as in Pound's poetry, seldom suffers from sterility—and the other to the upper: we have working-class prostitutes on the one hand and overrefined, frigid women on the other. Gender and class designations cross one another. At the same time, of course, women in Eliot's work are very often enigmatic, intimidating figures; this is certainly the case in "Prufrock." Putting all of this together we can see clearly that, in these poems, sexuality is never healthily integrated into a woman's sensibility—nor, we are given to understand, could such an integration ever really exist in Eliot's work. Perhaps that is why he is so nostalgic for the work of Donne and at the same time so completely unlike Donne in his imagination of the erotic. (The resemblance between the two men is really superficial, consisting largely of specific echoes of the earlier poet by the later one.) Eliot is recognizably a scion of the Puritan-Unitarian, New England strain that was in fact his birthright. His gender anxieties therefore reflect both his position in the Puritan tradition of Hawthorne *and* his position as a noticeably "modern" American writer. His working-class women may have a certain Hawthornian quality, modified by Baudelaire, as I have suggested. But the upper crust women of "Prufrock," their sophistication notwithstanding, are very much your modern Thurber women. (I am thinking, for example, of Walter Mitty's formidable wife or of Madge in the grim story "Whip-poor-will.") And J. Alfred Prufrock's masculine timidity and anxiety are altogether in the Thurber vein.[3]

The contrast between Eliot and Pound becomes unmistakable when we observe that Pound—who was, after all, born in Idaho—shows the effects only of the latter condition of modernity and almost none of the first condition of New England Puritanism. Sexuality *as such* is never gendered feminine in *Lustra,* nor are women enigmatic, intimidating figures. The difference between Pound and Eliot becomes still more obvious when we observe that, in *Lustra,* Pound's main nineteenth-century American precursor is Whitman, not Hawthorne. The male speakers of Pound's *Lustra* poems are perfectly in touch with their sexuality. They make Whitmanesque overtures to women and even propose to "mother" them, as in "Ortus." These poems show how relaxed Pound's male sexual personae can sometimes be with their often flexible gender identity—flexible, that is, in comparison to Eliot's men. Pound's male personae are never intimidated, cowed, or neurotic; they are never Thurber men.[4] But it is absolutely impossible—not to mention ludicrous—to imagine Eliot and his impotent male personae "dancing the dance of the phallus." It is as if his early poetry were constantly a Lawrentian diagnosis of his own male "deficiency." A catalog of the personae encountered in Eliot's poetry helpfully summarizes the problem. We have "Gerontion," that "old man in a dry month," and the dislocated, voyeuristic male speaker of "La Figlia che Piange." There is J. Alfred Prufrock, fraught with trepidations of male menopause, whose tormented love song ends in an especially sad sort of wet dream: "We have lingered in the chambers of the sea," he says of the mermaids who will never sing to him, "until human voices wake us and we drown." There is the young man of "Rhapsody on a Windy Night," whose sortie into a sexual wilderness concludes with the fragmentary, self-mortifying line: "The last twist of the knife." And there are the many barren voices of *The Waste Land,* in this case both masculine and feminine. In short, Eliot's personae are—to borrow Pound's terms in "The Garden"—almost always "exquisitely," "excessively" disaffected, bored, and impotent. Eliot is simply incapable of assuming the phallic vigor or the cherubic scorn of *Lustra.* He writes from *within* the aristocratic malaise to which Pound's Whitmanesque speaker in "The Garden" so noticeably offers himself as an exception. This marks a great difference between the two men and helps explain why *Lustra* and *The*

Waste Land, though they share so many concerns, are finally so utterly different in tone and disposition. Pound's work is in a major key and is satirical and Whitmanesque in emphasis; Eliot's is in a minor key and is tragic and gothic in emphasis.

How does Frost fit into these equations? In poems such as "Putting in the Seed" Frost takes on a remarkable phallic vigor and fertility, implicitly gendering poetic creativity masculine (and also heterosexual). The same emphases are felt in his account of "the figure a poem makes," as has often been noticed: "The figure is the same as for love," he says, and follows out a description delicately sexual, both in its imagery and its rhythm. "Putting in the Seed" depends upon a traditional, indeed ancient, figure: the phallus as a "plow" that makes fertile the "feminine" land. It is a poem about "husbandry," in every sense of the word: man is to woman as farmer is to field. Katherine Kearns has suggested that Frost's work generalizes this idea by associating imperatives of form and order with masculinity, and "barrierlessness," chaos, and insubordination with femininity (2). She concludes that for Frost "the work of manhood" is "to urge control on the uncontrollable, to impose upon its own 'femaleness'—that which embodied in women seems to be randomly destructive—moderation and orderliness" (21). Working from certain insights of French feminist theory, Kearns proposes to gender the dialectic that recurs throughout Frost's work, a dialectic in which "form" and "wildness" exist in indecisive antagonism. If in "Putting in the Seed" springtime planting and sexual insemination are analogues, then we may draw a broad conclusion: the conflict in Frost's poetry between insubordinate natural forces and the forms he imposes on them is always also, indirectly and residually, a conflict between the feminine and the masculine, or between feminine and masculine *subject positions:* to speak for order and culture is to speak as the Father, to speak for insubordination and nature is to speak as Woman. In a chapter about early agricultural myths, Simone de Beauvoir writes in *The Second Sex:* "The Other—she is passivity confronting activity, diversity that destroys unity, matter as opposed to form, disorder against order." De Beauvoir then quotes an apposite passage from Pythagoras: "'There is a good principle, which has created order, light, and man; and a bad principle, which has created chaos, darkness, and woman'" (80). These oppositions (though not necessarily these judgments) certainly govern "The Birthplace," a seldom-discussed lyric from *West-Running Brook:*

> Here further up the mountain slope
> Than there was ever any hope,
> My father built, enclosed a spring,
> Strung chains of wall round everything,
> Subdued the growth of earth to grass,
> And brought our various lives to pass.
> A dozen girls and boys we were.
> The mountain seemed to like the stir,
> And made of us a little while—
> With always something in her smile.
> Today she wouldn't know our name.
> (No girl's, of course, has stayed the same.)
> The mountain pushed us off her knees.
> And now her lap is full of trees.
>
> (*CPPP* 243)

Most remarkable is what "The Birthplace" omits to mention, as Kearns points out: the mother that presumably had something to do with "bringing" a dozen girls and boys "to pass." The poem concerns instead—and this quite literally—the Founding Father. "The Birthplace" seems written out of the dispensation de Beauvoir describes early in *The Second Sex:* "With the advent of patriarchal institutions, the male laid eager claim to his posterity. It was still necessary to grant the mother a part in procreation, but it was conceded only that she carried and nourished the living seed, created by the father alone" (8). Even so, the name of the mother is repressed only inefficiently in "The Birthplace," as Frost subtly acknowledges. In fact, her role is not so much repressed as *displaced* onto the mountain itself, which the father "husbands" and makes fertile, rather like the man in "Putting in the Seed," and which "pushes" the children off her "knees" once they have grown. The displacement (or repression) of the mother issues, I think, from fear: that is what the sardonic, quietly troubling smile of the mountain-mother is meant to suggest. She is enigmatic and only temporarily subject to mastery. In any case, the allegory could hardly be clearer. This homestead is an enclave of patriarchal order imposed on an unruly but nonetheless potentially productive feminine landscape. Moving to a higher level of abstraction we can see that the feminine, as "The Birthplace" implies, is only partly and ephemerally susceptible to masculine orders that would "subdue" it. The "stay" against wilderness figured in "The Birthplace" is but "momentary," a quality that associates it with "the figure a poem makes" in Frost's well-known formulation. The father of this poem is therefore, at least provisionally, also a "father-poet." So far as the father-poet is concerned, to bring a life to pass and to bring a poem to pass are cognate endeavors: both entail "a momentary stay against confusion."

But as always in Frost *something* escapes the father's government. In so gendering the opposition of culture to nature and of order to chaos, "The Birthplace" affiliates Frost's thinking with Hawthorne's, as I have sketched it out above—though not necessarily with Eliot's. In Frost's work the written word is promiscuous and metamorphic, as Katherine Kearns has argued; it is therefore also "feminine," at least as "The Birthplace" figures these things. The writing of poetry becomes the subordination to order—to the rule of the father—of this feminine unruliness. As de Beauvoir definitively puts it: "It is male activity that in creating values has made of existence itself a value; this activity has prevailed over the confused forces of life; it has subdued Nature and Woman" (65). Frost had certainly arrived at a "muscular" (or phallocentric) poetics, though he seldom danced the dance of the phallus *outright.* And yet he arrived at it only at a certain cost of which he remained, I believe, acutely aware: the "occlusion" of what was insubordinately "feminine" in his own temperament. Frost may associate his work as a poet with the work of the father-figures in "The Birthplace" and "Putting in the Seed." But he can also imagine himself as vulnerable in specifically "feminine" ways. His sexual personae remain relatively fluid and mercurial, as he often adopts "subject positions" marked by femininity, as Kearns might say. In his best writing Frost remains in play, as we shall see below in reading "The Last Mowing." He felt the tyranny of what he understood to be the masculine and is as often on the feminine side of the mountain in "The Birthplace" as on the masculine side of the father and the plow. He remains as much elusive as imperial. Kearns astutely writes: "The resolute 'masculine' combatant informed by the essential absurdity of the game he nonetheless plays, Frost generates poetic love from the lips with a wiliness that transcends the stereotypes of gender, even while his characters resolve themselves into just such manly men and hysterical women as one might expect" (51).

Frost's reasons for arriving at a muscular poetics differ somewhat from Pound's in *Lustra.* For Frost, human affection and sexual love—and also the poetic creativity associated with these things—find grounding in a sort of Lucretian naturalism: sexual attraction exists on a continuum with the natural forces even of magnetism and gravity. "A Prayer in Spring" says of the season it petitions: "For *this* is love and nothing else is love" (*CPPP* 22; my emphasis). "Love" is used here in a specifically Lucretian sense. The alliance of human sexual energies and the resurgent energies of spring, as when the sap rises, is unmistakable.

In "making love," that is, we fulfill the larger ends of nature and of God in nature; we become, in fact, a part of nature, no longer alienated from it. The reference in the last stanza of the poem to "God above," and to the "sanctity" he bestows on human couplings, suggests a further context of heterosexual marriage, which the poem apparently naturalizes. It would be difficult clearly to distinguish the specifically Lucretian elements of this poem's sexual ideology from elements more particular to Frost's American cultural situation. But it seems safe to say that Frost's poetry of masculine sexuality *promises* to transcend the arguments about gender and the poet's vocation that obviously limit Pound's more polemical lyrics in *Lustra.* This promise accounts for the lack of polemical energies in "Putting in the Seed," "The Birthplace," "A Prayer in Spring," "The Figure a Poem Makes," and related works—a lack all the more noticeable when we compare them to "Salutation the Second" or "Tenzone," in which Pound ostentatiously "dances the dance of the phallus." Moreover, the women represented in Frost's poetry typically have a coherence and integrity seldom encountered in Eliot's and Pound's writing. Eliot may pine for a love poetry such as Donne wrote, a poetry of a truly "*associated* sensibility." But we have it in full flower in many of Frost's lyrics, in which discourses of sexuality and courtship are in the largest sense always also philosophical and aesthetic in their concerns: he is a writer who might well have read Spinoza (or Lucretius), fallen in love, and understood the two experiences as "organically" unified.

All the same, Frost's poems of the 1910s are touched at times by an evident desire to *codify* gender rather than scrutinize it. His poems then seem oddly off balance. A good example of this occurs in the dramatic poem "The Death of the Hired Man," which depends upon sharply drawn and entirely reassuring distinctions between "feminine" and "masculine" responses to its central dramatic situation: the reappearance at the farm of an aged hired hand. In passages like the following, Frost's language, notwithstanding its colloquial idiom, loses the verve and tension of his finest writing in *North of Boston*—or at least it does to my ear:

> "Warren," she said, "he has come home to die:
> You needn't be afraid he'll leave you this time."
>
> "Home," he mocked gently.
>   "Yes, what else but home?
> It all depends on what you mean by home.
> Of course he's nothing to us, any more

> Than was the hound that came a stranger to us
> Out of the woods, worn out upon the trail."
>
> "Home is the place where, when you have to go there,
> They have to take you in."
> "I should have called it
> Something you somehow haven't to deserve."
> (*CPPP* 43)

The passage pretty much sums up what the poem thinks about gender: masculinity includes justice and reason; femininity, mercy and emotion. The poem is perfectly intelligible in these terms, which is probably why it earned the place of esteem it has always held in genteel American culture. "The Death of the Hired Man" is always *reassuring.* In later years Frost used to cheapen it somewhat with remarks such as these in a *Paris Review* interview: "In 'The Death of the Hired Man' that I wrote long, long ago, long before the New Deal, I put it two ways about home. One would be the manly way: 'Home is the place where, when you go there, They have to take you in.' That's the man's feeling about it. And then the wife says, 'I should have called it / Something you somehow hadn't to deserve.' That's the New Deal, the feminine way of it, the mother way. You don't have to deserve your mother's love. You have to deserve your father's. He's more particular. One's a Republican, one's a Democrat. The father is always a Republican toward his son, and his mother's always a Democrat" (*CPPP* 885). Even so rigid a scheme as this, when imposed on the poem, does little injustice to its complexities. To my ear, its lines are at times too fully accredited, too self-satisfactory, though it has beautiful moments. "The Death of the Hired Man" provides an example of a kind of thinking Frost describes, in a well-known letter to Louis Untermeyer, as "formulaic." More unstable and intriguing, with regard to questions of gender, are poems such as "A Hundred Collars," "The Grindstone," "The Last Mowing," and "The Code," which acquire a purchase on the language of gender not found in "The Death of the Hired Man." In the latter poem, the writing is perhaps too fully invested in that language; in the former poems, the writing *assesses* as well as speaks it and thereby suggests *un*-formulaic possibilities that lie beyond the boundaries of form and custom.

Intimations of a muscular poetics of the sort practiced by Pound occur often in Frost's prose writings. There, we find ample evidence of Frost's efforts to reposition the vocation of poetry within a specifically *masculine* arena and to develop a muscular poetics of his own. A good example of these efforts is "Some Definitions by Robert Frost," a collection of remarks that first appeared in a brochure released by his publisher under the title *Robert Frost: The Man and His Work* (1923) and which was afterwards reprinted in various publicity materials and on the dust jackets of his books. These brief remarks provide a fine example of a public persona that Frost often adopted as a poet. "Sometimes I have my doubts of words altogether, and I ask myself what is the place of them. They are worse than nothing unless they do something; unless they amount to deeds, as in ultimatums or battle-cries. They must be flat and final like the show-down in poker, from which there is no appeal. My definition of poetry (if I were forced to give one) would be this: words that have become deeds" (*CPPP* 701). This is an especially ingratiating example of Frost's "social repositioning" of poetry—an example of how, in certain situations, he "takes himself" as a writer. He speaks here in his most readily available voice, his most popular and highly socialized voice: assertive, honest, sincere, so direct as to doubt "of words altogether"—quite a remark for a *poet* to make. He will define poetry only if "forced" to do so, though this only begs a question: Who is forcing him to do it here (for define it he does)? The self-assured (if nonetheless embattled) tone *almost* discourages us from dwelling too much on the attractive vagueness of the claims actually being made in this passage. How is a poem *specifically* like a "battle cry" or an "ultimatum"? Why the martial metaphors? In what sense is a poem a "deed"?

In speaking of "ultimatums" and "battle cries" Frost seems instinctively to understand Burke's point in *Counter-Statement,* in the passage quoted above: "If the aesthetic had no *purpose* outside itself, the corollary seemed to be that the aesthetic had no *result* outside itself. Logically there was no cogency in such an argument, but psychologically there was a great deal." In "Some Definitions" Frost affirms the psychological cogency of this idea. Words, and by extension poems, are "worse than nothing unless they do something; unless they amount to deeds." His frame of reference and stoic tone recognizably belong to the competitive, masculine world of American business. We are on the battlefield, at the poker table. Women may write poetry but by the logic of gender they cannot write poetry of precisely *this* kind. Moreover, Frost's "definition" of poetry remarkably leaves out of account all the seductive, charming, sensuous, merely *pleasurable* satisfactions that the writing and reading of poetry afford—satisfactions that had been gendered "feminine" in American culture. If in America "poetry" named a vocation from which masculinity had been alienated, then definitions such as Frost's reposition poetry in such a way as to alienate *femininity* noticeably. Here, poetry is the sublimation of aggressive instincts—something like the "moral equivalent of war," to adapt William James's well-known phrase—as Frost's masculine poet-figure engages in what Theodore Roosevelt called "the strenuous life." I am thinking of remarks like the following, from Roosevelt's book of that title: "We need," he writes, "the iron qualities that must go with true manhood. We need the positive virtues of resolution, of courage, of indomitable will, of power to do without shrinking the rough work that must always be done" (257). The Rooseveltian rhetoric of Frost's definition of poetry apparently derives from ideals of masculinity common among American men in the early decades of the twentieth century. And on this head, Anthony Rotundo usefully explains that "the obsessions of male writing about manhood in the late nineteenth and early twentieth century—competition, battle, physical aggression, bodily strength, primitive virtues, manly passions—all were inversions of 'feminized' Victorian civilization" (253).

Implicit in Frost's very muscular definition of poetry is that it is a competitive endeavor in which an opponent is presumably vanquished. These ideas color the analogies Frost frequently drew between the writing of poetry and athletic performance. A fine example is his 1936 memorial tribute to Edward Morgan Lewis, a president of the University of New Hampshire who had pitched for the Boston Braves in the 1890s:

> He told me once . . . that he began his interest in poetry as he might have begun his interest in baseball—with the idea of victory—the "Will to Win." He was at an Eisteddfod in Utica, an American-Welsh Eisteddfod, where the contest was in poetry, and a bard had been brought from Wales to give judgment and to pick the winner; and the bard, after announcing the winner and making the compliments which judges make, said he wished the unknown victor would rise and make himself known and let himself be seen. . . . The little "Ted" Lewis sitting there beside his father looked up and saw his father rise as the victor. So poetry to him was prowess from that time on, just as baseball was prowess, as running was prowess. And it was our common ground. I have always thought of poetry as prowess—something to achieve, something to win or lose. (*Collected Prose* 149)

Better known are Frost's remarks in a 1956 article published in *Sports Illustrated*, an article that recalls the phrasing of "Some Definitions by Robert Frost": "Prowess of course comes first, the ability to perform with success in games, in the arts and, come right down to it, in battle. The nearest of kin to the artists in college where we all become bachelors of arts are their fellow performers in baseball, football and tennis" (*CPPP* 835). In thinking about his work in this way, Frost was typical of men of his generation. As Rotundo points out, "if contests mirrored life, life at the end of the nineteenth century seemed more and more to mirror a contest. Repeatedly, men of this era described their lives, and especially their work, in the language of competitive games." Of course, "an underlying structure of competition had, in fact, been built into men's work lives for some time," as Rotundo concedes. But by the latter years of the century "middle-class Americans had gone beyond the element of competition inherent in their economic and political systems. They had begun to *import* competition as a motivating device into activities that were basically solitary" (244). This is precisely what Frost's descriptions of poetry often accomplish, though they also accomplish much more.

But naming poetry as the stuff of battle-cries, ultimatums, or athletics is not entirely characteristic of Frost, as is clear from a letter he wrote to Louis Untermeyer in 1924: "I have come to the conclusion that style in prose or verse is that which indicates how the writer takes himself and what he is saying. . . . I own any form of humor shows fear and inferiority. Irony is simply a kind of guardedness. So is a twinkle. It keeps the reader from criticism. . . . Humor is the most engaging cowardice. With it myself I have been able to hold some of my enemy in play far out of gunshot" (*CPPP* 702–3). Frost perfectly describes his own poetic and epistolary style—how he "takes himself" as a writer, at least in this instance. Nothing could be further from the evasive genius of this "most engaging cowardice" than the talk, in "Some Definitions by Robert Frost," of ultimatums and battle-cries. In the letter to Untermeyer, Frost is thinking more of the *bluff* in poker than of the "showdown." And in sharp contrast to Frost's placement of poetry on a masculine battlefield are these remarks from a talk he gave in 1959: "My own idea of poetry isn't of its climbing on top of the earth. Nor is it of its sitting on top of the earth nor of its standing on top of the earth but of its reclining on top of the earth and giving way to its moods . . . like a spoiled actress, you know, the day after she has been on stage, reclining on top of the world and giving way to her moods" (*Collected Prose* 262). The calling of poetry is here associated not merely with femininity but with a particularly *campy* sort of femininity—a sexual persona Frost rarely adopted in print. With these other descriptions of the work of poetry before us, "Some Definitions of Robert Frost" seems all the more characterized, even *anxiously* so, by a virile masculine ethos.

Vocationally speaking, the assertiveness of the language in "Some Definitions" is itself already somewhat embarrassed. Frost seems to acknowledge that poetry is not *usually* "work" at all: "Sometimes I have my doubts of words altogether, and I ask myself what is the place of them. They are worse than nothing unless they do something." In this he may concede too much. Despite his assertive tone Frost essentially takes up the defensive position with regard to his vocation that Howells occupies in "The Man of Letters as a Man of Business."

One final observation is appropriate. In comparing Frost's definition of poetry in *Robert Frost: The Man and His Work* to the one given in the letter to Untermeyer we should bear in mind that the former is offered publicly, in the commercial context of his publisher's advertisement of his writing, while the latter is made privately to an intimate friend who was among his best readers. It is difficult to imagine Frost representing his art as a "most engaging cowardice" in any publicity brochure released by his publisher in 1923. The noticeably, even reassuringly *masculine* language of "Some Definitions of Robert Frost" perfectly and intuitively reflects his desire to socialize his art among the very broad constituency of the American "general reader"—a category that might include such "big bold" businessmen as Frost later spoke of in his 1938 letter to R. P. T. Coffin. When writing for purposes of establishing that constituency in the early years of his career, Frost probably instinctively acknowledged the anxious pressures of gendered vocational criteria. This may help explain his exaggeration of a masculine ethos that is nevertheless present, in an attenuated form, in many of his other definitions of poetry. The contrast I draw here between his remarks in the brochure and his remarks to Untermeyer may be yet another example of the contrast between the two audiences Frost was always trying to reach: a general readership who might not be alert to the subtle insubordinations of his strong writing and a much more elite sort of reader who undoubtedly would. Frost associated a certain flirtatiousness with poetry, and with the feminine, that simply cannot be assimilated to rigorously masculine vocational ideals, which is why his remarks in "Some Definitions" and his remarks in the 1924 letter to Untermeyer cannot be reconciled. A chain of opposed terms emerges here: public/private, seriousness/humor, masculine/feminine, committed/evasive, rational/emotional, self-controlled/self-indulgent, and orderly/chaotic. The first in each pair of terms bears on the "masculine" posture struck in "Some Definitions," the second on the "feminine" posture struck in the remarks about the "spoiled actress" or, as we shall see below, in "The Last Mowing."

Some such background as I am tracing helps explain why Frost's ideal audience, as Frank Lentricchia describes it, would be "a skeptical and even scoffing masculinized audience whose American cultural formation had made it resistant to poetic reception, but which might receive him in its depth if his were the verse of a writer who is all man and whose poetry does not present itself under the conventional genteel sign of poetry" ("Resentments" 275). His 1942 letter to Lawrance Thompson reveals that Frost believed, at least in certain moods, that he had achieved this aim. It contains another representative anecdote, which, like the one he told to R. P. T. Coffin in 1938, seems to sum up something significant about his own vocational ordeal: "Did I ever tell you how his daughter once caught a magnate reading my NoB [*North of Boston*] early one morning before he thought anyone was up. Why father she stinted, I thought you never read poetry. This isn't poetry he said crossly throwing it into the open fire. The great object of great art is to fool the average man in his first or second childhood into thinking it *isnt* art" (*Selected Letters* 499). The *idea* of art is itself the problem to be gotten around, quite as if poetry *as such* had been compromised beyond recovery as an institution of masculine resort. Frost's interest, here, is entirely in the "average *man*," not in the daughter whom he can, as a poet, simply take for granted. And this time the tables are very satisfactorily turned: the business "magnate," not Frost, is made to feel ashamed of "poetry." Frost does not reveal where he heard the anecdote, but he must have been oddly gratified to hear any businessman say of a book he had authored: "This isn't poetry." Hardly ideal, it is nevertheless considerably better than: "Hell. . . . My wife writes that stuff." The latter remark issues a categorical judgment about poetry's "feminine" irrelevance; the former remark makes a particular judgment about the newly gendered power of *North of Boston*, the book in which Frost had "descended" (as Frank Lentricchia would say) farthest into the masculine vernacular. In *Modernist Quartet*, Lentricchia speaks of the success Frost had "in breaking through the genteel lyric, as if through a cultural chastity belt, a vernacular descent from which [E. C.] Stedman and other genteel cultural critics had outlawed the conversational voice" (86). Frost would have agreed with his business magnate that *North of Boston* was not "poetry." He had arrived at a literary appeal that depended—as did also the art of Mark Twain, according to Van Wyck Brooks—on what I have called the humiliation of literariness itself.

The "Psychogenesis" of a Style: Frost in the "Villages" of America

I have been trying to set out the vocational and the stylistic equations that are of concern both to Van Wyck Brooks and Frost. An artist wants to socialize his art, but since the constituency he would reach seems hostile to the ideals he represents as an artist the only way he can socialize it is by means of a style that forces an important component of his sensibility into eclipse; his style is therefore animated to a degree by motives of self-defense and by a certain embarrassment associated with his vocation. I want to test this proposition in close readings of several letters and poems by Frost, all of which date from about 1913, when he at last began to establish a broad constituency for his poetry. Each of these works directly or indirectly imagines the male poet in America as an alienated, misunderstood, and even somewhat ridiculous figure. These works have particularly to do with the uncertain situation of the poet in what Frost and Pound called the "villages" of America—places that exist as much in imaginary space as in geographical space. That is to say, we can point to the villages of America on a map, but for writers like Pound and Frost they find their real grounding in a particular condition of mind and sensibility that might be called—to adopt Frost's cultural shorthand—"utilitarian," with all that word implies of petty bourgeois mores, capitalist conceptions of what constitutes "work," and philistinism. George Bernard Shaw once remarked that America is "a nation of villagers," and in *Civilization in the United States* the essayist on "The Small Town," Louis Raymond Reid, concurs: the culture of America, Reid argues, is a small town culture, whether we encounter it in Boston or Peoria. In the 1910s and 1920s the attitude a poet takes toward American "village" culture is a fine index of his attitude toward American culture as a whole; the former is often but a figure for the latter, as is clear from the letters and poems I examine in the following pages. After all, these documents date from the era that incubated and brought to birth *Winesburg, Ohio* and *Main Street.* I simply propose that we read Frost's letters and poems about American "villages" in the way we might read Anderson's or Lewis's books: as a species of cultural criticism.

I turn first to a letter that Frost wrote from England to his American friend Sidney Cox in May 1913:

> I like that about the English—they all have time to dig the ground for the unutilitarian flower. I mean the men. It marks the great difference between them and our men. I like flowers you know but I like em wild,

and I am rather the exception than the rule in an American village. Far as I have walked in pursuit of the Cypripedium, I have never met another in the woods on the same quest. Americans will dig for peas and beans and such like utilities but not if they know it for posies. I knew a man who was a byword in five townships for the flowers he tended with his own hand. Neighbors kept hens and let them run loose just to annoy him. I feel as if my education in useless things had been neglected when I see the way the front yards blossom down this road. So I can afford perhaps to yield a little to others for one spring in the cultivation of one form of the beautiful. Next year I go in for daffodils. (*Selected Letters* 71–72)

The English spring of 1913 was the time of the flowering of another kind of poesy: *A Boy's Will,* Frost's first volume of poems, published in London by the English firm of David Nutt. In this letter, Frost plainly tells a parable of his own career.[5] Once again he makes the point that poetry—the cultivation of *un*-utilitarian flowers—is not an accredited vocation for American men: "I like that about the English—they all have time to dig the ground for the unutilitarian flower. I mean the men. It marks the great difference between them and our men." In his subtle way, Frost makes a then-familiar point. Van Wyck Brooks writes in his 1922 essay "The Literary Life": "That old hostility of the pioneers to the special career still operates to prevent in the American mind the powerful, concentrated pursuit of any non-utilitarian way of life: meanwhile everything else in our society tends to check the growth of the spirit and to shatter the confidence of the individual in himself" (193). This had led, Brooks argues, to the social isolation in "utilitarian" Gilded Age America of artists, poets, and intellectuals, and he pursues this thesis at length in *The Ordeal of Mark Twain,* as we have seen. For his part (truly in the slacker spirit), Pound makes an outright virtue of unutilitarian idleness in "Further Instructions," a Whitmanesque lyric originally collected in *Lustra:*

Come, my songs, let us express our baser passions,
Let us express our envy of the man with a steady job and no
worry about the future.
You are very idle, my songs.
I fear you will come to a bad end.
You stand about in the streets,
You loiter at the corners and bus-stops,
You do next to nothing at all.
(95)

Frost is considerably less direct than Pound and Brooks as he continues in the letter to Sidney Cox: "I like flowers you know but I like em wild." This subtle remark acknowledges an antagonism between genteel styles in poetry—for example, the highly refined lyrics of *A Boy's Will*—and the "wild" vernacular poetry that Frost was then assembling into the collection that would soon become *North of Boston,* a book even utilitarian business magnates could read. A similar contrast may be intended between the Cypripedium, a rare orchid, and more common, "vernacular" flora such as daffodils; Frost, an avid botanist, no doubt had something like this in mind. But the main purpose of his letter obviously is to address the social *distinction* of the unutilitarian poetic vocation, not to distinguish between different styles of poetry. In contrast to the vocational letters we have so far examined, this one shows no outright bitterness or sarcasm about life under a "utilitarian" regime. Nor do we sense here the frustrations of the twenty years Frost had waited to establish himself in America as a poet. Whatever isolation or embarrassment he felt while "tending flowers with his own hand"—that is, while writing his idle songs—dissolves into these unpresumptuous remarks: "I am rather the exception than the rule in an American village. Far as I have walked in pursuit of the Cypripedium, I have never met another in the woods on the same quest."

Even so, in the letter to Cox, Frost refers to the same villages described quite differently in another letter written in 1913 to an English friend, the imagist poet F. S. Flint. Alluding to their first meeting at Harold Monro's Poetry Bookshop in London, Frost writes: "I was only too childishly happy in being allowed to make for a moment in a company in which I hadn't to be ashamed of having written verse. Perhaps it will help you understand my state of mind if I tell you that I have lived for the most part in villages where it were better that a millstone were hanged about your neck than that you should own yourself a minor poet" (qtd. in Walsh 86).[6] Here, the stigmata of Frost's vocational martyrdom are plainly evident. Presumably, he refers to his years in the village of Derry, New Hampshire, between 1900 and 1906, where he made a modest living as a farmer but chiefly subsisted on a small annuity from his paternal grandfather. He became convinced that the inheritance had made the townfolk jealous and disdainful. They did not think he worked for a living—a terrible thing for an American man. And what was worse, he wrote *poems.* Occasionally he did try to sell these poems, and for a while earned a little extra money writing short stories and articles for two New England poultry-farming journals, *Farm-Poultry* and the *Eastern Poultryman.* Years later he summed up his situation in conversation with the book collector Louis Mertins: "I suppose my grandfather was right, dead right. I had set up a claim to being a poet, but I was a complete failure—had wasted my life" (Mertins 65). He later recalls an encounter with the town butcher that convinced him to set aside his literary ambitions and find regular employment as a teacher at Pinkerton Academy in Derry:

> Well, in the summer of 1905, one day I drove Old Billy down to Derry depot with two of the kids with me, to get some meat for supper, we had to eat. The butcher came sneering out, knowing very well what I was after, and remembering my account-payable. He eyed the horse up and down, asking if anybody had a lien on him. That determined me as to what I should, or rather *must* do. It was my first clash with realism. There I was with four children and a wife to feed and clothe and doctor—something I was not knowing rascal enough to put across well, at all. I was thirty years old and as great a failure as anybody ever was at the turn of life. Up to that day I had sold exactly five poems. (Mertins 88)[7]

The strictures enforced by Frost's town butcher are perfectly familiar, as least as Frost represents them. Anthony Rotundo assesses them accurately enough: "The division of tasks between the sexes gave a man the power to determine the social status of his whole family," he explains in *American Manhood.* "It was *his* work that marked the place of his wife and children in the world. . . . No wonder he identified himself so fully with his work; in a social sense, he was what he achieved—and so were those he loved" (169).

In the letter to Sidney Cox, Frost transforms these hard vocational experiences into a kind of parable. He is a solitary but not terribly disgruntled quester after "the Cypripedium," or an "unutilitarian gardener." It seems safe to say that in the letter to Cox he intentionally overlooks the resentments expressed outright in the letter to Flint. The humor of the letter to Cox allows Frost to "vent his hatred" of the social conditions that were "thwarting his creative life," to borrow Brooks's somewhat overwrought phraseology in *The Ordeal of Mark Twain.* Frost writes with a twinkle, but the situation he describes, a strict divorce of "utilitarian" and "unutilitarian" values, was the occasion for deep and long-lived regrets. The consequences of a dis-integrated vocation and avocation are set out clearly in the letter to Cox. "Our men," Frost says, will not dig for posies "if they know it." We must suppose that they *will* dig for them if the unutilitarian fact can be called by another name. This is apparently meant as consolation, but its satisfactions remain ambivalent. The *idea* of poetry—not poetry itself—is the problem to be circumvented, as we have seen in Frost's 1942 letter to Lawrance Thompson: "The great object of great art is to fool the average *man* in his first or second childhood into thinking it *isnt* art."

This is precisely the difficulty, according to Brooks, that Mark Twain had faced. It is a peculiarly American cultural dilemma, in which the very term "art" is compromised and in which the serious literary artist achieves a sense of solidarity with a "general" audience only rarely and tenuously.

In Frost's account, then, American men are not completely insensible of the beautiful. They are in fact quite embarrassed by it. The proof is that they play practical jokes to keep that sensibility hidden—in themselves and among their company. In a 1924 letter to Louis Untermeyer, Frost suggests that "any form of humor shows fear and inferiority" and this clearly includes such practical jokes as these (*CPPP* 702). The kind of joking described in the letter to Cox is a means of keeping the odd "unutilitarian" in check, together with the countercultural values he potentially represents: "I knew a man who was a byword in five townships for the flowers he tended with his own hand. Neighbors kept hens and let them run loose just to annoy him." (I think of Brooks's observation that the American man prizes most the literary artist who degrades "as pretentious and absurd everything of a spiritual, aesthetic and intellectual nature.")

A certain habit of gendered self-admonition was in fact quite characteristic of American men, as is clear from the letters, diaries, and other writings quoted in Rotundo's *American Manhood.* I will give only one example here. Rotundo cites Artemis B. Muzzey, who suggests in *The Young Man's Friend* (1836) that the American man "is never . . . so uneasy as when seated by his own fireside; for he feels, while conversing with his kindred, that he is making no money. And as for fireside reading . . . 'he reads no book but his ledger'" (qtd. in Rotundo 175–76). So much for the absurd, "unutilitarian" flowers of poesy; for American men in the late nineteenth century, the "feminine" and the "unutilitarian" simply *were* the absurd. Rotundo makes a useful observation in discussing "the woman within" the American man: "The fear of womanly men became a significant cultural issue in the late nineteenth century, one discussed by men in a new, gendered language of manly scorn. Men in the late nineteenth century began to sort themselves out into hardy, masculine types and gentle, feminine types" (265). This kind of "sorting" is the subject of Frost's letter to Sidney Cox about his solitary quest for "the Cypripedium" and also, implicitly, of his letter to F. S. Flint about the martyrdom that (male) poets suffer in American villages. Neither letter is intemperate or excessively bitter, but there is no doubting the anxieties to which they direct our attention. Gender codes became a subject of urgent public concern in America during this period. The influential psychologist G. Stanley Hall published in 1908 an article entitled "Feminization in Schools and Home: The Undue Influences of Women Teachers." In it he makes the following claim: "[Gender] differentiation ought to be pushed to the very uttermost and everything should be welcome that makes men more manly and women more womanly; while, on the other hand, all that makes for identity [between them] is degenerative" (qtd. in Rotundo 269). One need not have subscribed to these views in order to have felt their pressure.

"The Last Mowing" bears interestingly on these questions. It precedes "The Birthplace" in *West-Running Brook,* in which both poems were first collected, and in fact constitutes a "feminine" alternative to that poem's "muscular" (or "phallocentric") vocational implications. Katherine Kearns has suggested that "the iambic foot becomes in Frost's poetry a kind of moral baseline, a strong voice. . . . The anapest and the dactyl become in this context not merely melodic variations but markers of weakness." Additionally, "feminine rhymes, with their implication of passivity, tend in this iambic context inevitably to designate a departure from seriousness or from control" (74). These are astute remarks, and in light of them we can see that "The Last Mowing" differs considerably from "The Birthplace."

> There's a place called Far-away Meadow
> We never shall mow in again,
> Or such is the talk at the farmhouse:
> The meadow is finished with men.
> Then now is the chance for the flowers
> That can't stand mowers and plowers.
> It must be now, though, in season
> Before the not mowing brings trees on,
> Before trees, seeing the opening,
> March into a shadowy claim.
> The trees are all I'm afraid of,
> That flowers can't bloom in the shade of;
> It's no more the men I'm afraid of;
> The meadow is done with the tame.
> The place for the moment is ours
> For you, oh tumultuous flowers,
> To go to waste and go wild in,
> All shapes and colors of flowers,
> I needn't call you by name.
>
> (242–43)

Instead of the iambic rhythms on which Frost usually depends, we have anapestic triplets lightly supporting three-beat lines: triplets within triplets for a delicately turned lyric waltz. We also find, significantly I think, fourteen feminine, that is to say unstressed, endings out of nineteen total lines. The levity of the meter and of the feminine endings contributes much to the tone of the poem as well as to our feeling about its speaker's identity and gender. We might first suppose that a child speaks, and that we are to understand the feeling of solidarity with the flowers—as against the "mowers and plowers"—as one of Youth against Age. But attending to the language of gender and to the gender of prosody suggests another, likelier possibility: that the speaker is marked more by femininity than by youth. We are certainly asked to think of the mowers and plowers that oppose the speaker as preeminently *masculine;* this is what the speaker most notices about them. And these men, these Frostian mowers and plowers, contend for dominion over the flowering field, as in a battle, with trees that are themselves proprietary martial figures who "march into a shadowy claim."

My sense is that Frost is himself engaging, here, in some literary cross-dressing, for when we consider "The Last Mowing" in light of the letter to Sidney Cox about "unutilitarian" gardening, yet another possibility presents itself: the speaker is not merely feminized but is also somehow made *vocationally* specific—at least subsidiarily. "The Last Mowing" speaks from and to that place in Frost's personality that had been forced into "occlusion" by the "utilitarian" imperatives of American masculinity. Like the poet of Frost's little parable in the letter to Cox, the speaker of "The Last Mowing" prefers her flowers wild and "*un*-utilitarian": "The place for the moment is ours / For you, oh tumultuous flowers, / To go to waste and go wild in." So far is the speaker from masculinity, as this poem seems to understand it, that she refuses even the mildly proprietary gesture of *naming* the flowers. Alone in the woods together with her "wasted" flowers, Frost's speaker is released, if only for a moment, from the dominion and oversight of men—and released, I would add, from the tyranny of *masculinity* itself. That is undoubtedly what this subtle, unprepossessing poem is about. The vocational letters to Sidney Cox and F. S. Flint help us understand why Frost did, on occasion, adopt a feminine sexual persona; they let us see what that persona *does* for him—what "occluded" aspects of his sensibility it expresses. "The Last Mowing" emerges, at least in part, as a kind of confession of his sins against masculinity, a confession the mere expression of which provides its own absolution. Reading this poem persuades me that the burly Rooseveltian postures Frost sometimes strikes in his accounts of the poetic vocation—for example, his claim that the poet's words "must be flat and final like the show-down in poker, from which there is no appeal"—are maintained through considerable, or at least noticeable, exertions. "The Last Mowing" registers the relaxation of those exertions and does so with a tact communicated as much in the poem's delicate form as in its theme. And if Frost identifies with "plowers and mowers," he is thinking not of the ones figured here but of the mower whom his speaker succeeds in "A Tuft of Flowers": this "mower in the dew" loves flowers so much that he "un-utilitarianly" leaves a tuft of them behind to "flourish" from "sheer morning gladness at the brim." It is a figure, as Frost liked to point out, for the work of the poet, and there is, within the terms of our culture, nothing particularly "masculine" about it.

In his subtlest vocational poems Frost arrives at a kind of androgyny: his mower-poets are always also ever so slightly feminine, as much on the side of the flowers of the field as on the side of the order that would "subdue" or harvest them. But this androgyny was hard to sustain in a cultural regime whose conception of gender was ferociously binary. Rigidly binary gender codes such as those G. Stanley Hall enforced had far-ranging cultural consequences, as Anthony Rotundo demonstrates: "The tender, reflective male and the tough, assertive one became cultural symbols. . . . The former not only bore the social stigma of femininity in a society that elevated gender separation to the highest level of principle, but he also was a threat to his nation and even to the progress of human civilization. To have too much of 'the woman within' was a personal problem for a man in the late nineteenth century. More than that, it made him a living symbol, a moral and social mistake" (270). The utilitarian neighbors of Frost's letter, and the unutilitarian gardeners against whom they jovially operate, are variations of opposed types quite familiar to Americans of Frost's generation. Given the developments Rotundo describes it is not at all surprising that Frost became a shrewd observer of embattled masculinity, as is evident in poems such as "The Grindstone," "A Hundred Collars," "The Code," and (more indirectly) in "The Last Mowing." The letters I have examined suggest that Frost existed at times in an *abstract* relation to the ideal of masculinity—a relation that enabled him to scrutinize the gender role he felt called upon to perform. "The Code" offers a fine example of this. Its title refers to the unstated rules governing relations among male farm laborers. Their "code" has everything to do with gender: it manages competitive masculinity, as this competition is expressed, for example, in what the laborers themselves refer to as the practice of "bulling." In "bulling," one man challenges the masculinity of another by driving him so hard at work that he overwhelms and therefore *humiliates* him. Poems like "The Code" make clear the extent to which gender identity had come to be deeply invested in a man's performance at work. Frost's letters about his own poetic vocation leave no doubt that he had himself made this investment.[8]

A subtler kind of self-examination than the one indicated in Artemis Muzzey's *Young Man's Friend* occurs in Frost's vocational writings. He does not sit by the hearth reproaching himself with ledgers, but he nonetheless engages in a little gender sorting of his own with respect to "the woman within." The remarkable complexity of his 1913 letter to Sidney Cox is that, with considerably more sophistication, Frost is playing the same game he describes. The humor of his letter ingeniously keeps his own "inner seriousness" as a poet in "occlusion," even as it indirectly celebrates his ultimate success in that role with the publication of *A Boy's Will* and with the preparation for the press of his second, much more "masculine" volume, *North of Boston.* He socializes his vocation by identifying himself—that is, by means of this borrowed rhetorical maneuver—with the "occupational psychosis" motivating these utilitarian villagers. He thereby strikes up an alliance. The irony is that the villagers are hostile to the same *unutilitarian* patterns of life that Frost, in effect, endeavors to recommend by tapping the resources of a utilitarian morality. "Utilitarian" villagers and business magnates resort to joking to manage their residual unutilitarian, "feminine" tendencies—these jokes "sort" the real men from the womanly ones; Frost similarly resorts to humor to protect and indirectly reassert the same values that his cultural adversaries set up for ridicule.

This complex rhetorical situation is indicative of the uneasy solidarity of literary artists and businessmen that I have already described in connection with Howells's essay "The Man of Letters as a Man of Business." None of the caginess and indirection found in the letter to Cox is present in the letter on the same vocational theme written to the *English* poet Flint, where Frost's grievance candidly shows: "I was only too childishly happy in being allowed to make for a moment in a company in which I hadn't to be ashamed of having written verse." Then again, in England the cultural situation of the male poet was quite different. Frost's letter to Sidney Cox is clarified by an observation of David Bromwich's regarding "Two Tramps in Mud Time." He refers to Richard Poirier's earlier remarks on the same work: "The whole poem has been tipped off balance by a touch of bad faith. At the bottom of it, Poirier believes, is a distrust of poetry. I agree but would add: a distrust of being seen to be a poet. The poem lets us see two tramps, and a man whom we know is a poet because he writes poems, this one among them. But Frost-as-poet is not, so to speak, figured in the poem" (118). Its humor notwithstanding, the letter to Cox very subtly shows the same discomfort at being seen to be a poet, a consequence of the fact that Frost adopts as much as rejects the utilitarian mores of the villagers he describes: he figures himself as a poet only indirectly. Frost's distrust is not simply of being seen to be a poet but also, in a sense, of *seeing himself* as a poet, which is why Frank Lentricchia is correct in speaking of Frost's "conscience": "For Frost and other young poetic modernists, manliness was quite simply the culturally excluded principle in a life given to poetry that made it difficult for the modern American male to enter the literary life with a clean conscience" (*Modernist Quartet* 92–93). This may account for the peculiar element of vocational self-incrimination I find in the letters to R. P. T. Coffin and Lawrance Thompson discussed already, as well as in the letter to Cox on posies. The anxieties these letters partly obscure and partly express derive from Frost's vocational troubles. Their good-humored, accommodating rhetoric reflects his decision to manage these troubles within, rather than without, what Kenneth Burke would call the utilitarian (and masculine) "occupational psychosis" of America. We have seen how Randolph Bourne and Van Wyck Brooks took for granted the culturally oppositional status of poetry in America. This indicates how difficult a task Frost set himself when he attempted to stretch a utilitarian "occupational psychosis" to accommodate the life of poetry or to stretch the life of poetry to embrace masculine, utilitarian habits of mind. He had a long way to go in America to bring poetry *agreeably* under the regime of what he happily called "the trial by market everything must come to."

The humor of the letter to Cox, not the candor of the one to Flint, would characterize most of Frost's public references to the artist's vocation in America.[9] Very characteristically, he remained throughout his career both the solitary poet ("Far as I have walked in pursuit of the Cypripedium, I have never met another in the woods on the same quest") *and* the village joker—both unutilitarian outsider and utilitarian insider. These contrary tendencies mark his desire to think of himself and of his vocation as at once exceptional and thoroughly ordinary, which perhaps confirms the sincerity of his remark to Louis Untermeyer in a 1924 letter: "Many sensitive natures have plainly shown by their style that they took themselves lightly in self-defense" (*CPPP* 702). Frost writes to Cox from England, but the way he "takes" himself is consistent with how he felt he must take himself in the New England villages—American, utilitarian villages—where he would soon, again, be digging as a man for "posies." In a telling aside, Brooks writes in *The Ordeal of Mark Twain:* "And as for Mark Twain, the protective coloration that enabled him to maintain his standing in pioneer society ended by giving him the position which he craved, the position of an acknowledged leader" (251). Read "utilitarian" for "pioneer"—Brooks would approve the substitution—and the analogy to Frost's own strategies of protective coloration becomes clear. Brooks speaks of the "psychogenesis" of Twain's humor. To a remarkable degree, the psychogenesis of Frost's style, and of his most memorable and celebrated public persona, was very much the same: the ordeal of the literary life in America.

"Good Hours": Frost's Accommodating Intransigence

I am trying to bring out the emotional and personal necessities behind some of Frost's most distinctive stylistic strategies and public personae to show how they are associated with the careful management of a felt quality of difference in his personality, a "difference" closely linked to his work as a poet and to certain anxieties about gender. I use the term "difference" as Frost himself uses it in his introduction to *King Jasper:* "How does a man come on his difference, and how does he feel about it when he first finds it out? . . . There is such a thing as being too willing to be different. And what shall we say to people who are not only willing but anxious?" (*CPPP* 741). It is perhaps a hard point for us to understand, given the position that the term "difference" now holds in writing about literature and culture. We must accept difference in ourselves, Frost suggests, with skepticism and suspicion. Advocacy of this skepticism perfectly complements his remarks on humor later in the same essay, as well as his allusion there to the "ordeal" of Mark Twain. Frost asks us to accept two related propositions: that "difference" occasions social anxiety and that literary style is a problem of "charm" and "bearability"—in other words, a problem of overcoming the frictions potentially associated with social difference. Clearly, this has much to do with Frost's own ordeal. He had come upon his "difference" as a poet, just as Twain had come upon his difference as a writer. In the letters to Sidney Cox, R. P. T. Coffin, and others, we see evidence of his efforts to accommodate that social difference to accredited vocational ideals in capitalist, patriarchal America. Throughout this study, I will be arguing that Frost could not remain satisfied with the purely "inward sense of vocation" that David Bromwich (rightly, it seems to me) associates with modern poetry (*Choice* 111). Frost's writing argues that vocation, even the poetic one, is necessarily and fortunately a matter of socialization—a matter of *consolidating* fellowship, not of escaping its consequences. This is why he ultimately defers to the very forces of social conformity that seem to trouble his letter to F. S. Flint.

I have said that Frost remained the village joker. By this I mean that he remained, and desired to remain, as much like the villagers described in the letter to Cox as unlike them—despite his potential difference as a poet. Frost wanted to find a way, in his poetry, poetics, and vocation, to balance and symbolize two tendencies: the tendency toward "conformity" on the one hand and toward extravagance and difference on the other. The pattern of wandering off from a community, as in pursuit of the "Cypripedium," and then of return to it recurs throughout his poetry. In keeping with this he constructs in his essays and letters on poetics a subtle and persuasive defense of formalist poetry, a defense that acknowledges even the necessities of "conformity," as he puts it in a 1934 letter to his daughter Lesley Frost Francis. Motives of "conformity"—he means both social and aesthetic conformity—must always in his view balance and play against impulses of extravagance, in both poem and poet. Hence a basic dialectic of "inner form," or "formity," and "outer form," or "conformity," lies at the very heart of his poetics, as I pointed out in the introduction to this study. This helps explain the peculiar mixture in Frost's literary personality of conservative inertia and of insubordination, qualities that derive from and also reflect what I have been calling Frost's vocational ordeal: a very personal experience of at once fitting in and standing out, of conformity and extravagance. I recognize in the term "ordeal," then, a broader range of meanings than Van Wyck Brooks gives it in his study of Twain. As I use it, the term should be understood to embrace the ordeal-like implications of Frost's own description in "The Constant Symbol" of the movements of the poet within the poem: "Every poem is an epitome of the great predicament; a figure of the will braving alien entanglements" (*CPPP* 787). This great predicament includes, as he puts it, the experience of the individualistic "discipline" of the self working against and within the "harsher discipline from without." These outer "disciplines" represent social forces of the sort subtly figured in Frost's vocational letters—forces that encourage us to conform to socially accredited patterns of living—as well as the "forces" and "inertia" specific to language and poetic form, as we shall see in chapters 2 and 3.

The better to illustrate these matters I turn now to a poem that registers Frost's deference to potentially unfriendly social authorities with extraordinary subtlety and grace. I refer to "Good Hours," published in 1915 as a coda to the first American edition of *North of Boston:*

> I had for my winter evening walk—
> No one at all with whom to talk,
> But I had the cottages in a row
> Up to their shining eyes in snow.
>
> And I thought I had the folk within:
> I had the sound of a violin;
> I had a glimpse through curtain laces
> Of youthful forms and youthful faces.
>
> I had such company outward bound.
> I went till there were no cottages found.
> I turned and repented, but coming back
> I saw no window but that was black.
>
> Over the snow my creaking feet
> Disturbed the slumbering village street
> Like profanation, by your leave,
> At ten o'clock of a winter eve.
>
> (102)

In *The Philosophy of Literary Form* (1941) Kenneth Burke speaks of the "citational bridges for linking the imagery within a poem to the poet's life outside the poem" (73). In "Good Hours" the "citational bridges" are plainly marked. The poem shares with the 1913 letter to Sidney Cox both theme and dramatic pattern: an odd man given to walking outward bound where his benighted townsfolk haven't the inclination to follow him. The poem refines the symbolic pattern of this sentence in the letter: "Far as I have walked in pursuit of the Cypripedium, I have never met another in the woods on the same quest." (Almost as if he were sending the same message twice, Frost enclosed a manuscript copy of "Good Hours" in the next letter he mailed to Sidney Cox after the vocational letter on "posies.") The analogy between the letter and the poem is in fact quite close: as we shall see, the distinction of the speaker in "Good Hours" marks him, within the imagery of Frost's writings at the time, specifically as a poet. There is, then, a movement outward bound in both the letter and the poem, but both also describe a return. As the foregoing discussion suggests, in the letter this return to community—to the company and sympathy of the villagers—is already implied in the conformist *style* with which Frost describes the wandering off itself. That is to say, his style shows that although he is an "unutilitarian" poet he can fluently speak the jocular language of "utilitarian" villagers. The style of "Good Hours" is more complex, but I will show that it too is as much concerned with a symbolic return to the village—and with an accommodation within its cultural boundaries—as with an extravagance from it.

In "Good Hours," Frost's characteristic humor qualifies the experience of solitude, keeping it from assuming a melancholy or pitiful cast. If he slyly adopts the utilitarian morality of the villagers in the letter to Cox, playing the same game that they play, he does something similar in "Good Hours," this time with plainly evident sarcasm and self-awareness: "I turned and *repented,*" the speaker says, as if in mocking acknowledgment that his extravagance marks a serious transgression. The ambivalence of this appeal to the villagers' consent is perfectly expressed in the sardonic politeness of the last quatrain:

> Over the snow my creaking feet
> Disturbed the slumbering village street
> Like profanation, by your leave,
> At ten o'clock of a winter eve.

The strategy is the same one taken in the short poem "In Neglect," first collected in *A Boy's Will:*

> They leave us so to the way we took,
> As two in whom they were proved mistaken,
> That we sit sometimes in the wayside nook,
> With mischievous, vagrant, seraphic look,
> And *try* if we cannot feel forsaken.
> (*CPPP* 25)

The speakers of both "Good Hours" and "In Neglect" make a show of being properly penitent about their vagrancy; they *try* to feel forsaken. Moreover, they call attention to the fact that they are making such a show: the tone emphasized by the italic in the last line of "In Neglect" works almost as plainly in "Good Hours."

When *A Boy's Will* was still in press, Frost described the biographical situation of "In Neglect" to Ezra Pound, who later made use of the story, much to Frost's consternation, in a published review of the volume: "There is perhaps as much of Frost's personal tone" in this poem, Pound wrote, "as in anything else" in *A Boy's Will.* "It is to his wife, written when his grandfather and his uncle had disinherited him of a comfortable fortune and left him in poverty because he was a useless poet instead of a money-getter" (*Literary Essays* 383). The details of the account are not entirely accurate, perhaps because Pound shaped them to meet his own concerns, perhaps because Frost himself misrepresented his situation.[10] But the spirit if not the letter of Pound's remarks seems faithful to the poem. "In Neglect," like the letters to Cox and Flint, is a strategy for handling difficulties associated with the poetic vocation. In turn, "Good Hours" addresses, much more subtly, the theme of the culturally "disinherited" poet. Richard Poirier remarks of "Good Hours": "The walker here imposes himself on the sleeping scene and on the other people as a poet living within, escaping from, and then returning to certain decorums" (*Robert Frost* 90). He later points out that "In Neglect" concerns more or less the same imposition: "The lovers are displaying precisely the capacities for imagination that can be released in Frost by the achievement of some dialectical, in-and-out relationship to decorum." Poirier rightly goes on to suggest that this dialectical play probably has, in this poem as in "Good Hours," specifically vocational implications, for "by the phrase 'the way we took' the poem means his [Frost's] chosen but . . . precarious vocation as a poet, a 'neglected' one" (102).

One source for the envoi to "Good Hours" may lie in Robert Browning's dramatic monologue of a culturally dislocated painter, "Fra Lippo Lippi." The poem begins with a line perhaps echoed in the last quatrain of "Good Hours":

> I am poor brother Lippo, by your leave!
> You need not clap your torches to my face.
> Zooks, what's to blame? you think you see a monk!
> What, 'tis past midnight, and you go the rounds,
> And here you catch me at an alley's end
> Where sportive ladies leave their doors ajar?[11]

Of course, the speaker in "Good Hours" is up to nothing so indiscreet as Fra Lippo Lippi's visit to the alley's end. His countercultural transgression has nothing to do with "sportive ladies," and it is only ten o'clock, not "past midnight." His townsfolk are not even interested enough in his extravagance to be scandalized by it. "Poor brother Lippo" at least has *occasion* to deliver a line ("by your leave") that, in the mouth of Frost's speaker, carries a noticeably impotent irony: no one arrests him, no one is there for him to ask leave of. The speaker's self-conscious repetition of the possessive verb "have" six times in the first nine lines of Frost's poem only emphasizes what he points out to begin with: he has "no one at all with whom to talk." Or rather, he has only "such company" as he can glimpse through "curtain laces." There is the "sound of a violin" and "youthful," apparently engaging faces. These townspeople are by no means especially dull or listless, even if they do go to bed before ten. And yet despite all this the sarcastic address of the last eight lines shows that the poem is touched by something like a lack of sympathy. That is what most intrigues me, both for what it indicates about Frost's problem of vocation and for what it can tell us about the larger problem of relations between village intellectuals and "Middle Americans."

Given the vocational theme of "Good Hours," and given its possible allusion to Browning, another irony becomes apparent: Frost's speaker certainly cannot abash the philistine villagers by announcing, as the artist Fra Lippo eventually does, that the "Cosimo of the Medici" is his patron. In democratic, utilitarian America, no aristocracy or plutocracy patronizes artists; nor do grandfathers, as Frost apparently told Pound when discussing "In Neglect." The "trial by market," as Frost puts it in several letters and poems of the mid-1910s, is the only resource for poets and businessmen alike. In short, Frost was attempting to work through—and Pound merely to denounce—an American cultural situation in which intellectuals and artists had become "estranged," as Andrew Ross puts it in *No Respect: Intellectuals and Popular Culture* (1989). Ross explains that in America this situation has its origins "in the historical lack of an intelligentsia whose cultural authority and prestige could be relatively autonomous from the economic prestige valorized by a business culture"—or by what Frost called the "trial by market everything must come to." By contrast, "in Europe, the power and authority of the cultural establishment . . . endured historically because of its accumulation of *precapitalist* prestige, originally endowed by aristocratic patronage" (62–63)—in other words, by the patronage of such families as the Medicis, whom Pound (after Fra Lippo) loved to cite. Such was the cultural problem with which the American poet and intellectual was faced.

The matter of overriding interest to me is how Frost manages this vocational theme. He may intend a pun on poetic "feet" in the lines: "Over the snow my creaking feet / Disturbed the slumbering village street." Frost makes similar puns elsewhere, and the reference in "Good Hours" to "creaking feet" seems to emphasize the vocational context of the poem. The idea that poetry (his "creaking feet") somehow "disturbs" the peace of such villages as the one depicted here is evident enough from the letters to Cox and Flint. Any derogatory force in the epithet "creaking," at least insofar as it is applied to poetic "feet," is probably satirically borrowed, so to speak, from the villagers themselves.

Frost took great care in assembling and ordering his poems into collections and I find it significant that he affixed "Good Hours" to the first American edition of *North of Boston* almost as a coda. (The poem had not appeared in David Nutt's English edition.) Not listed in the table of contents, it is set off from the rest of the book spatially by a blank page and typographically by italic type.[12] The main body of the volume takes no notice of "Good Hours," which may be a bibliographical means of shoring up the themes I have identified in the poem. Much of *North of Boston* was written in New England by a poet who at times, apparently, could feel estranged from the people he was writing about and living among. Frost's placement of "Good Hours" in the first American edition is therefore particularly fitting. It stands in relation to the volume as a whole just as its last two stanzas stand in relation to the poem as a whole. In effect, the bibliographical gesture of framing what Frost calls in the dedication "this book of people" with "Good Hours" gently but precisely qualifies the fellowship of poet and villagers, just as the sardonic gesture "by your leave" qualifies what was after all only the imaginary fellowship of the speaker's walk "outward bound": "I thought I had the folk within." In this respect "Good Hours" functions as a kind of synecdoche for *North of Boston* and therefore makes an appropriate end piece: we can take the part for the whole.

Of course, for Frost it was not so much a question literally of living in New England villages as it was a question of becoming a poet within the "occupational psychosis" that those villages may be taken to represent. I do not wish to confine the significance of "Good Hours" to its biographical situation, but its complex tone does seem to derive from the same cluster of tensions in Frost's imagination that shaped such incompatible treatments of his problem of vocation as the letters to Flint and Cox. With regard to its author, it, too, answers the question posed in the introduction to *King Jasper:* "How does a man come on his difference, and how does he feel about it when he first finds it out?" Unless we take these social tensions and resentments into account, such words as "repent" and "profanation," with their associated energies, are likely to seem incongruous given the situation with which the poem has most immediately and literally to do: a nighttime walk through a quiet New England village. My arguments, then, depend upon our reading "Good Hours" as one among many parables of his experience in American villages that Frost told in the 1910s and upon our taking for granted that the concerns of these other parables—which Frost usually relayed in letters—are carried over into this short lyric, as obviously I believe they are.

Kenneth Burke writes, in *Attitudes toward History:* "One 'owns' his social structure insofar as one can subscribe to it *wholeheartedly* by feeling the reasonableness of its arrangements, and by being spared the need of segregational attitudes" (330; my emphasis). The works I have been examining are efforts on Frost's part imaginatively to own his "utilitarian" social structure, to feel "the reasonableness of its arrangements." He had to strike an alliance, achieve an integration. But I emphasize "wholeheartedly" in the above quotation because, as should by now be clear, Frost's subscription to a utilitarian morality, and to the marketplace of what he called "casual readers," though genuine, was not entirely satisfactory for him. With William Dean Howells, he may have acknowledged that in America the only "solidarity" derives from "business." But his work shows a persistent awareness of the divergent "intentions and tastes and principles" (as Howells puts it) that potentially disturb that solidarity. Frost was not spared the need for "segregational attitudes," an epithet that I would apply to his strategies of rhetorical intransigence and subtlety. There is a certain pathos in this need, which Burke nicely catches: "An ideal world would be one in which one's allegiance to the reigning social criteria . . . could be paid without disaster. One would shape his mind as an individual with reference to the shape of the total collective pattern. Insofar as he cannot do this, to that extent he is 'dispossessed,' even if he enjoys material wealth" (*Attitudes* 330). Frost's 1913 letter to Flint frankly expresses this dispossession. By contrast, charming and bearable though it certainly is, the cagey rhetoric of "Good Hours"—like that of the 1913 letter to Sidney Cox—affirms and accepts that dispossession in addition to expressing it, and herein lies its ambivalent complexity: it is about intransigence, but also about propriety and accommodation. Frost seems to recognize that the solitary transgression of his speaker is rather overdramatized: the poem is quite aware of the postures it adopts, whether postures of transgression, repentance, or apology. This self-awareness affords the poem a certain latitude, a certain amount of play.

The form, tone, and theme of "Good Hours" all symbolize, so to speak, accommodation. In a *Paris Review* interview, Frost says: "I'm always interested, you know, when I have three or four stanzas, in the way I *lay* the sentences in them. I'd hate to have the sentences all lie the same in the stanzas" (*CPPP* 890). "Good Hours" certainly bears this out. Frost casts the poem into four superbly managed quatrains and the movement of the sentences within and across the boundary of the poetic line is wonderfully subtle. Through the first twelve lines the syntactic and grammatical units more or less coincide with the metrical units. There is little enjambment, and no special stress calls the slight effects of enjambment that do occur to our attention. This consistency is further reflected in the homogeneity of the subject-verb-object syntax, with nine of the first twelve lines hinging on the initial subject "I." These patterns, these "conformities," are finally broken in the last quatrain, in which the feeling of release is gently impressive. Even as the speaker "repents" his social and geographical vagrancy—his wandering out of bounds at ten o'clock—Frost resorts to a specifically metrical sort of extravagance or wandering: an enjambed sentence broken across the boundaries of four lines. As a poetic maneuver this reinforces the vocational intransigence of what is, after all, only a mocking sort of apology anyway:

> Over the snow my creaking feet
> Disturbed the slumbering village street
> Like profanation, by your leave,
> At ten o'clock of a winter eve.

The elegant grammar complements the speaker's officious air of apology and provides a satisfying stylistic contrast to what has gone before. When the speaker is literally out of bounds, the poem itself remains *in,* metrically speaking; as he returns, the poem itself begins to wander—to play against the conformity of the poetic line and also against the conformity of the relatively plain syntax on which the lyric has so far relied. In other words, Frost violates the boundary of the poetic line, and of the grammatical patterns of the first three quatrains, only when his speaker recrosses the line back into the village *physically* with his return and also *sympathetically* with his apology. These tendencies toward extravagance and toward conformity remain perfectly balanced in the poem. In both theme and form, "Good Hours" depends equally upon dispositions of intransigence and dispositions of propriety. The coincidence of these two values suggests the psychological function that the poem may have fulfilled for Frost. It negotiates a compromise, an accommodation of difference to conformity, whether we mean *social* difference and conformity or *metrical* difference and conformity. And these two kinds of conformity, as a poem like "Good Hours" suggests, are essentially complementary in Frost's work. Social and poetic ordeals are never entirely distinct.

It has often been suggested that Frost's poems of wandering and return can be read as allegories of his own work as a poet within the confines of poetic form. "Good Hours" obviously belongs in this category, and I am trying to show how it dramatizes Frost's investigation not simply of the processes of poetry but of the *social* ordeal of the poetic vocation itself. I dwell on the poem in such detail because it perfectly illustrates the integration in Frost's thinking of these several questions: What is it like to write a poem? What is it like to *be* a poet?—or, more particularly, to be a male poet in America in the early decades of the twentieth century? What is the relation of poets and poetry to society more generally? And, finally, in what way does poetry simply provide a specific instance of a more general human experience of the interplay of liberty and constraint, of social difference and correspondence? In short, a poem like "Good Hours" brings out with special clarity Frost's ordeal, in the multiple senses I assign the word in the introduction to this study. There is the social ordeal of coming to know one's "difference," as Frost says in the introduction to *King Jasper*, and of learning how to accommodate that difference to social constraints; and there is the artistic ordeal of accommodating self-expression to the limiting, highly socialized "disciplines" of language and poetic form.

It is worth considering a bit further certain social implications of the apology made in the last quatrain of "Good Hours." In his fragmentary essay "On Truth and Lies in an Extra-Moral Sense," Nietzsche speaks of "the duty [to truth] which society imposes in order to exist." "To be truthful," he suggests, "means to employ the usual metaphors. Thus, to express it morally, this is the duty to lie according to a fixed convention, to lie with the herd and in a manner binding upon everyone" (47). Nietzsche is ridiculing the social contract, and I find it useful to read the language of penitence in "Good Hours," and to consider the contracts that the poem at once parodies and renews, in light of his remarks. This is all the more useful considering that, through Mencken's influence, as I suggest in the introduction, Nietzsche did much to shape American intellectuals' troubled sense of their relation to American culture as a whole in the early years of the twentieth century.

"Good Hours," let us say, is *forthrightly* an experiment in employing "the usual metaphors" and "lying" with "the herd": in this case, a herd of utilitarian American villagers. Very dutifully, in fact, the speaker lies according to "fixed convention." He sardonically acknowledges a particular decorum and in so doing accepts the social mores upon which that decorum is based: "I turned and repented . . ." The difference ironically repented represents more than the rather inconsequential difference of a man keeping late hours in a proper New England village. As I have suggested, it apparently symbolizes the more important "difference" of the poet, a figure who, like the "disinherited" couple of "In Neglect" or like Browning's "Fra Lippo Lippi," potentially challenges the "utilitarian" values and customs of the society this village must be taken to represent.

Frost and Nietzsche may treat the same theme—the duty to lie in the usual manner of the herd—but they differ remarkably in tone. Nietzsche allows himself the luxury and simplicity of outright dyslogism. Frost never does, with the result that his tone can be extraordinarily complex, *especially* when his subject is his own troubled standing as a poet. In writing "Good Hours" he is, I think, acutely aware and suspicious of any claim to real distinction, let alone outright superiority, that the poem might seem to be making on behalf of the culturally exceptional figure. Any antagonisms that underlie the poem are ultimately mollified by its refusal to accept easy or ready-made metaphors for his alienation—such metaphors, for example, as an allusion to "Fra Lippo Lippi" might afford a writer of Pound's more Nietzschean temperament. Pound, for his part, felt perfectly comfortable making invocations such as the following, from "Salvationists": "Ah yes, my songs, let us resurrect / The very excellent term *Rusticus*" (*Personae* 100). The term means "boorish," "provincial," or "backward," and Pound never had any trouble telling the provincial from the central. By contrast Frost's village "songs"—and there are a great many—carefully avoid that very excellent term *rusticus*. The impatient sarcasm of the envoi to "Good Hours" seems to me as much directed toward the speaker's somewhat overdrawn posture of transgression as toward the complacent proprieties we might suppose the provincial, rustic villagers themselves to cherish. Frost was not grinding any axes.

Consider the following lines from "A Hundred Collars," another poem collected in *North of Boston*. Here, Frost quietly satirizes the figure of the intellectual—in this case Dr. Magoon, a Ph.D.—not the "rustics" who may at times speak against him:

> Lancaster bore him—such a little town,
> Such a great man. It doesn't see him often
> Of late years, though he keeps the old homestead
> And sends the children down there with their mother
> To run wild in the summer—a little wild.
> Sometimes he joins them for a day or two
> And sees old friends he somehow can't get near.
> They meet him in the general store at night,
> Preoccupied with formidable mail,
> Rifling a printed letter as he talks.

They seem afraid. He wouldn't have it so:
Though a great scholar, he's a democrat,
If not at heart, at least on principle.
(*CPPP* 49)

"A Hundred Collars" presents yet another treatment of the intellectual as an alien in the villages of New England. (One can readily imagine how differently Pound would have handled this situation by reading his poem "In Durance.") And it is probably redeeming that Frost does not allow himself the satisfaction of snobbery—far from it: in fact, the poem is an exercise in self-examination, as Frost clearly identifies to some extent with the unappealing Dr. Magoon. By contrast, Pound's Whitmanesque postures in *Lustra*—and his rigorous code of *pour épater les bourgeois*—can be uncommonly engaging, but they are also probably too easy and unreflective. Frost consistently remains as much interested in *sustaining* the solidarity of the artist and his difficult constituency—whether that constituency comprises his poetic subjects or his readers—as in highlighting any tensions that may be supposed to exist between them. In the introduction to *King Jasper* Frost calls this sense of solidarity "correspondence," suggesting that all poets ought to achieve it, a matter to which I will return in chapter 2.

The better to bring this out I refer again to Kenneth Burke, who clearly learned much from Nietzsche. In *Attitudes toward History,* Burke suggests that the Catholic church "was exceptionally cunning in founding its collectivist structure on the foundations of guilt. It formulated a doctrine of 'original sin,' holding that the individual could not be saved until he had been socialized" (163). He explains further that the mechanism of salvation-by-socialization supports not simply the ideology of the Catholic church, but is to be found ordering any cohesive social arrangement; inevitably, individuals accommodate their peculiar temperament and outlook to socially accredited patterns of living. The ideal of "Reason" itself is grounded in this accommodation of private desires to "public" resources of justification:

> That is: the only way in which one *can* rationalize a private act is by reference to a public effect (showing that it is "good" for someone beyond the self, that it is to be tested by reference to a field varying in scope, such as family, class, or nation). And since the individual mind is formed by incorporating such social materials, the social rationalization induces a sense of individual shortcomings, leading to a sense of guilt insofar as his private act is felt as a departure from its ideal.
>
> In this way, there is implicit in reason the need for "justification" (which is *per se* the evidence of guilt). In the aesthetic sphere, the same

> tendency is manifest in the individual's manipulation of the public materials for purposes of appeal ("style" and "form"). (164n)

We have seen already how literary style became, for Frost, a matter of what he called "charm" and "bearability." Burke would range these qualities under the heading of "appeal." We have also seen how Frost's various vocational writings "manipulate public materials" in service to this appeal. This manipulation may take a number of forms, of which Frost shows us several in the letters and poems discussed above. Brooks points to still another in his study of Twain. The main point is that some degree of alienation, or of what Burke calls dispossession, necessarily attends socialization in these terms. "Public" resources like reason and language potentially alienate an individual from herself by *shaping,* and thereby anticipating and "falsifying," her experience. Upon feeling this alienation in speaking or writing—that is, in attempting to conform our experience to the highly socialized and gendered resources of language—we say that we cannot find words for our thoughts. We feel it in social situations when we find no efficient, or at least negotiable, public outlet for essentially private aspirations. At times like this, to adopt Frost's terminology, some component of our personality is forced into "occlusion"—at least if we would remain "charming" and "bearable," rather than rebellious and oppositional. With this point in view we can perhaps discern a deeper irony in "Good Hours." In sublimating its vocational theme the poem may pay tribute to the same economies of social guilt that it apparently repudiates. It presents a subtle example of how people may come—to borrow again Terry Eagleton's perceptive remark—"to invest in their own unhappiness." As I see it, Frost essentially "staves off" his vocational "confession"—just as he does in the anecdote he tells to R. P. T. Coffin about the businessman on the train. David Bromwich's above-cited remark about "Two Tramps in Mud Time" therefore probably applies here as well: "Frost-as-poet is not, so to speak, figured in the poem," even though the evidence is strong that his status as a poet is very much a motivating concern in "Good Hours."

Acknowledging these effects of "social guilt" in Frost's vocational poems and letters helps us understand his remarks on the "fear of Man" in the introduction to *King Jasper:* "And there is the fear of Man—the fear that men won't understand us and we shall be cut off from them" (*CPPP* 741–42). Frost found this fear salutary—even redemptive, as I will argue in chapter 2. Insofar as we are susceptible to it, the "fear of Man" keeps us from straying too far apart from the herd—from wandering too far out of bounds past bedtime. The fear of being "cut off" from others is therefore the very medium of social cohesion and conformity. Referring to what he called the "extreme modernists," Frost once said to an interviewer: "They do not care whether their communication is intelligible to others" (*Interviews* 80). The remark is informed by the "fear of Man," a fear, at bottom, of an inner voice uncorroborated by external, *social* authority. Frost's ambivalence about the strategies of his "unintelligible" contemporaries is therefore quite consistent with his unwillingness to repudiate socializing forces that had failed readily to accommodate his difference as a poet. He could not, as Pound could, fashion a frame for rejecting the morality or "mores" of American culture; he fashioned a frame for accepting them instead. This suggests how much he valued the ideal of social cohesion, especially given the fact that in this case it comes at a price. He variously named that ideal "correspondence," or fitting "into the nature" of Americans, terms that I discuss in detail in chapter 2. It will do here to cite his remarks in "The Constant Symbol": "The ruling passion in man is not as Viennese as is claimed. It is rather a gregarious instinct to keep together by minding each other's business. Grex rather than sex. We *must* be preserved from becoming egregious" (*CPPP* 787).

In the final pages of this chapter, I want to study more closely Frost's differences from the American poet who most clearly marked the extravagant, egregious road that Frost did not take. The distinctive strategies of "Good Hours" are sharply brought out when we compare it to another poem on the same theme, written at about the same time, by Pound. I refer to "The Rest," cited already, which offers a very different representation of the artist in the villages of America. Pound's poem promises a safe social space for the poet, a space where he need undergo no ordeal such as we have been discussing. Pound significantly speaks from Europe, not from the margin of a sleepy New England hamlet, and his tone is as public and unequivocal as Frost's is equivocal, private, and subtle:

> O helpless few in my country,
> O remnant enslaved!
>
> Artists broken against her,
> A-stray, lost in the villages,
> Mistrusted, spoken against,
>
> Lovers of beauty, starved,
> Thwarted with systems,
> Helpless against the control;

> You who can not wear yourselves out
> By persisting to success,
> You who can only speak,
> Who can not steel yourselves into reiteration;
>
> You of the finer sense,
> Broken against false knowledge,
> You who can know at first hand,
> Hated, shut in, mistrusted:
>
> Take thought:
> I have weathered the storm,
> I have beaten out my exile.
>
> (93–94)

Pound wrote "The Rest" in 1913, the year he met Frost. Both poets were living in England at the time. In "The Rest" it is as if the figure in "Good Hours" walked "outward bound" that "winter eve" and never came back. "Pound-as-poet," to adapt once again David Bromwich's useful phrase, is most definitely "figured in the poem." There is no *occluded* seriousness here at all; nothing is held in reserve or balanced by "inner humor." The seriousness is all "up front," with the result that the tone of the poem is simply not complex enough to hold in suspension the various constituencies for whom Frost attempted to write. "The Rest" is a poem addressed to poets and it appeals entirely to their sense of election. It is what Mencken speaks of in *Prejudices: Third Series* (1922): a call "to the corn-fed *intelligentsia* to flee the shambles, escape to fairer lands, throw off the curse forever" (13). Frost wrote for the intelligentsia, corn-fed and otherwise, but he also wrote for general readers of "all sorts and kinds" (as he put it). These readers, together with the magazine editors and anthologists who reflected their tastes, could only have been put off by Pound's poem. It was of course designed to put them off.

I have pointed out that the pattern in "Good Hours" is one of wandering and return. We saw how this pattern mirrors the balance the poem achieves between its complementary attitudes, in style and theme, of intransigence and accommodation. And here, comparison to "The Rest" is especially instructive. "The Rest" is in free verse and therefore presents a marked stylistic contrast to the impeccably measured quatrains of "Good Hours." Pound's lines are not tempered by meter. Nor is their tone, a homogenous sort of chanting, tempered by the irony and circumspection that have, to an extent, "occluded" the meaning of Frost's lyric. The contrast in tone matches the contrast between the different constituencies for whom the two poets are performing, so to speak. In a sense, Pound is sure of his dinner, like the cocky young boy in Emerson's "Self-Reliance" (*Essays* 261). He writes as if for a constituency he can take for granted, a constituency that holds in common with him certain (somewhat exalted) ideas about the status of art and artists; this is not a poem meant to charm the unconverted. Nothing like this is indicated in Frost's lyric, which declines to address its vocational theme directly. Hence its more guarded, protean demeanor, and its ironic air of conciliation.

In the literary-historical context of 1913, a poem like "The Rest," simply by virtue of its free verse form, registered a protest against the conformities of the large-circulation American literary magazines. "The Rest" is a plea for little magazines, not big ones. Of course, the large-circulation American magazines—the *Atlantic Monthly* is a good example—would soon regularly feature Frost's poetry, and it was his express purpose, at the time, to be in them. Indeed, Frost feared that Pound's reviews of *A Boy's Will* and *North of Boston,* commendatory of his work though they were, would damage his prospects with prominent American editors. He wrote in January 1915 to Sidney Cox: "Another such review as the one [by Pound] in Poetry [of *North of Boston*] and I shan't be admitted at Ellis Island. This is no joke. Since the article was published I have been insulted and snubbed by two American editors I counted on as good friends" (*Selected Letters* 148). He has in mind such remarks as the following. Pound is reflecting on the fact that Frost's first two books appeared under an English imprint: "It is a sinister thing that so American . . . a talent as Robert Frost should have to be exported before it can find due encouragement and recognition. . . . But the typical American editor of the last twenty years has resolutely shut his mind against serious American writing" (*Literary Essays* 384).

"The Rest" is a poem of "impatience," to adapt Frost's terminology in the introduction to *King Jasper,* whereas "Good Hours" is a poem of "patience." And the free verse form of "The Rest" is as well suited to its theme of grievance and protest as the regulated form of "Good Hours" is suited to its theme, as I would say, of accommodation. "The Rest" perfectly exemplifies what Frost calls, in the 1934 letter to his daughter Lesley Frost Francis, the "doctrine of Inner Form." It rebels against the "conformities" of inherited poetic discipline, and, more importantly, against the social "conformities" with which those poetic disciplines had come to be associated in Pound's mind and in Frost's. That is to say, the "thwarting systems" and "controls" of which "The Rest" speaks are equally social and aesthetic. Its emancipatory imagery therefore perfectly complements its "free" verse style. "The Rest" is manifestly an ordeal poem ("I have weathered the storm"), even as it promises the poets it addresses a kind of cultural liberation in exile. Or to adapt Frost's phrase in a 1938 letter to R. P. T. Coffin: Pound promises a "world safe for art"—a kind of cultural separatism that Frost never desired.

In *Attitudes toward History,* Burke relates an anecdote about a British prime minister that has some bearing on the present discussion: "A member of his party, with a young son, asked the minister to find the son a position. The minister asked about the son's qualifications. 'Well, he is very modest,' said the father. 'Modest!' exclaimed the minister; 'What has he done to be modest about?' The anecdote draws its logic from the springs of 'ironic humility'" (48n). Burke borrows the phrase "ironic humility" from William Empson's *Some Versions of Pastoral,* and "Good Hours" (with its "by your leave") offers a variant of it. Burke explains: "Empson's analysis of Gray's reference to the flower 'born to blush unseen / And waste its sweetness on the desert air' discloses the ways in which the poet, confronting the rise of the get-ahead philosophy that went with the mounting industrial-commercial pattern of England, provides resignation for the man who has not found a *carrière ouverte aux talents,* and yet would feel himself of good quality" (49). Frost is writing in America at the other end of the "industrial-commercial pattern" with its "get-ahead" philosophy. He writes in the period of its maturity rather than of its mounting. "Good Hours" embodies an effort on his part, similar to the one Burke identifies in Gray's "Elegy," to achieve "resignation" and yet "feel himself of good quality" within a utilitarian regime. A problem of vocation is, after all, a problem of finding a *carrière ouverte aux talents.* Poems like "Good Hours" and Gray's "Elegy" perhaps make those problems easier for poets—and the unutilitarian intellectuals who read them—to bear. Any feelings of embarrassment that may lie behind "Good Hours" are redeemed, by means of irony and humor, into something like a sense of superiority, however provisional or qualified—a sense of being better than the establishment even when the establishment ignores you: hence its "ironic humility." It is not going too far to suggest that Frost has poems like "Good Hours" in mind when he writes to Louis Untermeyer in 1924: "Irony is simply a kind of guardedness" (*CPPP* 702).

"The Rest," like "Good Hours" and Gray's "Elegy," is an effort to manage the sense of social estrangement I have described. But while Frost and Gray are accommodating, the expatriate Pound is basically factional, which explains the hortatory, divisive rhetoric of "The Rest" as well as of his essays and reviews of the same period. His writing exploits, rather than ameliorates, social division. Much more Nietzschean in this respect than Frost, Pound "debunks" the "social guilt" that these other poems finally appease even if they appease it only ironically. But as Burke points out, "one cannot 'debunk' guilt completely without arriving at a disintegrative, anti-social philosophy" (*Attitudes* 164–65n), and this stricture certainly applies to Pound. In rejecting the guilt upon which the socialization of American writers seemed to depend, he did in fact arrive at a "disintegrative," us-against-them rhetoric. In "The Rest," the tribute the artist pays in "forming himself" (to borrow Burke's words) to "match the cooperative ways of his society" (*Rhetoric* 39) is described dyslogistically as "slavery," while Pound (characteristically, for those years) assumes the role of emancipator. The poem has its roots in what Richard Poirier calls the "central mythology" of modernism: "the idea that innovation in the arts is a form of cultural heroism" (*Renewal* 112).

"Good Hours," like "In Neglect" and the vocational letters I have cited, plays about the fringes of this central mythology. But it already adopts an ironic, skeptical attitude toward its own potentially countercultural energies. Frost himself seemed to understand his temperamental inclination toward accommodation rather than toward "cultural heroism." Prompted by a reading of Juvenal, he wrote to his friend and former editor Lincoln MacVeagh in December 1933: "A little irony is good medicine for the blood; but the out-and-out satire of Menken Dreiser and [Sinclair] Lewis I should hate to join them in—I shouldnt know how to join them in because I am conscious of my resentments as being merely personal and so not to be trusted to build a cause on" (*Selected Letters* 401). He could have added Pound to this list, who certainly trusted his resentments enough to build a cause on. Indeed, Pound would apparently go even further than Mencken, as this aphorism from *Pavannes and Divagations* suggests: "Mencken did not overestimate the dangers of boobocracy. Unfortunately he thought, or pretended to think, it was funny" (231). And as for Sinclair Lewis: Pound's indictment of the villages of America in "The Rest" certainly may stand alongside *Main Street.*

Frost is on record regarding the latter book in a 1921 letter to Louis Untermeyer. He writes, he lets us know, from "out here in the country": a kind of symbolic address. "Small towns do buy books," he says, "so what in Hell are the writers kicking about? Count me as in favor of reforming a whole lot of things downward. I keep hearing of Lewis wanting to better small town people. I'm for bettering or battering them back where they belong. Too many of them get to college" (*Frost to Untermeyer* 127). Frost had lately been house-hunting in the small town of Monson, Connecticut, where he was alarmed to discover a "bevy" of college boys "swatting" one another with copies of the liberal weekly the *New Republic*. Recollection of this in the letter to Untermeyer inspires him to respond to Lewis's sardonic preface to *Main Street*, which drily declares small-town America "the climax of civilization." "That this Ford car might stand in front of the Bon Ton Store," Lewis writes, "Hannibal invaded Rome and Erasmus wrote in Oxford cloisters. What Ole Jensen the grocer says to Ezra Stowbody the banker is the new law for London, Prague, and the unprofitable isles of the sea; whatsoever Ezra does not know and sanction, that thing is heresy, worthless for knowing and wicked to consider" (6). Another of Frost's parables of the writer in American villages, the 1921 letter to Untermeyer amounts to a wry, polemical *apologia* for small-town culture:

> 'Twas graduation at the Academy; everyone was shuffling reverently in white and black to some exercise that I as an outsider couldn't be expected to know the importance of. I didn't want to be an outsider. I was just on the point of mounting the Soldiers Monument and applying in a loud voice to the community at large to be taken in as soon as possible and treated as an insider when I ran bang into my bevy of twenty college boys all obviously out of tune with the village and not the least in the mood of its pitiful little function. They probably thought they were laughing at each other but what they were really laughing at was the notion of their ever having taken the Academy Graduation as an end and aim. At their colleges they had commencements, and there were even things beyond commencements: Rhodes Scholarships if you won them might take you to Oxford where you might hope to acquire a contempt beyond any contempt for small things you could show now. They knew now that there was nothing here that they would not some day be able to scorn. I fled them as I had fled their like thirty years before at Dartmouth. . . . To Hell with these memories! I went free from the Little Collegers like Sinclair Lewis ages ago. (*Frost to Untermeyer* 128)

The village parables we have so far examined date from the period before Frost's return to America in 1915. The parable of 1921 is another matter. It is already embedded in the very public "culture wars" of Frost's own day—wars that conditioned much of what he later said about the nature of poetry, as I argue in chapter 2. By the time he wrote this letter, the smug rural-sage persona that sometimes troubled the better angels of his nature had made its advent in Frost's poetry. (A good example of this is "Christmas Trees," collected first in *Mountain Interval* [1916], Frost's third book, and his first to be published initially in America.) His antagonism to the cultural and literary avant-garde, which he assumed upon his return to America in 1915, was already beginning to harden through stress of overdefinition: Frost had been culturally driven into a corner, or so he felt. By 1937 these developments would secure his perfect alienation from both the independent radical Left—as exemplified in the rejuvenated *Partisan Review*—and the modernist literary establishment, which, whatever their differences, were united in scorn for the "Middle American" villages with which Frost declared himself in tune.

But in 1921 all of that is still in the future. And it is hard not to be won over by Frost's comical boosterism in the letter to Untermeyer, as when, Garrison Keillor–like, he *almost* mounts the Soldiers' Monument. The letter develops to a new stage the pattern of the 1913 letter to Sidney Cox about "posies." There, one infers that Frost is out of tune with the villagers. But rather than rebel against them he adopts the humor of his cultural antagonists: he is both in and out of the game. In 1921 it is the intellectuals—the village atheists—that gall Frost, not the rotarians. In this later version of the story Frost once again emerges as neither atheist nor true believer—as neither unutilitarian nor utilitarian: just as before, he is both in and out of the game. He transcends the cultural opposition between village intransigence and village accommodation, and this affords him the detachment of an affectionate humor that, in his hands, never shades off into condescension: "'Twas graduation at the Academy; everyone was shuffling reverently in white and black to some exercise that I as an outsider couldn't be expected to know the importance of." It is a very different sort of attitude from the Lewisesque one taken by Louis Raymond Reid in his essay "The Small Town" in *Civilization in the United States:* "There has lately taken place in the villages throughout the country a new movement that has civic pride as its basis. It is the formation of boosters' clubs. Everybody is boosting his home town, at least publicly, though in the privacy of the front porch he may be justly depressed by its narrowness of opportunity, its subservience to social snobbery, its intellectual aridity. . . . 'Boost our Town' shout banners stretched across Main Street. Is there not something vitally poignant in such a proud provincialism?" (293).

The difficulty is that Frost would eventually wear the mask of the village booster too readily, and often without the ironies latent in such village parables as "Good Hours." Notice that he casts the later village anecdote—the one related in the letter to Untermeyer—in an autobiographical frame, linking up his 1921 heresies with his earlier declaration of independence from the "little collegers" of Dartmouth. In either case, conformity to the rhythms of village life symbolizes for Frost a particular kind of nonconformist intransigence with regard to what he takes to be the literary-intellectual establishment. For this reason, we should understand the development of Frost's style not only in the context of his experience in American villages—as we so far have—but in the context also of his engagement in debates *about* the experience of literary artists in American villages, a somewhat more complicated matter. That is to say, his persona of small-town booster was perhaps not so much the *cause* of his antagonism with the intellectual avant-garde as it was the *product* of that antagonism, and the voicings of that persona mark his dissonance with writers such as Sinclair Lewis and Mencken as much as his consonance with the "villagers" themselves. The small-town believer was very much a mask—another kind of "protective coloration." At times Frost wore this mask lightly and well, as in the 1921 letter to Untermeyer, or as in "Good Hours," with its wry, apologetic air. But sometimes he did not, as in poems such as "Christmas Trees" and "New Hampshire." His changeable, often ironic relationship to that "mask" is very much an index of the uneasy solidarity of the literary artist and his compatriot American villagers.

Pound swatted his friends with copies of Mencken's *Smart Set,* if not of the *New Republic.* In "Salutation the Second" he enjoins his songs to "dance shamelessly" with "an impertinent frolic," to "salute" the "grave and the stodgy" with "[their] thumbs at [their] noses" (87): *pour épater les bourgeois,* as always. His posture is steadfastly countercultural. Frost could never bring himself to this pass, as my reading of "Good Hours" suggests. At times he felt culturally dislocated. But he never really felt culturally *oppositional.* Time and again his descriptions of the work of poetry affiliate it with apparently ordinary patterns of life in "Middle America." There is seldom anything truly *distinguished* about the poet's vocation in his accounts of it. On the contrary, he will speak of poetry, in his "'Letter' to *The Amherst Student*" (1935), as but one instance of the general human tendency to create form and order where none had existed: "The artist, the poet might be expected to be the most aware of such assurance. But it is really everybody's sanity to feel it and live by it. Fortunately, too, no forms are more engrossing, gratifying, comforting, staying than those lesser ones we throw off, like vortex rings of smoke, all our individual enterprise and needing nobody's cooperation; a basket, a letter, a garden, a room, an idea, a picture, a poem" (*CPPP* 740). One can hardly imagine a less intimidating account of the poet's vocation. Frost speaks almost as if poems were made on rainy days out of what the grammar school teachers used to call "construction paper." We are very far here from poetry as "the lordliest of the arts," to recall Pound's phrase. At other times, Frost associates poetry with the play and intimacy of casual conversation, as in "Education by Poetry": "Poetry provides the one permissible way of saying one thing and meaning another. People say, 'Why don't you say what you mean?' We never do that, do we, being all of us too much poets" (*CPPP* 719–20). And as I have pointed out, Frost happily consigned poets—no different in this regard from businessmen—to what he called "the trial by market everything must come to." These generous definitions of poetry implicate us all, and what is more, they implicate us *as Americans:* their appeal is culturally specific. I suggested at the outset of this chapter that Frost works symbolically to integrate the poet's vocation into sanctioned rhythms of American life, even while holding his cultural intransigence in reserve. By 1921 poetry had indeed become his means charmingly and bearably to fit "into the nature of Americans."

I propose, at this point, a tentative hypothesis regarding the development of modernism, to which I have been helped by Kenneth Burke's chapter "Style" in *Permanence and Change* (1935). There was a time when a quorum of American poets and writers came to believe that the prevailing patterns of "village" living allowed them no social outlet for their aspirations as artists, and also as men and women. They felt a sea change in the relation between their own sensibilities and the social institutions and morality available to accommodate them. They gave up trying to reconcile these opposed forces and instead began to define and then to emphasize a new morality, together with a new set of symbols and attitudes that would support it. They conducted teach-ins in little magazines. It was a time of great manifestoes, and for a while the linkages between social dispossession and literary innovation seemed perfectly clear. If a writer lacked the courage of her resentments, these linkages showed themselves in small, furtive ways, as when she troped an accredited cultural "vocabulary" for purposes of expressive irony; that is what happens in "Good Hours." If the writer did have the "courage" (and for this she usually needed company), these linkages showed themselves much more starkly, as in "The Rest," and as in the movement among American writers that we now call, perhaps with some prejudice in their favor, "*high* modernism."

The building up of the high modernist canon in America in the years following World War II may well reflect the need on the part of literary critics to have their own vocational and social dislocations, vis-à-vis the members of Mencken's "booboisie," both echoed and affirmed.

Dwight Macdonald's criticism from the 1950s and early 1960s about the bankruptcy of "middle-brow" American culture certainly leaves this impression. Andrew Ross has argued persuasively that critics like Macdonald sought, in the 1950s, to protect the integrity of "high" culture against the contagion of "middle-brow" education and entertainments; this became especially urgent as the student population in colleges and universities grew at an unprecedented pace in the two decades following World War II. And it is still somehow more self-flattering to read "difficult" writers like Eliot and Pound than it is to read a so-called "popular" one like Frost. Anyone who is alert to it must have encountered this attitude in the academy. Frost remarked in a 1947 talk at Amherst College: "I had a questionnaire the other day from an editor. He asked, 'What in your opinion is the present state of middle-brow literature in America?' That was new slang to me. I'd got behind a little bit, being off in the country. I hadn't heard of 'middle-brow' before. What he meant to say was, 'You old skeezix, what's the present state of your own middle-brow stuff?' There was something invidious, I am sure, in that" (*CPPP* 797).

There was some sign in the 1980s of a modest readjustment of sympathy against "high" modernism. But anyone with an investment in Frost's institutional prestige may well have greeted with chagrin what otherwise might chiefly have been amusing. I refer to Vice President Dan Quayle's 1992 campaign attacks, anti-intellectual in character, on "cultural elites" in "faculty lounges." This makes "cultural elitism" downright attractive. The political prestige of Quayle's brand of anti-intellectual populism has not declined in the years since 1992. And one hopes that conservative speechwriters do not start discovering Robert Frost, with his remarks about "the trial by market everything must come to" and his attacks on the progressive intellectuals of his own day. They would be singularly well-equipped to "understand him wrong" (as Frost himself liked to say), and to miss the subtler aspects of his response to the "utilitarian" morality of American "villages."

When politicians accuse "cultural elites" of being "out of touch" with "mainstream America," their motives are often unrespectable. But academic intellectuals dismiss the charges at their peril. Criticism of "cultural elites" comes not only from conservative political consultants but also, with various motivations, from right-leaning journalists such as Roger Kimball, George Will, and Richard Bernstein; from liberal scholars such as David Bromwich and Andrew Delbanco; from liberal philosophers such as Richard Rorty and John Searle; and from radical libertarians such as Camille Paglia. It is a broad field, and more politically varied than is sometimes supposed. Largely through Kimball's agency, the suspicions and resentments of the "booboisie" have given rise to a new character in the melodrama of American cultural politics: the overpaid, arrogant "tenured radical"—overpaid, that is, either *not* to teach our young men and women or else overpaid to teach them hatred of values cherished by god-fearing parents everywhere. In an article in the Modern Language Association's journal *Profession 93*, the Victorianist George Levine makes much the same point that I make here about how literary study in higher education is perceived. He enjoins his colleagues in the academy to take "far more seriously than they at present do the disparity between their sense of what constitutes useful work in English and what the state and most people who send their children to universities think such work is" (44).

The accusations of writers such as Roger Kimball hurt precisely because they have the ring of *half*-truth. Undoubtedly there has existed a lack of sympathy—a kind of bad faith—between the progressive, highly educated classes and "Middle America." This situation neither arose with H. L. Mencken nor disappeared at his wake. In a 1994 article in *Harper's* entitled "The Revolt of the Elites," Christopher Lasch speaks of the "venomous hatred that lies not far beneath the smiling face of upper-middle-class benevolence." He suggests that "middle Americans, as they appear to the makers of educated opinion, are hopelessly dowdy, unfashionable, and provincial. . . . Simultaneously arrogant and insecure, the new elites regard the masses with mingled scorn and apprehension" (40–41). I think he is largely correct. And it is not at all surprising that for their part "Middle Americans" return the scorn and apprehension. Their suspicions are in part what helps politicians such as George Bush, Dan Quayle, Phil Gramm, and Newt Gingrich win elections. During the 1994 midterm elections, for example, the strategy was very much revived by the Republicans, who spoke often of how "liberal elites" were "out of touch" with "mainstream America." The day after those elections, as if in explanation of the Democrats' defeat, Gingrich called Bill Clinton and his wife Hillary Rodham Clinton "counter-culture McGoverniks," an epithet that unfortunately packs a considerable punch. In a speech at the 1992 Republican National Convention, Gingrich claimed that the Democratic party "despises the values of the American people" and advances a "multicultural nihilistic hedonism." Surely God has raised up in Gingrich a worthy mouthpiece for Mencken's "booboisie." And it should surprise no one that in a lecture series entitled "Renewing American Civilization," Gingrich singles out Mencken for derision, under the thoughtful heading "Mencken Despised People." Gingrich associates Mencken with the progressive academic intellectuals of the late 1980s and early 1990s, and though many of those intellectuals may be astonished to find themselves placed in Mencken's orbit, there is a compelling cultural logic to Gingrich's grievance: intellectuals in America, of whatever convictions, have most often been countercultural figures—members of what Pound, in "The Rest," called the "remnant enslaved, or of what Mencken preferred to call "a meager and exclusive aristocracy" (*Prejudices: Third Series* 13).[13]

I have described Frost's problem of vocation. I am suggesting now that his problem is in some sense *our* problem of vocation as academic intellectuals. His ordeal is ours, and perhaps quite literally: the mistrust between academic intellectuals and legislators—those instruments of Mencken's "booboisie"—may soon issue in legislative oversight of faculty teaching loads and curricula at taxpayer-supported colleges and universities and in standardized programs of assessment issued "top-down," as they say. A few state legislatures are already getting down to brass tacks. As Michael Bérubé points out in *Public Access* (1994), "What truly endangers the future of higher education . . . are the PC wars in tandem with the growing mad-as-hell taxpayer outrage at the professional autonomy of faculty, an outrage most effectively expressed as the demand that universities curtail professional research and require more undergraduate instruction from their employees" (22). Criticism of the professoriate succeeds so well because, as Bérubé argues, the conditions under which college professors work—a relatively large amount of personal and intellectual autonomy, flexible schedules, job security, generous benefits packages—contrast so markedly (and so regrettably) with the conditions under which most Americans labor. They think we have it easy, and in a certain way we do, which means that any perceived cultural arrogance toward them on our part—and conservative publicists from Quayle to Lynn Cheney to Dinesh D'Souza do not hesitate to supply them with examples of this—seems merely gratuitous and goes down very bitterly indeed. The general feeling seems to be—as George Levine and other writers imply—that amends are somehow in order. Progressive intellectuals in the academy have often been in the business of carelessly burning cultural bridges. Now they must learn to get along—Mencken's satisfactions be damned—even in the "villages" of America. Intellectuals may have often felt "mistrusted, spoken against," to borrow a phrase from Pound's "The Rest." But so have the "booboisie."

Newt Gingrich accuses academics of being captive to the radical Left; Richard Bernstein contends that they are in thrall to a "modish leftism." There is relatively little truth in the charges, but that does not seem to matter. "General readers" and voters often simply *assume* such accusations and contentions to be true. All the burden of proof lies with the academy. Why is this the case? Partly because Americans have been quietly suspicious of intellectuals all along. Frost's, Pound's, and Brooks's accounts of their vocational troubles in American "villages" attest to the longevity of these suspicions. The embattled situation of the humanities in the academy is thus a consequence of two contributing factors: on the one hand, an enduring strain of anti-intellectualism in "utilitarian" American culture and, on the other, an enduring elitist sentiment among intellectuals themselves. These two factors help explain one another and are reciprocal rather than merely coincident.

As I have intimated, these questions have a bearing on canon formation as well. One would expect any canon established by literary intellectuals obliquely to reflect their felt relation to the larger society. I want to suggest one specific way in which this oblique relationship developed in the years following World War II. Dwight Macdonald's argument in "Masscult and Midcult" provides a case in point, as other commentators have suggested. Macdonald's essay is a polemic against cultural totalitarianism and the tyranny of—as Frost would unabashedly say—"the trial by market everything must come to." For Macdonald, denouncing the abuses of "masscult" and "midcult" art was a necessary complement to denouncing those of state totalitarianism. "The question of Masscult," he writes, "is part of the larger question of the masses. The tendency of modern industrial society, whether in the USA or USSR, is to transform the individual into the mass man" (*American Grain* 8). To Macdonald, masscult and midcult in America and bureaucratic socialism in the USSR seemed all part of the same totalitarian developments, and in the 1940s and 1950s he struggled to maintain a third camp position independent of capitalist and communist extremes. Perfectly in keeping with this was his championing of a "high" modernist art that, notwithstanding its variety, had never been congruent with the imperatives of the literary marketplace. So, Macdonald's anarchistic politics perfectly complemented his "high-cult" allegiances; the two things symbolized one another. In "Masscult and Midcult" he explains that

> with the French Revolution, the masses for the first time made their entrance onto the political stage, and it was not long before they also began to occupy a central position in culture. Grub Street was no longer peripheral and the traditional kind of authorship became more and more literally eccentric—out of the center—until by the end of the nineteenth century the movement from which most of the enduring work of our

> time has come had separated itself from the market and was in systematic opposition to it. This movement, was, of course, the "avant garde" whose precursors were Stendhal and Baudelaire and the impressionist painters, whose pioneers included Rimbaud, Whitman, Ibsen, Cezanne, Wagner, and whose classic masters were figures like Stravinsky, Picasso, Joyce, Eliot, and Frank Lloyd Wright. (20)

Macdonald goes on to explain that the significance of the modernist avant-garde was that "it simply refused to compete in the established cultural marketplaces" (56). And there you have it: the canon and genealogy of high modernism as a counterforce to the capitalist mass marketplace and as the vanguard opposition to the "booboisie," with its "midcult" and "masscult" tastemakers. Frost could win no place on such a syllabus, of course, though Macdonald expressed qualified admiration for his work. Frost had spent far too much time "barding around," as he liked to say; he had given us all to understand that he accepted "the trial by market"; and after all, *A Further Range* (1936) had been a selection of the Book-of-the-Month-Club—as efficient a middle-brow credential as one could desire, at least as Macdonald saw it. Michael Bérubé, following Andrew Ross, sums up the situation well: "What really 'consolidated' modernism, in the late 1940s and 1950s, was a conglomeration of strange modernist bedfellows, as critics of the anti-Stalinist left lined up with critics of the right in a bi- or multi-partisan agreement that nothing could resist the twin evils of totalitarianism and mass culture—nothing except the transcendent masterpieces of the modernist 'avant-garde'" (131). Moreover, this avant-garde was then "retrospectively theorized" as a literature "whose force lay in its resistance to institutionalization"—despite the fact that it had itself become, by this time, "institutional" (130).

Given the often unhappy relation of high culture to "Middle America," the fate of relatively "popular" poets in the academy—poets whose constituency crossed over (as *Billboard* would say) into something like *general* cultural appeal—may have something to do with just who, at any given time, is most successfully cashing in on populist rhetoric. Sometimes the political Left has, as for example during the "Popular Front" years of the mid- and late 1930s. Then, high modernist poets were chastised from the hard Left as decadent, elitist, and bourgeois and from the liberal center simply as elitist. But these days, in the mid-1990s, the political Right seems to own whatever prestige attaches to "the popular." Look once again (perhaps) for academic writers to seek out ways to symbolize countercultural moods—to emphasize their difference from *boobus Americanus*; the inclination to do so is often hard to resist. How else are we *fully* to explain the peculiar fact that progressive democratic intellectuals continue to form such strong and passionate *personal* identifications with figures such as Pound and Eliot—Macdonald is the archetypical example of this—as opposed to a merely "scholarly" interest in them? These poets held political convictions that are eccentric at best, abhorrent at worst, and that in any event compare unfavorably to Frost's Jeffersonian libertarianism—whatever its many limitations. In *Repression and Recovery: Modern American Poetry and Cultural Memory* (1989), Cary Nelson suggests that in the postwar years the elevation of Pound, particularly, was occasioned by, and also helped sustain, a rigid New Critical distinction between "the political" and "the poetic." This is surely the case, and documents defending the award of the Bollingen Prize to the *Pisan Cantos* bear Nelson out. And yet I think that Andrew Ross and Michael Bérubé help us see how other motivations were also in play—namely, the desire on the part of literary intellectuals to contain "popular" art. The imaginative alliance in the late 1930s and later decades between a basically progressive intellectual establishment—best represented, say, by the constituency of the reorganized Trotskyist *Partisan Review* of the late 1930s and early 1940s—and the reactionary "high" modernist writers looks extraordinary if we do not see it at least partly in this light. Alliances of this sort enable intellectuals and literary critics to symbolize countercultural feelings by identifying with figures who are noticeably elite and embattled, not "democratic"—with figures who are above all innocent of the sins of possessing "middle-brow" appeal and of doing their cultural work within the corporate limits of American villages.[14] This is precisely the function that a cultural bridge-building poet like Frost can never fulfill. His admonitory example as a literary intellectual offers academics little excuse for not making themselves intelligible and persuasive even to natives in the villages of Middle America. (In this, Frost is curiously like Walt Whitman, and significantly unlike Dickinson, perhaps our greatest poet of intransigence.) Apparently we have not yet learned how to socialize our vocation, nor how, with Frost, to ask even an ironic by your leave when we scandalously stay out past ten o'clock at night.

In a March 1995 article in the *New Yorker,* Andrew Delbanco points out that "universities have an obligation to keep alive the spirit of blasphemy that has always been a part of the true life of the mind" (8). He also points out that universities are basically conservative entities, drawing monies, as they do, from the very people and institutions against whom they (rightly) blaspheme. Such is the peculiar position of the university. Where does Frost come down on this question? He was hardly a stranger to blasphemy—as any careful reader of him knows. But in public he most often struck a much more "accommodationist" stance, as I have suggested. In a commencement address at Dartmouth College in 1955 he advised his audience of graduating students (perhaps belatedly) not to "get converted" at college, as he put it—to hold firm to the convictions they had brought with them to college in the first place (*Collected Prose* 235–44). In moods like this, he resumes the stand he takes in the 1921 letter about those irreverent, village-atheist college boys, swatting themselves with copies of the *New Republic*. And as "Good Hours" suggests, when Frost undertakes an extravagance—an impiety or heresy—he usually *somehow* asks leave to do it, whether in his tone, his bearing, or his attitude. In that way, as a writer within the academy, and as a thinker on the margin between the "ordinary" and the "extravagant," Frost represents the balance of inertia against heretical energies that Delbanco considers the health of the university.

In a column in the winter 1994 *MLA Newsletter* Patricia Meyer Spacks, then president of the MLA, draws an unsurprising conclusion: "The escalating competition for increasingly inadequate public funding has reminded many academics of another obligation—to represent their profession more attractively and more accurately to the public at large" (3). To the same effect, George Levine speaks of the necessity for academics "to reconcile our training and professional satisfactions with our institutional and social obligations to the people whose money we take" (44). Michael Bérubé suggests in *Public Access* that "the political, cultural, and social context of academic 'theoretical' debates needs to be broadened and 'popularized.' . . . If we're going to be PC, politically committed, then we'll also have to be PI, persuasively inclined" (37). And in an article in *Profession 94*, Erik D. Curren enjoins graduate programs in English to "examine not only questions that are interesting to academic intellectuals but also ways to translate our interests into the language of undergraduates or intelligent nonacademic readers." He goes on to point out that "the most important benefit of working with a larger audience in mind is that it would mount an advocacy of academic work that is sorely needed in the face of attacks by conservatives and public questioning of the value of what we do. . . . If we do not want the study of modern languages to be downsized out of recognition, all academics . . . should be willing to explain to the public why modern language scholarship and teaching should be supported by tax and tuition monies" (60). The day of the public intellectual may once again arrive in America, and the reason for her advent is quite possibly economic. Recalling the opening pages of this chapter, I am inclined to suggest—with Levine, Spacks, Bérubé, and Curren—that academics will either have to learn to "flatter the mob," as Pound uncharitably says, or at least how to remain "charming" and "bearable" in its presence, as Frost says much more agreeably. And of course the second alternative is really the only desirable and practical one. We must discover how to be at once accommodating and intransigent. Frost's poetry may be ubiquitous in the classroom. But the forms of cultural accommodation that his poetry practices and to a great extent recommends have never really been in favor in the academy since he died, and even before. It affirms Frank Lentricchia's wistful remark in *Modernist Quartet:* "Frost wanted to be a poet for all kinds, but he mainly failed. He is [in the academy] the least respected of the moderns. Pound wanted a few fit readers, and he got them" (76).[15]

2 *Robert Frost and the "Fear of Man"*

> I had, I believe, no more public spirit than a policeman or an archbishop, but I was full of lust to function, and before I was twenty-five it was already plain that my functioning would take the form of a sharp and more or less truculent dissent from the *mores* of my country. By the time I set to work on my [George Bernard] Shaw book I was already becoming known, in the narrow circle I then inhabited, as one to whom the American spectacle, American ideas and ideals, the great body of Americans themselves, were predominantly more amusing than inspiring, and less admirable than obscene.
>
> —H. L. Mencken, *My Life as Author and Editor*

> Beyond my belief in myself, beyond another's critical opinion of me, lies this. I should like to have it that your medal is a token of my having fitted not into the nature of the Universe but in some small way at least into the nature of Americans—into their affections is perhaps what I mean.
>
> —Robert Frost, 1939 speech

IN AMERICA, ANTHONY COMSTOCK IS to literary modernism (at least to certain denominations of it) what Judas is to Christianity: his bad faith made the whole thing possible. This is of course an overstatement. But it corrects an omission in literary histories of the period. In understanding the motives of literary expatriatism and of the modernist avant-garde—and therefore also the cultural politics of the

American literary modernists—we must consider in some detail the climate for the arts in America in the period between 1874 and 1920, when Frost, Pound, Eliot, Stevens, Mencken, and others were born, raised, and came into their own. Comstock probably did as much as any single man or woman to make that climate what it was. What made it possible for Pound *reasonably* to say in 1912 that in America artists were "mistrusted, spoken against," as he puts it in "The Rest"? The answer is complex, but "Anthony Comstock made it possible" is a good enough place to start, as is clear from Mencken's survey of the now largely forgotten vice crusader's works in "Puritanism as a Literary Force" (1917), an essay of which Pound was particularly fond.

A good example of the moral style in question here is Comstock's chapter "Artistic and Cultural Traps" in his 1883 tract *Traps for the Young:*

> The more seductive the bait, the more numerous are the victims. To please the eye, to charm the ear, or to enter any of the senses is often the easiest way to the heart. That "appearances are deceitful" is especially true whenever Satan sets a trap for his victims. . . . So "art" and "classic" are made to gild some of the most obscene representations and foulest matters in literature, regardless of their results to immature minds. . . . "Fine art" has lent its charms to pictures of lust, intensifying their power for evil, and finding an apology for them before the public. In every genuine work of art there is much to please. A thing of beauty is pleasant to recall. The charms lent by the artist render it more ensnaring, by hiding the reality and results. You cannot handle fire and not be burned, neither can the black fiend Lust touch the moral nature without leaving traces of defilement. Again, in "literature," authors whose pens seemed dipped in the sunlight of eloquence have vividly portrayed scenes of licentiousness; or satirically personated the life of the libertine and his conquests; or recorded the histories of ancient rakes; or gratified their own low-born or degraded natures by making pen-pictures of their own lascivious imaginings. . . . Many "classical" writers, as the word goes to-day, have gained fame by catering to the animal in man, expending high genius in their efforts to deify this "companion of every other crime." (168–69)

In this hygienic discourse the terms "art," "classic," "fine art," "literature," and the like are so thoroughly compromised by infection as to be safely handled only within the quarantine of quotation marks—punctuation that contributes greatly to the paragraph's supercilious air of the pedant. Designations such as "art" are taken to be mere impostures, ruses by which licentious "artists" secure an unwitting audience for lewd works of art. Here, we are beyond the point of any dialogue with "cultural elites," as the contemporary heirs to Comstock sometimes style American artists and intellectuals. The discourse of Comstockery can only denounce; it cannot negotiate—as Mencken learned to his chagrin. This, then, was the country that the modernists fled with stories about how they had "lived for the most part in villages where it were better that a millstone were hanged about your neck than that you should own yourself a minor poet." And these words are Robert Frost's, not Pound's.

Looking back on this epoch it is easy to suppose that Comstockery was little more than a sideshow, without real consequence or prestige. But Comstock and his agents were responsible for instigating thousands of prosecutions against authors, editors, and publishers. The more militant Comstocks created a chilly atmosphere in which magazine and book editors seldom took risks. "As a practical editor," Mencken writes in "Puritanism as a Literary Force," "I find that the Comstocks, near and far, are oftener in my mind's eye than my actual patrons. The thing I always have to decide about a manuscript offered for publication, before I give any thought to its artistic merit and suitability, is the question whether its publication will be permitted . . . whether some roving Methodist preacher, self-commissioned to keep watch on letters, will read indecency into it. Not a week passes that I do not decline some sound and honest piece of work for no other reason." He continues in a passage that explains much about American literary expatriatism: "I have a long list of such things by American authors, well-devised, well-imagined, well-executed, respectable as human documents and as works of art—but never to be printed in mine or any other American magazine. . . . All of these pieces would go into type at once on the Continent. . . . But they simply cannot be printed in the United States, with the law what it is and the courts what they are" (*A Book of Prefaces* 277). This is a remarkable concession from perhaps the most intrepid major American magazine editor of the period. One can well imagine how the Comstocks affected less Nietzschean tempers than his.[1]

To this cultural environment Frost chose, in 1915, to accommodate himself, animated by the ambition to reach the "general reader who buys books in their thousands." This resolution set him apart from Pound and the more intransigent expatriates, as well as from the cultural critics at home who were their fellow travelers, if only in thought. There were, let us say, three paths open to the American writer in the 1910s: expatriatism, the route marked out by Pound and those who followed him into exile; what we might call "domestic expatriatism," the route marked out by Mencken, who declared in *A Book of Prefaces* that he remained in America simply because the spectacle of the "booboisie" was supremely entertaining; and finally what I would call "principled domesticism," the route marked out by Frost, who—astonishingly, it must have seemed to Pound—resolved to make himself at home in America as a poet. As I hope to show, this resolution came to be associated intimately with Frost's descriptions of (and apologia for) a poetics of "conformity," as he once termed it—the adherence to a more or less conventional poetic form and a more or less conventional literary audience and marketplace, even as the avant-garde evolved through *vers libre,* Imagism, Vorticism, and other innovations. The latter writers published almost exclusively in "little magazines." Frost, for his part, suggested that "nothing is quite honest that is not commercial" and sought publication in large-circulation magazines such as the *Atlantic Monthly.*

This chapter considers how Frost's decision to write in America for a broad audience both affected and grew out of his theories of poetry. I regard his defense of correspondence and conformity in poetry as a kind of cultural criticism—as a mode of practicing cultural politics. I also aim to show that Frost's writings about poetic form are decidedly "overdetermined"—motivated by many things, of which cultural politics is only an obvious example. His motives seem by turns to be political: form as a kind of conservation, a check against radical personal and social "difference." Or philosophical: form in poetry as acknowledgment of the intrinsic constraints to which grammar and prosody—and the larger forces of which they may be taken as symbols—inevitably make us subject, no matter what we do to "free" ourselves and our writing. His motives are also quite possibly (though obliquely and residually) Christian: form as an expression of humility or of the subordination of individual vagaries to social and communal authorities—an Eliotic idea that I take up again in chapter 3. And, finally, Frost seemed to be working also from personal and familial motives: form as a stay against "insanity" and "confusion," as he memorably put it. This last line of inquiry takes into account the relation in Frost's writings between the stabilities of poetic form and the stabilities of sanity—a relation with specific biographical roots that I trace out in the concluding section of this chapter.

England in the Grip of Frost: Literary Expatriatism and Poetic Form

In the summer of 1921 Van Wyck Brooks asked Frost to write an essay for publication, presumably in *The Freeman,* which Brooks then edited. Frost refused, and if in fact the requested article was to have appeared in *The Freeman*, his refusal is understandable. On August 10, just a few weeks before Frost would write his letter of refusal, Brooks published an essay in *The Freeman* titled "Our Lost Intransigents." It reviewed a recently published edition of William James's letters and few things could have made Frost more reluctant to submit prose to Brooks than these remarks about a philosopher he revered: "It is our American philosophers and poets who are at fault for the stagnancy of our life; and indeed to explain the lapse, the defection, the fatuity of the most recent generation of intellectuals one need go no farther back than their acknowledged master, William James" (*Van Wyck Brooks: The Early Years* 238). Many of the writers who contributed to *The Freeman* were of the expatriate school from which Frost had already set himself apart. In the early 1920s, Harold Stearns—editor of *Civilization in the United States* (1922), an iconoclastic volume of cultural criticism to which Brooks contributed—published a regular letter from Europe in its columns. And it is interesting that two critics who later would author several of the most unforgiving attacks on Frost began their careers at *The Freeman* under Brooks: Malcolm Cowley and Newton Arvin.[2]

Whatever the occasion might have been for Frost's letter of refusal to Brooks, its ironies are subtle, even a little biting: "I am no such Puritan as to enjoy resisting temptation. It is hard for me to refuse you: but I must. I used to say prose after thirty; then in the thirties, prose after forty. Still distrusting myself at forty odd, I now say after fifty. Out of what we don't know and so can't be hurt by, poetry: out of knowledge, prose. Wait til I get wisdom; wait til I sell out and move to 'the place of understanding,' by which Solomon (or was it David?) must have meant Chicago—the Middle West anyway."[3] Brooks had published his own first volume of prose at the green age of twenty-three: *The Wine of the Puritans* (1909). What he thought of Frost's arch humility we can only wonder. And yet the teasing here is mostly affectionate. The two men admired one another.

About the time he wrote this letter, Frost's little-known contribution to a historical pageant called *The Pilgrim Spirit* was being published. The lyric was set to music for the pageant under the title "The Return of the Pilgrims" but Frost referred to it simply as his "puritan poem" (he would later incorporate certain key lines from the poem into "The Gift Outright"). Frost rather jealously defended the Puritans against the attacks (from H. L. Mencken, among others) that Brooks's first book, *The Wine of the Puritans*, had been instrumental in setting afoot. And in his first remark to Brooks, Frost apparently parodies the stock Puritan: someone who, a little hypocritically, actually *enjoys* self-abnegation. Perhaps he also parodies the view that poetry is somehow trivial or harmless: "Out of what we don't know and so can't be hurt by . . . " Wryly, and probably simply to goad his friend, Frost adopts a view of poetry that he no doubt knew Brooks would despise. It is the sort of view Brooks attributed to philistine midwesterners, such as when, in "The Culture of Industrialism," he chides our "orthodox literary men" who "cannot rise above the tribal view of their art as either an amusement or a soporific" (110).

Frost is not to be taken at his word in any event: "getting wisdom" suffers somewhat by comparison to "sel[ling] out" and moving, ultimately, to "the Middle West," where Frost was to take up his position in the fall of 1921 as Poet in Residence at the University of Michigan. But Frost's irony is probably at the expense of Brooks—not Michigan or Ohio. In 1920 Brooks's study *The Ordeal of Mark Twain* had appeared, with its argument that the cultural poverty of the Middle West, together with the gentility of the East, had stunted Twain's genius, as it had stunted the genius of an entire generation of American writers. In his letter to Brooks, Frost probably obliquely refers to *The Ordeal*—a book he seems to have known well—as much as to anything else. Brooks's view of the Middle West in the early 1920s shows plainly in a letter he wrote to Waldo Frank from Carmel, California, where he had settled in 1918. At the time, he was struggling to complete *The Ordeal of Mark Twain:* "You have no idea . . . how little the ideas of the last twenty years have penetrated across the continent. . . . Never believe people who talk to you about the West, Waldo; never forget that it is we New Yorkers and New Englanders who have the monopoly on whatever oxygen there is in the American continent!" (Hoopes 130). Frost is a considerably less anxious easterner when he writes in January 1920 to Sidney Cox, who had accepted a teaching position in Missoula, Montana: "The further from New York the better for a whole lot of reasons. Out there there ought to be something new for you to get the hang of for yourself. In New York there is next to nothing that somebody else hasn't already got the hang of for you. New York's as completely formulated as Abraham Lincoln. The last Englishman to arrive knows as much about it as the most pains-taking Greenwich Villager is ever likely to know" (Evans 136). As I will argue later in this chapter, skepticism about the Greenwich Village set would color Frost's essays on poetics, indirectly bringing into them some of the cultural debates hinted at in his 1921 letter to Brooks.

At issue in these documents is less the virtue of the Middle West than of American culture more generally. And Frost's contention in his letter to Cox that there was little new in the cultural criticism of the New York intellectuals—writers associated with the *Seven Arts* and *The Freeman,* for example—doubtless had some validity. Brooks's arguments about America in books such as *The Ordeal of Mark Twain* are in fact at least as old as Alexis de Tocqueville's *Democracy in America,* first published in 1835. Tocqueville writes:

> I know no country in which, generally speaking, there is less independence of mind and true freedom of discussion than in America. . . . No writer, no matter how famous, can escape from [the] obligation to sprinkle incense over his fellow citizens. Hence the majority lives in a state of perpetual self-adoration; only strangers or experience may be able to bring certain truths to the Americans' attention.
>
> We need seek no other reason for the absence of great writers in America so far; literary genius cannot exist without freedom of the spirit, and there is no freedom of the spirit in America. (254–56)

Brooks was simply the first to apply such ideas systematically in a study of American letters. In his view the decades between the Civil War and World War I were "the age when presidents were business men and generals were business men and preachers were business men, when the whole psychic energy of the American people was absorbed in the exploitation and the organization of the material resources of the continent and business enterprise was virtually the only recognized sphere of action." He describes the result with Nietzschean animosity: "The mere assertion of individuality was a menace to the integrity of what is called the herd: how much more so that extreme form of individuality, the creative spirit, whose whole tendency is skeptical, critical, realistic, disruptive!" (*Ordeal* 77, 85). And about what he terms "the normal Americano," H. L. Mencken writes in *Prejudices: Third Series:* "With the concept of wrongness, of course, he always confuses the concept of mere differentness—to him the two are indistinguishable. Anything strange is to be combatted; it is of the Devil" (27–28). Mencken, Brooks, and many other intellectuals felt that they inhabited an America in which any sort of dissent—intellectual, artistic, political, or moral—was promptly punished by severe social disapproval, and quite possibly by legal sanctions as well.

Mencken's and Brooks's allegations may seem to us extreme. But then again they may not: one must bear in mind that this episode of American history is unique for its suppression of civil liberties. In the late 1910s, periodicals publishing antiwar sentiments ran considerable risk of being denied use of the mails. The Comstock Postal Act had been on the federal books since 1873, and in the 1910s the Comstocks continued to foster numerous suits against, and frequent public defamation of, journalists, publishers, magazine editors, and novelists. Legal codes criminalizing obscenity were written so broadly as to inspire blatantly irresponsible prosecutions. Any language held by a jury to "arouse a libidinous passion . . . in the mind of a modest woman" was legally actionable.[4] Even the report of the Chicago Vice Commission was barred from the mails since it quoted and described "obscene" materials. The pressure was such that publishers began to write clauses into contracts extracting guarantees that manuscripts contained no scandalous language, the effect of which was to make authors bear all liability for any future litigation. Mencken took signal part in several battles with Comstockery, most notably in defending Dreiser's *The Genius* against suppression.

This was also the era out of which sprung Prohibition, beginning with the Webb-Kenyon Interstate Liquor Act of 1913 and culminating in the Volstead Act of 1919. Legislative efforts to control "sexual irregularity," as Mencken put it, resulted in passage of the Mann Act in 1910 and somewhat later in the adoption of the New York Adultery Act. In short, the 1910s and early 1920s were an era in which majoritarian tyranny seemed to men and women of Brooks's, Pound's, and Mencken's sensibility not merely a likely prospect but a fait accompli. By 1922 Mencken could write, with considerable evidence in his favor: "A minority not only has no more inalienable rights in the United States; it is not even lawfully entitled to be heard" (*Prejudices: Third Series* 294). Citing the case of Eugene Debs, who was imprisoned on charges that he encouraged resistance to the draft, Mencken points out that "a citizen who happens to belong to a minority is not even safe in his person: he may be put into prison, and for very long periods, for the simple offense of differing from the majority" (295). The Supreme Court, Mencken concludes, echoing the language of the *Dred Scott* decision, "has gradually succumbed to the prevailing doctrine that the minority has no rights that the majority is bound to respect. As it is at present constituted, it shows little disposition to go to the rescue of the harassed freeman" (297). This was but another symptom, Mencken thought, of a militant, resurgent Puritanism. "In brief," he wrote in 1917, "the new will to power, working in the true Puritan as in the mere religious sportsman, stimulated him to a campaign of repression and punishment perhaps unequalled in the history of the world, and developed an art of militant morality as complex in technique and as rich in professors as the elder art of iniquity" (*A Book of Prefaces* 240–41). Mencken goes on to cite damning statistics taken from a popular biography of Anthony Comstock. All told Comstock undertook 3,646 prosecutions, winning 2,682 convictions; he was estimated by supporters to have destroyed fifty tons of books, 28,425 pounds of stereotype plates, 16,900 photographic negatives, and 3,984,063 photographs (*A Book of Prefaces* 254n). This historical context helps explain why Mencken and Brooks identified "that extreme form of individuality" with "the creative spirit" and also why countercultural literary work acquired, for them, an aspect of heroism and martyrdom—a development exemplified nowhere better than in the poetry and essays of Pound in the mid- to late 1910s. This libertarian, countercultural ideal of the creative spirit eventually, and quite sharply, set Mencken, Brooks, and like-minded writers apart from Frost, as theorists of aesthetics and as interpreters of American culture. (An interesting chapter in the history of American literary modernism might be written about the connection between political challenges to free speech, personal liberties, and a free press in the 1910s and the advocacy by writers such as Pound, Brooks, Cowley, and Mencken of radical aesthetic libertarianism.)

In any event, the truculence of Brooks's arguments in *The Ordeal*—as when he speaks of a "creative spirit, whose whole tendency is skeptical, critical, realistic, disruptive"—makes clear the reason that so many of his generation saw no alternative but to sail for Europe. To them the very possibility of sustaining the "creative spirit" seemed to require emigration from America. The "anguish" of such artists, Mencken wrote in 1922, "fills the Liberal weeklies, and every ship that puts out from New York carries a groaning cargo of them, bound for Paris, London, Munich, Rome and way points—anywhere to escape the great curses and atrocities that make life intolerable for them at home" (*Prejudices: Third Series* 9). In 1912 Frost himself departed for England, where he would remain until 1915. But he apparently never intended to live in exile. In fact, he was quite self-conscious, sometimes even a little cocky, about his position as an American poet sailing for England (the "land of *The Golden Treasury*," as he later called it, alluding to Francis Turner Palgrave's anthology of English lyric poetry). In "Pan with Us," collected in *A Boy's Will* though written earlier, Frost offers something of a declaration of independence, reminiscent of the literary nationalism of the antebellum years:

> He tossed his pipes, too hard to teach
> A new-world song, far out of reach,
> For a sylvan sign that the blue jay's screech

> And the whimper of hawks beside the sun
> Were music enough for him, for one.
> (*CPPP* 32)

The subject of these lines is poetic diction. Not the precise, saccharine music of the pan pipe shall animate the New World poet's lines, the speaker is saying; instead, he shall write with the natural clamor and fuss of the jay's voice and the hawk's. There is a Whitmanesque touch in this, and perhaps a Jamesian one as well. (In *Essays in Radical Empiricism* James says that reality is "game flavored as a hawk's wing.")[5]

Among Frost's first letters home from England was this one to his friend Susan Hayes Ward, wherein he offers what is essentially another setting of "Pan with Us":

> Here we are between high hedges of laurel and red-osier dogwood, within a mile or two of where Milton finished Paradise Lost on the one hand and a mile or two of where Grey lies buried on the other. . . . To London town what is it but a run? Indeed when I leave writing this and go into the front yard for a last look at earth and sky before I go to sleep, I shall be able to see the not very distinct lights of London flaring like a dreary dawn. If there is any virtue in Location—but don't think I think there is. I know where the poetry must come from if it comes. (*Selected Letters* 52)

We should read these remarks in the context of the work in which Frost was then engaged, the preparation of *A Boy's Will* for publication. In *A Boy's Will* we hear echoes of Longfellow, from whom Frost borrows the title of his volume; we probably sense as well the presence of Yeats, from whose *The Wind among the Reeds* Frost apparently borrowed the device of attaching glosses to the titles of his poems. There are also evocations of Shakespeare, whose "Let me not to the marriage of true minds" contributes a phrase to "Into My Own," itself a variation on the Shakespearean sonnet form; of Wordsworth, inasmuch as "Ghost House" quietly recalls certain passages of "Tintern Abbey" and is haunted by the Romantic gothicism of the 1790s; of Marvell, whose "mower" poems stand behind "Mowing" (which echoes also Coleridge and Andrew Laing), "The Tuft of Flowers," and other poems; of Hardy, whose influence is no doubt felt in "Love and a Question"; and of Dickinson, who clearly provided the stanzaic model for "Stars"; and so on.[6] This brief list suffices to suggest that although the opening sequence of poems in *A Boy's Will* concerns a retreat from society, it is certainly not a retreat from the society of Frost's literary precursors. The "land of the *Golden Treasury*" is everywhere evident here. And we should regard *A Boy's Will* as we do the earlier books of Pound: as an effort on Frost's part to find a voice among his poetic predecessors, not only of the nineteenth century but of earlier ones as well. The important difference is that Frost is altogether quieter about this effort—and also less anxious—than is Pound.

A good example of Frost's way of addressing these matters occurs in the poem "My November Guest":

> My Sorrow, when she's here with me,
>   Thinks these dark days of autumn rain
> Are beautiful as days can be;
> She loves the bare, the withered tree;
>   She walks the sodden pasture lane.
>
> Her pleasure will not let me stay.
>   She talks and I am fain to list:
> She's glad the birds have gone away,
> She's glad her simple worsted gray
>   Is silver now with clinging mist.
>
> The desolate, deserted trees,
>   The faded earth, the heavy sky,
> The beauties she so truly sees,
> She thinks I have no eye for these,
>   And vexes me for reason why.
>
> Not yesterday I learned to know
>   The love of bare November days
> Before the coming of the snow,
> But it were vain to tell her so,
>   And they are better for her praise.
>
> (*CPPP* 16–17)

The remarkable music of this poem engages effects of consonance, assonance, and internal rhyme so pronounced as nearly to make a tongue twister of such lines as the following: "The beauties she so truly sees, / She thinks I have no eye for these." I often stumble over these lines in reading them aloud, and their elastic sounds are not typical of Frost's best-known work. Indeed, in a Fourth of July 1913 letter to John Bartlett—a kind of literary Declaration of Independence from England—Frost writes: "You see the great successes in recent poetry have been made on the assumption that the music of words was a matter of harmonised vowels and consonants. Both Swinburne and Tennyson arrived largely at effects in assonation. But they were on the wrong track or at any rate on a short track" (*CPPP* 664). "My November Guest" is a notable success in exactly this outworn assonant vein. And yet even as it depends upon the music associated with the "short track" laid out by Swinburne and Tennyson, the poem depends perhaps more importantly on what by 1913 Frost was calling "sentence sounds." In fact, Frost cites "My November Guest" in one of his better-known letters on sentence sounds, in which he is attempting to distance himself decisively from the Tennysonian-Swinburnian mode. "Take My November Guest," he writes, again to John Bartlett. "Did you know at once how we say such sentences as these when we talk? She thinks I have no eye for these. / Not yesterday I learned etc / But it were vain to tell her so" (*CPPP* 676). The sounds Frost points to here are impeccably conversational and have nothing to do with "harmonised" vowels and consonants.

In illustrating his theory of sentence sounds, then, Frost directs attention to a poem that deftly performs the old nineteenth-century music of Tennyson. This suggests how comfortable Frost already had become in working his own distinctly modern voice in among the voices of his English and American precursors. In a poem like "My November Guest," as in *A Boy's Will* more generally, there is harmony and merger among these several musics; nowhere is there evidence of the various purges and strict reforms of outmoded poetic diction that Pound suffered himself to undergo between 1908 and 1916. "My November Guest" obliquely accomplishes in tone and manner what Pound's well-known poem "The Pact" accomplishes by outright address to Walt Whitman: it strikes a bargain with literary precedent. In "The Tuft of Flowers," another poem from *A Boy's Will,* Frost's speaker tacitly addresses the laborer who preceded him in mowing the field: "'Men work together,' I told him from the heart, / 'Whether they work together or apart'" (*CPPP* 31). It has often been suggested that "The Tuft of Flowers" is an allegory of literary fellowship, and the poem certainly offers a useful way to characterize Frost's relation to his precursory poetic laborers. As if to bring home his point about the mutuality of literary dependence and independence, Frost follows "The Tuft of Flowers" with the considerably more assertive "Pan with Us," in which, as we have seen, that allegory is made explicit. One can readily see how the dialectic of society and solitude explored in *A Boy's Will* is also the dialectic of tradition and the individual talent.

This dialectic interested Frost nearly as much as it did Eliot. In 1925 he wrote an introduction for an anthology of poetry by Dartmouth College students. In it he offers the following parable about the poet's development:

> No one given to looking under-ground in spring can have failed to notice how a bean starts its growth from the seed. Now the manner of a poet's germination is less like that of a bean in the ground than of a waterspout at sea. He has to begin as a cloud of all the other poets he ever read. That can't be helped. And first the cloud reaches down toward the water from above and then the water reaches up toward the cloud from below and finally cloud and water join together to roll as one pillar between heaven and earth. The base of water he picks up from below is of course all the life he ever lived outside of books.
>
> These, then, are the three figures of the waterspout and the first is about as far as the poet doomed to die young in everyone of us usually gets. He brings something down from Dowson, Yeats, Morris, Masefield, or the Imagists (often a long way down), but lifts little or nothing up. If he were absolutely certain to do as doomed and die young, he would hardly be worth getting excited over in college or elsewhere. But you can't be too careful about whom you will ignore in this world. Cases have been known of his refusing at the last minute to abdicate the breast in favor of the practical and living on to write lyric like Landor till ninety.
>
> Right in this book he will be found surviving into the second figure of the waterspout, and, by several poems and many scattered lines, even into the third figure. "The Heritage," "Sonnet," "I Have Built a Vessel," and "The Wanderer," good as they are of their kind—accomplished and all that—are of the first figure and frankly derivative. They are meant to do credit to anyone's reading. But "The Letter," "The Village Daily," "For a Salvationist," and best of all, "The Ski Jumper," at least get up the salt water. Their realism represents an advance. They show acceptance of the fact that the way to better is often through worse. In such a poem as "Underneath Sleep" the pillar revolves pretty much unbroken. (*CPPP* 709)

A Boy's Will is exactly such a record of Frost's negotiations with his predecessors. It is easy to see how so richly allusive a volume might, in a sense, have begun as "a cloud of all the other poets" Frost ever read. More particularly, the atmosphere in which these poems subsist and take their inspiration issues, it might reasonably be said, chiefly from Palgrave's *Golden Treasury,* which is after all alluded to in "Waiting: Afield at Dusk" (*CPPP* 24). But if *A Boy's Will* first gathered itself together and was published in what Frost called "the land of the *Golden Treasury,*" it nonetheless has other, more native roots; the atmosphere may be English but the soil is American and in certain respects peculiar to Frost. In "My November Guest," as I point out, we hear Frost's own distinctive voice blending with the voice of the Tennysonian-Swinburnian strain he was even then setting himself against; here, the "pillar" revolves pretty much unbroken, as Frost carries something down from the cloud of all those other poets while drawing up something of his life lived outside of books. This movement was made complete in *North of Boston,* his second and most revolutionary book.

The movement from the *Golden Treasury* down into his own life was also a movement that spanned the Atlantic, as a poem like "Pan with Us" suggests with its moderately expressed literary nationalism. *A Boy's Will* is a kind of treaty, negotiated by Frost, harmonizing English and American poetries. And his tactful, diplomatic touch in addressing these negotiations should not obscure the fact that he took them quite seriously. In a 1913 letter home to Ernest Silver—head of the Plymouth, New Hampshire, Normal School where Frost had taught in 1911—Frost quotes a recent headline from an English paper: "One morning early in December the papers were out with scare heads like this: ENGLAND IN THE GRIP OF FROST. I accept the omen, says I, I accept the omen. Better than that Frost should be in the grip of England" (*Selected Letters* 59). In 1913 Frost confided to the English poet F. S. Flint that he had lived in American villages where "it were better that a millstone were hanged about your neck than that you should own yourself a minor poet." But his ambition was nothing less than to return to America and own himself a major poet in the villages of *New* England, where even Amy Lowell feared to tread. The foregoing examples show that Frost was able to consider with equanimity and good humor potentially embattled questions about literary nationalism and originality, which, to him, presented occasions for play and irony, not occasions for the considerably more anxious blandishments of Pound.

Frost's decision to repatriate himself in 1915 would resonate in his poetry and in his essays on poetics. In 1934, he wrote a long letter to his daughter Lesley Frost Francis—quoted already in the introduction to this study—describing his encounter with the New Movement poets in England in the mid-1910s and giving as well an account of the poetic theories of their successors. He refers to Herbert Read, author of *Form in Modern Poetry* (1932), whose name he misspells: "You'll find in Reed his [Pound's] latest descendant a full statement of the doctrine of Inner Form, that is to say the form the subject itself takes if left to itself without any considerations of outer form. Everything else is to have two compulsions, an inner and an outer, a spiritual and a social, an individual and a racial. . . . Everything," Frost adds with scorn, "but poetry according to the Pound-Eliot-Richards-Reed school of art" (*CPPP* 735). The previous chapter should be enough to suggest how social "compulsions" and "conformities" can temper the career not of the poem only but also of the poet—at least in America. And among the most interesting suggestions in Frost's letter is that social and aesthetic problems are one and the same. He is thinking at once of the "subject" of a poem and of human "subjectivity" itself when he remarks: "Everything" has "two compulsions, an inner and an outer, a spiritual and a social, an individual and a racial."

The "doctrine of Inner Form," as Frost styles it, dates from as early as 1912. Clearly Pound has something like it in mind in *Patria Mia,* an essay very much concerned with the intersection of the social and the aesthetic, as well as with American literary expatriatism:

> I met a man in New York. He is over thirty, he has never had time to get "educated." I liked some of his lyrics. I said, "Give me some more and I'll take 'em to London and have 'em published."
>
> I found the rest of his work, poem after poem, spoiled. I said: "Why do you do this and this?" He said: "They told me to." I said: "Why have you utterly ruined this cadence, and used this stultifying inversion to maintain a worn-out metre that everyone is tired of?"
>
> Same answer. I said: "Why do you say what you don't mean to get more rhymes than you need?" He said: "They told me it was paucity of rhyme if I didn't."
>
> Then he read me the chorus of a play—in splendid movement. The form was within it and of it. And I said: "Mother of God! Why don't you do that sort of thing all the time?" And he said: "Oh! I didn't know that was poetry. I just did it as I wanted to—just as I felt it."
>
> And of course, the way to "succeed," as they call it, is to comply. To comply to formulae, and to formulae not based on any knowledge of the art or any care for it. (*Selected Prose* 113)

The chief question Pound asks about a poem is this: "Does it comply with the laws inherent in itself?" And he contends that American editors are all but incapable of asking it: "They are meticulous to find out if a thing conforms to a standard, like the carpenter who sawed off the books. But they have no interest whatever in ascertaining whether new things, living things, seeking for expression, have found for themselves new and fitting modes wherein to be expressed" (114). He objects to the same forces of social conformity, here manifested in the realm of poetics, that had made "the mere assertion of individuality . . . a menace to the integrity of . . . the herd," as Brooks writes in *The Ordeal of Mark Twain.* Or as Pound has it: "The way to 'succeed,' as they call it, is to comply."

Clearly, then, the doctrine of Inner Form reaches beyond the limits of aesthetics. Pound's struggles against American editors caused that doctrine to become attached, in his imagination, to the artist's higher integrity. It came to symbolize a purity of purpose and a sacrifice much more than merely aesthetic. Recall how he transforms and elevates his debate with American editors and American culture in "The Rest," quoted above in connection with Frost's poem "Good Hours":

> O helpless few in my country,
> O remnant enslaved!
>
> Artists broken against her,
> A-stray, lost in the villages,
> Mistrusted, spoken against.

Pound probably does not intend that we take these metaphors of enslavement and martyrdom too much in earnest—things were not quite *that* bad. But nevertheless he borrows their prestige. And taking all things into account, Pound's suggestion that American intellectual and cultural life was both regimented and a little vicious is not without basis, as I have already suggested. The 1910s were undoubtedly an era of majoritarian abuses, an era in which freedom of the press suffered at the hands of the Comstock antivice movement and the censors of the postmaster general. Prudish, genteel magazine editors therefore worked hand in glove—or so it seemed to Pound and Mencken—with censors of considerably more sinister aspect. "The Rest" is thus to be accounted for in part by the situation Mencken describes in "Puritanism as a Literary Force": "No other nation has laws which oppress the arts so ignorantly and so abominably as ours do, nor has any other nation handed over the enforcement of the statutes which exist to agencies so openly pledged to reduce all aesthetic expression to the service of a stupid and unworkable scheme of rectitude" (253). Mencken then cites a 1914 publication authored by Comstock himself, titled *MORALS, Not Art or Literature*—capitals in the original, as Mencken drily indicates. As he points out, the Comstock movement was but another manifestation of a persistent "national suspicion of the arts" (254), which I have considered at greater length in chapter 1. In any event, "The Rest" is altogether concerned with aesthetic and cultural *non*-"compliance," to use Pound's term in *Patria Mia*. Through such strategies as these the doctrine of Inner Form acquired a moral and political necessity, even an air of heroism. And although it is one of Pound's less satisfying lyrics, "The Rest" illustrates quite well the sort of thing I want to trace in Frost's own work: the means by which aesthetic strategies assume ethical and moral significances.

Brooks, like Pound, favored metaphors of slavery in talking about these matters. He writes in "The Literary Life in America," his contribution to *Civilization in the United Sates:* "Let us call it local patriotism, the spirit of the times, the hunger of the public for this, that or the other: to some one of these demands, these promptings from without, the 'normal' American writer always allows himself to become a slave. It is the fact, indeed, of his being a slave to some demand from without that makes him 'normal'—and something else than an artist" (165). One way to describe Frost's career is to say simply that he hoped to show how an American poet might be at once "normal" *and* an "artist." Self-fulfillment alone was by no means enough for him; he wanted also to fulfill what Brooks calls the "promptings from without." In this he shows how unsatisfactory, for him, was the modernist ideal of a "purely inward sense of vocation," to borrow David Bromwich's phrase in *A Choice of Inheritance.* In his essays and letters on poetics Frost variously calls these promptings "compulsions," "conformities," "commitments," and "disciplines," and we should bear in mind always that these commitments are equally the social ones identified by Brooks *and* the aesthetic ones described by Pound and Herbert Read. The dialectic of "conformity" and "formity" figured in Frost's letter may also be taken to represent—as "My November Guest" helps us see—Eliot's dialectic of tradition (or "conformity") and the individual talent (or "formity").

This dialectic has much to do with the question of expatriatism. In a 1944 essay, "The American Literary Expatriate," R. P. Blackmur describes what he calls the "psychological values" of expatriation:

> There is the value connected with the relationship between the outsider and the insider, the unique and the representative, as groups and individuals feel it, which may be expressed, when it is an imbalance, in the outward act of expatriation. This is the case with both James and Eliot.
>
> There is also the parallel value connected with the balance or imbalance between anarchy and order, the rebellion against or the reliance upon imposed external forms, whether cultural, political, or economic, in terms of which groups frame their response to society, and which again, when the imbalance is severe, may be expressed dramatically in expatriation. Both James and Eliot seem in the terms of their expatriation to symbolize such imbalances. (*Lion and the Honeycomb* 74)

All writers probably feel the pressures of this rebellion against or reliance upon "imposed external forms" of culture. Frost felt it no less than

Eliot, Pound, or James, but unlike them he chose repatriation—reliance upon, rather than all-out rebellion against, the imposed external forms of American culture. I have suggested in chapter 1 that a number of Frost's vocational poems and letters are subtle efforts to accommodate his "unutilitarian" difference as a poet to a "utilitarian" American morality, to use his own terminology; that is to say, these works reflect his efforts to balance his status as a cultural outsider against his status as an insider, in Blackmur's terms. And the pressures of poetic form in his verse became, as he saw it, the constant symbol of the cultural pressures and commitments he was unwilling to abjure. He came to value his own performances in life and in poetry for the success with which he accepted and mastered these pressures: "Every single poem written regular is a symbol great or small of the way the will has to pitch into commitments deeper and deeper to a rounded conclusion and then be judged for whether any original intention it had has been strongly spent or weakly lost; be it in art, politics, school, church, business, love, or marriage—in a piece of work or in a career. Strongly spent is synonymous with kept" (*CPPP* 786).

American writers have often described the difficulties of their careers in the apparently impersonal terms of aesthetics. One of the best-known examples occurs in Henry James's *Hawthorne,* originally published in the English Men of Letters series in 1879. James writes: "It takes so many things, as Hawthorne must have felt later in life, when he made the acquaintance of the denser, richer, warmer European spectacle—it takes such an accumulation of history and custom, such a complexity of manners and types, to form a fund of suggestion for a novelist" (351). Blackmur suggests, as have a number of later critics, that James is really making an "apologia for his own action" (*Lion and the Honeycomb* 64)—that is, for his choice of expatriation. I am suggesting that Frost's writings on poetic form are, in part, a kind of apologia for his alternative action: his choice of repatriation and his conjoined decision to write in traditional poetic form for "the general reader who buys books in their thousands." The point is well made by Kenneth Burke in *The Philosophy of Literary Form* (1941): "Critical and imaginative works are answers to questions posed by the situation in which they arose. They are not merely answers, they are *strategic* answers, *stylized* answers. . . . So I should propose an initial working distinction between 'strategies' and 'situations,' whereby we think of poetry (I here use the term to include any work of critical or imaginative cast) as the adopting of various strategies for the encompassing of situations" (1). Simply put, Frost and Pound had adopted opposed strategies for encompassing the same situation: the admittedly difficult literary life in an America populated—as Pound, Mencken, and Brooks would say—by Comstocks, genteel editors, and philistines. The difference between Frost and Pound may be summarized as follows: Pound sought to resist American cultural (and marketplace) influences on his work while in America and to cultivate European influences on his work while in Europe, whereas Frost sought to resist, or simply to control and monitor, English influences on his work while in England: England in the grip of Frost indeed. And as we shall see presently, Frost's essays on poetics define poetry so as to transfigure the often difficult cultural and personal choices he had made into something satisfying and rational. It is a process of impersonalizing personal struggles until they feel natural and inevitable.

The "Greenwich Village Idea" and Frost's "Constant Symbol"

An "ethic of self-fulfillment," as F. W. Dupee called it, remained always at the heart of Brooks's writings, even after he had by and large repudiated the militancy of his early essays on American culture. Dupee points out that in this respect Brooks was representative of a good many writers of his generation for whom the figure of the artist had "supplanted the muckraker as the standard intellectual type; consciousness of self was cultivated in place of class consciousness; and writers set out to express and assert and fulfill themselves" (564). Perfectly self-realizing poets writing perfectly self-realizing poems: that was what these critics hoped to bring about, all differences among them allowed.

Mencken's influence is very much in evidence here. In *The Philosophy of Friedrich Nietzsche* (1908) and in essays of the 1910s, he had helped establish the ideal of a nonconformist, "Dionysian" creative spirit, an ideal largely derived from Nietzsche's writings. Mencken summed up his position in an essay published in 1922 in the *Smart Set:* "As for me, my literary theory, like my politics, is based chiefly upon one main idea, to wit, the idea of freedom. I am, in brief, a libertarian of the most extreme variety. . . . The essence of sound art is freedom. The artist must be allowed his impish impulse, his revolt, his perversity. He stands in fundamental opposition to Philistine correctness; if he is bound by it he is nothing" (*Smart Set Criticism* 24–25). Given these sentiments, it is easy to see why Mencken gave such a warm welcome to the Imagists—the poets whom Frost associated with the libertarian doctrine of Inner Form. In a May 1915 omnibus review of new books of poetry Mencken had this to say about them (he had been reading the anthology *Des Imagistes*): "Rebellious ladies and gentlemen, making faces at orthodoxy in all its forms! It is Miss Lowell who speaks for them. 'Away,' says she, 'with didacticism, rhyme schemes, hobbling metres, ancient forms.' The aim of poetry is 'to head-up an emotion until it burns white-hot'—and that sort of heading-up is not to be done in corsets, hoop-skirts, straight-jackets" (*Smart Set Criticism* 87). The latter items symbolize not simply the constraints of social class and propriety but of aesthetic form as well.

Mencken sometimes sounds merely descriptive when setting out in his study of Nietzsche the opposition of "Apollonian" and "Dionysian" dispositions. But his sympathies unmistakably lie with the latter. Dionysians aim, he says, "to live under the most favorable conditions possible," "to adapt themselves to changing circumstances, and to avoid the snares of artificial, permanent rules" (*Nietzsche* 72). These ideals clearly inform what Malcolm Cowley calls, in his memoir *Exile's Return* (1934), the "Greenwich Village Idea," two principles of which bear closely on the present discussion: "The idea of self-expression.—Each man's, each woman's, purpose in life is to express himself, to realize his full individuality through creative work and beautiful living in beautiful surroundings. . . . The idea of liberty.—Every law, convention or rule of art that prevents self-expression or the full enjoyment of the moment should be shattered and abolished" (60). This Greenwich Village Idea, energized by Menckenian-Nietzschean polemics, complements the more strictly aesthetic doctrines of such theorists of inner form as Herbert Read, who writes in *Form in Modern Poetry* (1932): "[Organic form] is the form imposed on poetry by the laws of its own origination, without consideration for the given forms of traditional poetry. It is the most original and most vital principle of poetic creation; and the distinction of modern poetry is to have recovered its principle" (11). Read completes the picture that Mencken, Pound, and Brooks had severally begun. In his account, the "creative spirit" is itself generally libertarian, while *modern* art, more specifically, is self-consciously based on the recovery of libertarian ideals.

Frost's letters of the late 1910s and early 1920s show that he was much exercised by the Greenwich Village intellectuals described in Cowley's memoir. He had served as contributing editor to the short-lived progressive magazine the *Seven Arts* (1916–17), which was apparently inspired by Brooks's essay *America's Coming of Age* (1915). James Hoopes writes in *Van Wyck Brooks: In Search of American Culture* (1977): "When Waldo Frank wrote to enlist Brooks for the new magazine which he and James Oppenheim were planning, he called *America's Coming of Age* the 'prolegomena to our Future Seven Arts Magazine'" (110). Brooks accepted a position on the magazine's advisory board. Other major contributors were Mencken, Randolph Bourne, Brooks, Untermeyer, Floyd Dell, and Max Eastman. Frost's satirical poem "New Hampshire" (1923) registers quite clearly his encounters with literary radicals both in and out of Brooks's circle. In a review of *New Hampshire* John Farrar even praised the poem (somewhat extravagantly) as "the best poised and wisest diatribe against current literary smartness" (Wagner, *Critical Reception* 57). Evidently, Frost considered his work as in some sense an answer to the "Greenwich Village Idea." His contemporaries certainly saw it in this light.

Whether or not "New Hampshire" is an especially wise diatribe against the smartness of the Greenwich Village set, Frost's poetics do in fact present a coherent and subtle alternative to the libertarian ideals of those same intellectuals. Brooks's celebration of a socially subversive "creative will," for example, stands in the deep background of Frost's arguments in what seems to me his greatest essay in poetics, "The Constant Symbol" (1946). He offers an analysis therein of Shakespeare's sonnet twenty-nine:

> Suppose [the poet] to have written down "When in disgrace with Fortune and men's eyes."[7] He has uttered about as much he has to live up to in the theme as in the form. Odd how the two advance into the open pari passu. He has given out that he will descend into Hades, but he has confided in no one how far before he will turn back, or whether he will turn back at all, and by what jutting points of rock he will pick his way. He may proceed as in blank verse. Two lines more, however, and he has set himself in for rhyme, three more and he has set himself a stanza. Up to this point his discipline has been the self-discipline whereof it is written in so great praise. The harsher discipline from without is now well begun. He who knows not both knows neither. His worldly commitments are now three or four deep. Between us, he was no doubt bent on the sonnet in the first place from habit, and what's the use in pretending he was a freer agent than he had any ambition to be. (*CPPP* 789)

It is clear from the rest of the essay that when he says "*self*-discipline," stressing the first word rather than the second, Frost refers to individual will, as opposed to the will of other forces "from without." He is not thinking, for example, of "repression." This is brought out even more clearly in an early manuscript of the essay held in the Barrett Collection of Alderman Library at the University of Virginia: "This is the self discipline from within where of so much is written. He goes relatively undisciplined who knows no other whose impulse has not tempted him out into the harsher discipline of the world." Brooks, Pound, and Herbert Read had all written in great praise of self-discipline in this sense and in scorn of the harsher discipline from without. In speaking of self-discipline Frost uses the term much as Brooks does in "The Literary Life": "The country literally swarms with half-artists, as one may call them, men and women, that is to say, who have ceased to conform to the law of the tribe but who have not accepted the *discipline* of their own individual spirits" (197; my emphasis). The doctrine of Inner Form justifies these remarks: to become a whole artist is wholly to give one's self over to the discipline of one's individual spirit, as against the discipline of the law of the tribe. But references to Brooks notwithstanding, Frost probably refers in "The Constant Symbol" more particularly to Read's *Form in Modern Poetry,* which offers a definition of "personality" (as opposed to "character") firmly grounded in such a conception of self-discipline as Brooks defends in the passage just quoted. Read stresses "the idea of a free disposition . . . of the sensations and memory—the sensual being":

> This being is given coherence, is defined or outlined, by a judgment which is innate. The ego is a synthesis of the sensations, is generated by conscious experience, by that inward perspective which Montaigne exercised so freely for our delectation. The judgment is not imposed on the sensations from without, as if by an external agency—that is the process of repression which results in character; judgment emerges from the history of our sensations, is elected by them, and the coherence of personality is indeed the coherence of a natural process; not the coherence of an arbitrary discipline. (28–29)

The passage perfectly states what Frost called the doctrine of Inner Form, and it brings out in sharp relief the difference between his poetics and Read's. Read emphasizes "*innate*" judgment, "*inward* perspective," and the coherence of "natural process" rather than of "arbitrary discipline"; Frost emphasizes "the harsher discipline from without."

Frost believed that exercises in poetic form are a means of reasserting the *kind* of control we tend to lose over such worldly commitments as have overcome the speaker of Shakespeare's sonnet. In this sense, the writing of poetry has specifically therapeutic benefits, as I will explain later. Frost writes in the "'Letter' to *The Amherst Student*" (1935): "Anyone who has achieved the least form to be sure of it, is lost to the larger excruciations. I think it must stroke faith the right way. The artist, the poet might be expected to be the most aware of such assurance. But it is really everybody's sanity to feel it and live by it" (*CPPP* 740). The speaker of Shakespeare's sonnet would certainly understand this because in thinking of his lover he finds something like redemption from the larger excruciations: "For thy sweet love rememb'red such wealth brings / That then I scorn to change my state with Kings." And that redemption, in the broader argument of the sonnet sequence, becomes indistinguishable from the writing of the sonnets themselves. Poetry is a means of community for the lovers, often their only means; it is their way of overcoming the confusions of time and in this case also of disgrace. The genius of Frost's phrase "worldly commitments," and of his analysis as a whole, is that it expresses equally the formal and the thematic problems in the sonnet, and for that matter in all sonnets—all poems "written regular," as he says earlier in the essay (*CPPP* 786). In speaking of "*his* worldly commitments," Frost refers at once to Shakespeare and to the figure in his sonnet: form (Shakespeare's commitments) and theme (his speaker's commitments) "advance pari passu." The larger argument of the essay is simply a generalization of this idea: "Every poem is an epitome of the great predicament; a figure of the will braving alien entanglements" (*CPPP* 787).[8] One of the implications of Frost's commentary seems to be that poetry is not simply a figure of this entanglement but also a means to address it—even, as in Shakespeare's sonnets, symbolically to overcome it.

And yet, any satisfaction gained by such means will necessarily be partial and momentary. It is as if Frost deconstructs Shakespeare's sonnet. In his reading, the sonnet itself becomes a brilliant but finally unsuccessful attempt to take fortune in hand. The "worldly commitments" in the little theater of the poem prove too much for the "individual will," even *this* "Will":

> He had made most of his commitments all in one plunge. The only suspense he asks us to share with him is in his theme. He goes down, for instance, to a depth that must surprise him as much as it does us. But he doesn't even have the say of how long his piece will be. Any worry is as to whether he will outlast or last out the fourteen lines—have to cramp or stretch to come out even—have enough bread for the butter or butter for the bread. As a matter of fact, he gets through in twelve lines and doesn't know quite what to do with the last two. (*CPPP* 789)

Implicitly in this sonnet, and explicitly in the sequence of which it is a part, poetry is proposed, again, as a means to master fortune. But as Frost sees it, the poetry itself is in this case finally unmasterable. And the control over fortune extravagantly promised on behalf of poetry in the sonnets is of course impossible. In Frost's view this is no disgrace: the forms of poetry almost always outlast anyone's ability to master them. The moment a poet makes his commitments to rhyme, line, and stanza, these commitments begin to restrict and redirect the progress of his intention—his "will"—in the poem. Shakespeare "doesn't even have the say of how long his piece will be." And the "harsher discipline[s] from without," already "well begun" at line four—at which point stanzaic form is established—get the better of the poet in the couplet, just as other, still harsher disciplines have presumably overwhelmed the speaker of his poem. Shakespeare—as the major leaguers say—is letting the ball play him: "As a matter of fact, he gets through in twelve lines and doesn't know quite what to do with the last two." He does not have enough butter for his bread.

For these reasons, Pound and the poets and critics associated with him came to distrust form *as such.* It seemed *insincere* to them, too contingent; it seemed to do too much of the work in the poem. Herbert Read writes in *Form in Modern Poetry:* "When an organic form is stabilized and repeated as a pattern . . . the intention of the artist is no longer related to the inherent dynamism of an inventive act, but seeks to adapt content to predetermined structure" (9). Or as Frost would say: the poet finds himself "either cramping or stretching to come out even." Later in the same book Read points out that "it was with the school which [T. E.] Hulme started and Pound established that the revolution begun by Wordsworth was finally completed. Diction, rhythm and metre were fully emancipated from formal artifice, and the poet was free to act creatively under laws of his own origination" (59). Here is Frost's own more matter-of-fact description of the problem: "One of the first things Pound thought of was that rhyme and meter made you use too many words and even subsidiary ideas for the sake of coming out even" (*CPPP* 734). The question that Pound, Hulme, and the Imagists had asked was a simple one: To what extent may poetry be writing itself? This leads to the more general question that many critics and poets have raised more recently: To what extent may language be "speaking" us?

In *Language as Symbolic Action* (1966), Kenneth Burke points out that language has unconscious motives or purposes, to which anyone speaking it is in some sense merely incidental; in Frost's terminology, such motives fall under the heading of "conformity" or of the "harsher discipline[s] from without." There are grammatical motives, as when the "object" of a sentence is "motivated" by a transitive verb or as when a particular kind of subject motivates and delimits the choice of verb, and so on. Then there are the higher-level motivations of syntax, such as when patterns like "antithesis" and "balance" begin to motivate word choice; diction, rhyme, meter, and stanza are complications of this motive. We may even speak of the motivation of a prevailing style, as Euphuism motivated writing and speech in the 1590s or as Augustan "balance" motivated writing in Pope's day. Obviously, we move, here, into a kind of middle ground where strategic or personal motivations begin to operate, since such structures as characterize Euphuism may be consciously adopted for a particular end; and in Frost's terminology such motivations as these come under the general heading of "formity" or "*self*-discipline."

But we are perhaps given to overestimating the amount of conscious motivation involved in such stylistic decisions, owing to our historical and literary distance from the period in question. We speak after the fact, viewing the *effects* of certain stylistic strategies as motives for their use, as when the mere fitness of a device to achieve a particular end is taken as evidence of design. To some extent, one quite probably learns, say, Augustanism simply by coming of age literarily in the 1720s, somewhat in the sense, to put it perhaps too simply, in which one learns particular grammatical and syntactical habits as a child; the structures by which we organize our thoughts are never entirely, or even chiefly, peculiar to us. Doubtless a style may feel as natural to its true contemporary as it feels merely strategic to us, coming of age, as we have, under an altogether different stylistic regime. Style is, among other things, the lens through which a writer looks out on or addresses the world, and until she moves beyond its perspective she is unlikely to see her style for the filtering lens it actually is. When a style seems thus "natural" to a poet writing under its influence, it is probably at least partly inappropriate to speak in terms strictly of her conscious motivation; to a degree, she may very well be "spoken" by the style. This seems to be the point of Frost's remarks about Shakespeare's choice of the sonnet form: "Between us, he was no doubt bent on the sonnet in the first place from habit, and what's the use in pretending he was a freer agent than he had any ambition to be?"

In working out his theories of Imagism in the mid-1910s, Pound had tried to make his contemporaries acutely conscious of the Victorian and Georgian styles they had come of age speaking; the consciousness-raising passage quoted above from *Patria Mia* is a perfect example of this. But for his part, Frost saw that the difficulties really only begin with rhyme, meter, and stanza. Beyond these lie the more profound "forms" of vocabulary, grammar, and "diary," as he puts it in "The Constant

Symbol": "To the right person it must seem naïve to distrust form as such. The very words of the dictionary are a restriction to make the best of or stay out of and be silent. . . . Form in language is such a disjected lot of old broken pieces it seems almost as non-existent as the spirit till the two embrace in the sky" (*CPPP* 790). This is another way of suggesting that form is a kind of linguistic "unconscious." "Form in language" only *seems* "non-existent"; we are always already within its embrace. Frost understood that Pound and the Imagists had brought only a small part of this formal unconscious to light; their therapies had been incomplete.

Earlier in "The Constant Symbol" Frost writes: "Texture is surely something. A good piece of weaving takes rank with a picture as decoration for the wall of a studio, though it must be admitted to verge on the arty. There is a time of apprenticeship to texture when it shouldn't matter if the stuff is never made up into anything. There may be scraps of repeated form all over it. But form as a whole! Don't be shocking! The title of his first book was *Fragments*" (*CPPP* 786). The reference may be to the last section of Eliot's poem *The Waste Land,* with its often-quoted line: "These fragments I have shored against my ruins." If so, Frost probably points to this mild paradox: Although Eliot's poem lacks a general, broad form traditional to English literature, it nevertheless depends upon a great many formal devices. It is in fact a rich repository of poetic forms, "scraps" of which are "repeated all over it": rhyme, meter, stanza, the English sonnet, assonance, patterns of recurrent imagery, and such overarching thematic forms as the grail quest. In view of this, Frost may have thought Eliot somewhat evasive when he spoke of the "fragments" he had "shored against [his] ruins." Reading the poem closely we constantly discover the many ways in which it is precisely *not* fragmentary. Indeed, in his notes to the first book edition of *The Waste Land,* Eliot himself suggests several broad thematic forms or patterns that bind together this "fragmentary" poem. But setting aside for the moment the possibility that Frost refers particularly to *The Waste Land,* it is nevertheless easy to see his general point. When the modernists exhibited distrust of form *as such* they had often been quite naive—at least to Frost's way of thinking about the matter. If it is true, as he seems to believe, that poets inevitably enter into myriad small-scale formal commitments, then on what *principle,* finally, can they properly object to form *as a whole?* As Frost would have it, writing poetry is a veritable education in how deeply committed to form poets have always already become. And what is the use in pretending that poets are freer agents than they actually are?

It fell to Charles Olson to understand the latency of form in language as well as Frost did. His response was to perfect, in a sense, the doctrine of Inner Form, taking it much further than Pound and the Imagists had. Consequently, his essay "Projective Verse" (1950) provides an especially useful contrast to "The Constant Symbol." He is discussing poetic form: "Which brings us up, immediately, bang, against tenses, in fact against syntax, in fact against grammar generally, that is, as we have inherited it. Do not tenses, must they not also be kicked around anew, in order that time, that other governing absolute, may be kept, as must the space-tensions of the poem, immediate, contemporary to the acting-on-you of the poem? . . . The conventions which logic has forced on syntax must be broken open as quietly as must the too set feet of the old line" (*Selected Writings* 21). In brief, Olson is asking "how far a new poet can stretch the very conventions on which communication by language rests" (*Selected Writings* 21). That question marks the consummation of the doctrine of Inner Form, and over against it I would set Frost's alternative question about Shakespeare's behavior in "When in disgrace with Fortune and men's eyes": "What's the use in pretending he was a freer agent than he had any ambition to be?" Significantly, Frost speaks of "ambition" rather than, say, of "capability." It may well be impossible, as he believed, that anyone should escape the harsher disciplines from without. But for him there is really no reason to *hope* that one could, no reason to make it one's ambition. If Olson, Pound, and Read distrusted form as such, Frost distrusted the idea that the poem ought to, let alone *must,* develop strictly according to "the laws of its own organization, without consideration for the given forms of traditional poetry" (Read 11). And I want next to investigate how, in Frost's poetics, the concept of "conformity" acquires what I would call a normative value.

The "Fear of Man"

I have suggested that Frost's criticism of the "doctrine of Inner Form" speaks of more than merely technical poetic concerns. This is brought out clearly in his discussion of "difference" in his introduction to Edwin Arlington Robinson's *King Jasper:* "There is such a thing as being too willing to be different. And what shall we say to people who are not only willing but anxious? What assurance have they that their difference is not insane, eccentric, abortive, unintelligible?" (*CPPP* 741). In chapter 1, I discussed this passage in connection with what I call the "accommodating" rhetoric of Frost's poetry, but it has much broader implications. These remarks on the "fear of Man," and the introduction to *King Jasper* more generally, reflect Frost's efforts to set himself apart from the poetry of high modernism and from the cultural criticism that he apparently associated with the doctrine of Inner Form. And in this Frost's introduction to *King Jasper* perfectly complements "The Constant Symbol."

"That is where the extreme modernists are defeating themselves," Frost remarked in a July 1931 interview. "They do not care whether their communication is intelligible to others. It suffices that it has significance only to its creator. They desire, also, to play always on the insane fringe of things" (*Interviews* 80). These remarks are elliptical. But a fairly general argument may be inferred from them. In Frost's view, it was probably no accident that so much "extreme" modernist poetry took cultural impotence and desolation for its theme. The modernists themselves had undertaken elaborate stylistic strategies to break off "their communication," as he puts it somewhat vaguely. It must have seemed to Frost presumptuous, then, to claim—as Eliot did, for example—that the difficult, esoteric *style* of modernist poetry must itself be the index of some larger cultural malaise. As a number of readers have observed, it is just as likely that an artist's own feelings of alienation lay at the bottom of it all. This is of course putting the matter rather crudely. But it at least suggests why Frost is often willing to speak of "extreme" modernism as almost a form of pathology—as an existence on "the insane fringe of things." The logic of Pound's career may well have seemed inevitable to him, if he was ever given to thinking about the matter symbolically: alienation, expatriation, extreme modernism, arrest and imprisonment on charges of treason, and at last (so the courts ruled, at any rate) insanity. Frost does not explain what he means when he says that the "extreme modernists" play on the "insane fringe of things." But in 1931 he might have been thinking of political extremism, very far to his right. Pound's fascination with the social-credit theories of Clifford Hugh Douglass was leading him to support Mussolini. A few years later he would compose a tract that drew favorable analogies between the policies of Jefferson and the Italian dictator.

Frost's suggestion that "extreme modernism" verges on the pathological would soon be echoed by socialist realist critics associated with the Communist Popular Front. These critics charged that modernists such as Joyce were decadent, obscure, dangerously skeptical, socially unprogressive, and so on. Similar claims date from Mike Gold's rather severe manifesto in *The New Masses,* "Proletarian Realism" (1930): "[Proletarian realism] has nothing to do with the sickly mental states of the idle Bohemians, their subtleties, their sentimentalities, their fine-spun affairs. The worst example and the best of what we do not want to do is the spectacle of Proust, master-masturbator of the bourgeois literature. . . . We are not interested in verbal acrobats—this is only another form for bourgeois idleness. The Workers live too close to reality to care about these literary show-offs, these verbalist heroes" (206–7). By the end of the decade, even Brooks—now repented of his youthful iconoclasm—was criticizing the literary avant-garde. In a remarkable speech delivered at Columbia University in 1941, Brooks drew a distinction between "primary" and "secondary" writers. The primary writer "bespeaks the collective life of the people," concerns herself with "the great themes . . . by virtue of which the race has risen—courage, justice, mercy, honor, love," and believes in the "idea of progress." The secondary writer, by contrast, writes merely for coteries, obsesses herself with matters of form and aesthetics as against content and theme, manifests a fascination with the "death-drive," and is skeptical about notions of "progress" (qtd. in Macdonald, *Memoirs* 213). Most of the secondary writers Brooks names happen to be the "extreme" modernists of whom Frost apparently speaks: Joyce, Proust, Pound, Eliot, Mallarmé, Stein. I mention Brooks's address to show that Frost's response, in the 1930s, to the more aesthetically radical of the modernist writers was by no means remarkable; it was to find support, by the late 1930s, from both left-wing literary critics like Gold and liberal centrist ones like Brooks (an odd literary alliance that incidentally mirrored the subsequent military alliance of the Soviet Union and America). Dwight Macdonald drew the analogy between Brooks's position and that taken by Stalinist socialist realists in a lacerating review of Brooks's Columbia University address published in the *Partisan Review.*[9] And after 1937 the "extreme modernists" found a vigorous champion in the rejuvenated *Partisan Review,* edited by Philip Rahv, William Phillips, and Macdonald. These men were independent Trotskyist radicals and were quite hostile to the politics and the literary regime of Stalinism, as well as to the liberal bourgeois American culture that Macdonald would later contemptuously term "midcult." (Frost's "midcult" constituency—*A Further Range* had been a Book-of-the-Month-Club selection in 1936—probably suffices to explain Macdonald's lack of interest in his work, despite the fact that Frost's libertarian politics, as expressed in *A Further Range,* very much resembled Macdonald's after about 1946.)

In any event, as Brooks's remarks about "coterie" literature and the "collective life of the people" suggest, especially important in this ongoing debate was the question of the modern poet's constituency: For whom did she write? Indeed, the question has a long, contentious history in American literature. As his remarks in the 1931 interview suggest, Frost associates "unintelligibility" in form with a potentially dangerous eccentricity in theme and point of view. For him the great means for steadying down or moderating this eccentricity is audience itself: the artist has to socialize himself and his work; he has to accede in some way to the more or less rigid prescriptions of social engagement. In fact, American writers have often thought about their audience in something like moral terms. In a survey of the literary marketplace in the midnineteenth century, and of the pressures it exerted upon American authors, William Charvat writes:

> It was Emerson, as usual, who saw in true perspective the dilemma of the author in the age of Barnum, Beecher, and Bonner. When a "stout Illinoisan" walked out on his lectures, he reflected that "the people are always right (in a sense), and that the man of letters is to say, These are the new conditions to which I must conform. . . . He is no master who cannot vary his forms and carry his own end triumphantly through the most difficult." The time was, indeed, a difficult one for the artist, but it was not impossible. He needed only faith and humility to see that though he himself must serve Mammon as well as God, the people served God as well as Mammon. (315–16)

Such was the ameliorating genius of Emerson, but also of Frost. Emerson uses the term "conform" here precisely as Frost uses it in the 1934 letter to his daughter Lesley. There is "formity" to be considered, but there is also "conformity"; and in "The Constant Symbol" Frost essentially contends that "he who knows not both knows neither." Emerson makes the same point: "He is no master who cannot vary his forms and carry his own end triumphantly through the most difficult." Mastery for both writers meant mastery through and by means of what Frost calls the "harsher discipline[s] from without," disciplines that include, particularly for Frost, conformity to the sensibility of a broad community and literary marketplace, as against what Brooks calls a "coterie" audience.

The community in question here is the rather large and indistinct general audience, so-called: Emerson's "stout Illinoisan" and Frost's readers who buy books "in their thousands." Pound, together with H. L. Mencken and the cultural critics of the 1910s, had little but disdain for the audience "of all sorts and kinds" that Frost claimed he was trying to reach. In *Prejudices: Third Series* (1922) Mencken says of the men and women who form the large constituency that Frost sought to establish: "The American people, taking one with another, constitute the most timorous, sniveling, poltroonish, ignominious mob of serfs and goose-steppers ever gathered under one flag in Christendom since the end of the Middle Ages, and . . . they grow more timorous, more sniveling, more poltroonish, more ignominious every day" (10). And he writes with his usual merry contempt in *Notes on Democracy* (1926): "By 1828 in America and by 1848 in Europe the doctrine had arisen that all moral excellence, and with it all pure and unfettered sagacity, resided in the inferior four-fifths of mankind" (*Chrestomathy* 156). These ideas had characterized Mencken's thought since he published his study of Nietzsche in 1908. Within six or seven years, largely because of his efforts, they were truisms among a certain class of writers in America and abroad. Mencken recalls in *My Life as Author and Editor:* "In the days before the war my *Smart Set* reviews got steadily increasing notice, and it came to be a sort of common assumption that I was the chief fugleman of a new criticism, principally aimed at overturning the old American idols. Already in December, 1912, *Current Literature,* the *Time* of the era, was speaking of me as 'a distinguished Baltimore Nietzschean'" (41). In 1913 Mencken, Willard Wright, and George Nathan attempted to launch a magazine under the name *Blue Weekly.* Wright, Mencken later recalled, "wrote a sort of salutatory announcing that it was to be violently against virtually everything that the right-thinking Americans of the time regarded as sacred, from Christianity to democracy" (40).

One consequence of these general developments was an assault upon the democratic faith. In the essay "The New Sculpture" published in 1914 Pound, a frequent correspondent of Mencken, was able to take for granted that the artist "has dabbled in democracy and he is now done with that folly" (qtd. in Wolfe 28). And in "Notes toward a Definition of Culture," published much later, Eliot argues the point that "equalitarianism" and "culture" are conflicting ideals. This vein of cultural criticism reached a kind of epitome in Dwight Macdonald's 1962 collection *Against the American Grain,* in which he suggests that "all great cultures" are "elitist affairs, centering in upper class communities" (56). Such ideas often appear in Pound's work, as in *Hugh Selwyn Mauberley,* in which his attitude toward the civil religion of democracy is made quite plain:

> Faun's flesh is not to us,
> Nor the saint's vision.
> We have the press for wafer;
> Franchise for circumcision.

All men, in law, are equals.
Free of Pisistratus,
We choose a knave or an eunuch
To rule over us.

(*Personae* 187)

The cultural politics here are impeccably Menckenian (or Macdonaldesque). Without a strongman like Pisistratus to dominate us we choose—that is to say, the "booboisie" chooses—either a rascal or a weakling. That Pisistratus was also a patron of the arts probably further explains the reference: "Look (Pound seems to be saying) what has become of the arts under 'democracy,' in which newsprint, ingested as the wafer at a communion rail, 'transubstantiates' into that peculiar ruse of modern liberal democracies—'independent' thought." One can readily see why, in *Jefferson and/or Mussolini,* Pound advocates the placement of limitations on suffrage. Mencken's Nietzschean aristocratic political theories naturally complement Pound's aristocratic aesthetics of inner form: self-realization, self-will, and *self*-discipline are the essential components of both.[10] Taking much the same line, the historian and cultural critic Albert Jay Nock argued in a September 1922 column in *The Freeman,* to which the previous year Frost had playfully declined to contribute: "Democracy is easily victimized; it falls a ready prey to catchwords and claptrap; it is therefore guided by sentiment and not by reason. It chooses its agents badly, bringing to the top the lightest of demagogues. It progressively vulgarizes its civilization through putting a general premium of public favor upon mediocrity and pliability."[11] The occasion for these reflections, as Nock points out, was Mencken's publication of the essays he eventually collected in *Notes on Democracy* (1926). Typical of Mencken's arguments in that book is the observation that "Democratic man is quite unable to think of himself as a free individual; he must belong to a group, or shake with fear and loneliness" (*Chrestomathy* 157).

In the essay "The New Poetry Movement" collected in *Prejudices: First Series* (1919), Mencken singles out for notice Louis Untermeyer's influential early study *The New Era in American Poetry,* a book that helped shape the developing debate about American modernism. Mencken has much good to say about the book. But he balks at Untermeyer's suggestion that the impulse of the new poetry is democratic. Poetry had once been, Untermeyer argues, "the most exclusive and aristocratic of the arts, appreciated and fostered only by little *salons* and erudite groups" (qtd. in Mencken, *Prejudices: First Series* 92). Now, he suggests, reforms in diction and subject matter had brought poetry closer to a common, even a mass appeal—a development he associates with what he calls the "inherent Americanism" of the new verse. Clearly, such an account of modernism, had it succeeded, would have placed Frost and Sandburg at the center of the map rather than Eliot, Pound, and Stevens. Mencken objected to this, and his argument with Untermeyer foreshadows later debates about the genealogy of modernism. "The new poetry," he writes, "is neither American nor democratic. Despite its remote grounding in Whitman, it started, not in the United States at all, but in France, and its exotic color is still its most salient characteristic. . . . The deliberate strangeness of Pound, his almost fanatical anti-Americanism, is a mere accentuation of what is in every other member of the fraternity" (*Prejudices: First Series* 92). From this point Mencken derives a general principle, which would later be echoed by Dwight Macdonald in "Masscult and Midcult," an essay that very much reflects the consolidation in the 1940s and 1950s of the high modernist canon. "No sound art," Mencken argues, "could possibly be democratic. . . . The only art that is capable of reaching *Homo Boobus* is art that is already debased and polluted—band music, official sculpture, Pears' Soap painting, the popular novel." He concludes with an echo of Hamlet's speech to the players: "What is honest and worthy of praise in the new poetry is Greek to the general" (94). So much for Frost's aspirations in the 1913 letter quoted in the introduction to this study, in which he echoes the same speech from *Hamlet* to very different effect: "There is a kind of success called 'of esteem' and it butters no parsnips. It means success with the critical few who are supposed to know. But . . . I want to be a poet for all sorts and kinds. I could never make a merit of being caviare to the crowd the way my quasi-friend Pound does."

Sentiments like these lodged Frost very much in Louis Untermeyer's democratic camp. And he would eventually answer Mencken, Pound, the "extreme modernists," and those holding similar views in his 1935 introduction to *King Jasper.* There, after surveying the New Movement and modernist poetry of the 1910s and 1920s, Frost forthrightly defends—contra Mencken and company—what he calls "the fear of Man." If in "The Constant Symbol" Frost hopes to renew and redeem the meaning of discipline, in the introduction to *King Jasper* he hopes to teach the writers of his generation the felicities of fear. At the same time, and in a complementary gesture, he suggests the possible dangers of too much freedom and independence of mind. His remarks affiliate him with the democratic poetics advanced by Untermeyer and set forth a theory of "correspondence" in poetry that attaches peculiar significance to the poet's ability to reach a general audience. Here, as in "The Constant Symbol," Frost is surely responding to the radical individualism of Mencken and Brooks and to the corresponding elitist "difference" of such modernists as Pound and Eliot.

Frost begins:

> It may come to the notice of posterity (and then again it may not) that this, our age, ran wild in the quest of new ways to be new. The one old way to be new no longer served. Science put it into our heads that there must be new ways to be new. Those tried were largely by subtraction—elimination. Poetry, for example, was tried without punctuation. It was tried without capital letters. It was tried without metric frame on which to measure the rhythm. It was tried without any images but those to the eye; and a loud general intoning had to be kept up to cover the total loss of specific images to the ear, those dramatic tones of voice which had hitherto constituted the better half of poetry. It was tried without content under the trade name of poesie pure. It was tried without phrase, epigram, coherence, logic and consistency. It was tried without ability. I took the confession of one who had had deliberately to unlearn what he knew. He made a back-pedalling movement of his hands to illustrate the process. It was tried premature like the delicacy of unborn calf in Asia. It was tried without feeling or sentiment like murder for small pay in the underworld. These many things was it tried without, and what had we left? Still something. The limits of poetry had been sorely strained, but the hope was that the idea had been somewhat brought out. (*CPPP* 741)

The parenthesis in the first sentence is quietly snide. Experimentation in poetry may not "come to the notice of posterity" because, we must suppose, posterity will no longer read experimental poets. Or perhaps all the fuss will seem, from the elevated perspective of posterity, no experimentation at all. Frost refers to "our age," to "our heads." But his voice remains aloof enough to suggest at once that he is speaking about the extravagances of *other* writers. He is writing already from the elevated perspective of posterity, a suggestion that is only affirmed when he humorously assumes the role of priest: "I took the confession of one who had had deliberately to unlearn what he knew. He made a back-pedalling movement of his hands to illustrate the process." Frost was apparently a man more sinned against than sinning, and the list of poets from whom similar confessions are due is considerable: Cummings ("it was tried without capital letters"), Pound, Eliot, Amy Lowell ("it was tried without metric frame on which to measure the rhythm"), Vachel Lindsay, Sandburg ("a loud general intoning had to be kept up to cover the total loss of specific images to the ear"), Paul Valery (poesie pure), Williams, perhaps, and Stein ("it was tried without phrase, epigram, coherence, logic and consistency"), and so on. The passage is meant to be funny, and it is. In the middle of it Frost lets fall this deflating sentence: "It was tried without ability," which, like the parenthesis in the first sentence, has an effect somewhat more comprehensive than may at first seem to be the case.

But the best achievement of the writing is its control. The age may have "run wild in its quest," but Frost's tone in describing it is not at all wild. It ranges from statement ("those tried were largely by subtraction—elimination") to understatement ("and then again it may not") to overstatement ("I took the confession"), as Frost argued all good writing should. The essay has at least this much in common with "the better half of poetry": it certainly offers "specific images to the ear," and in that sense is not merely a sentence against the follies of other writers but an exhibition of how things ought alternatively to be done. The anaphora ("it was tried") underscores Frost's accumulating boredom and amusement and works against the claims for novelty made by each of the experimental poets he dismisses. And yet, he does not really dismiss them. His argument is merely that what they were attempting in so many different ways had nothing to do with real poetry after all. "These many things was it tried without, and what had we left? Still something." This is in keeping with the tone of the opening paragraph and of the essay as a whole. It is written as if by a poet for whom theoretical debate is, let us say, not really of the essence.

Of course, the tone of the essay has also been making us impatient for some solution to the literary infirmity of modernity, or "*new* ways to be new." As all good satirists must, Frost demolishes only so that he may rebuild. He offers, beginning in paragraph two, what amounts to his own theory of poetry. And the power of the writing in the second and third paragraphs is certainly remarkable, all the more so as they follow the smug survey of modern poetry given in the first:

> Robinson stayed content with the old-fashioned way to be new. I remember bringing the subject up with him. How does a man come on his difference, and how does he feel about it when he first finds it out? At first it may well frighten him, as his difference with the Church frightened Martin Luther. There is such a thing as being too willing to be different. And what shall we say to people who are not only willing but anxious? What assurance have they that their difference is not insane, eccentric, abortive, unintelligible? Two fears should follow us through life. There is the fear that we shan't prove worthy in the eyes of someone who knows us at least as well as we know ourselves. That

> is the fear of God. And there is the fear of Man—the fear that men won't understand us and we shall be cut off from them.
>
> We began in infancy by establishing correspondence of eyes with eyes. We recognized that they were the same feature and we could do the same things with them. We went on to the visible motion of the lips—smile answered smile; then cautiously, by trial and error, to compare the invisible muscles of the mouth and throat. They were the same and could make the same sounds. We were still together. So far, so good. From here on the wonder grows. It has been said that recognition in art is all. Better say correspondence is all. Mind must convince mind that it can uncurl and wave the same filaments of subtlety, soul convince soul that it can give off the same shimmers of eternity. At no point would anyone but a brute fool want to break off this correspondence. It is all there is to satisfaction; and it is salutary to live in the fear of its being broken off. (*CPPP* 741–42)

Frost's voice comprehends a range that would sound inconsequent or off key coming from a lesser writer. He writes by turns with humor, with extraordinary grace, even with something approaching mystery: "Mind must convince mind that it can uncurl and wave the same filaments of subtlety, soul convince soul that it can give off the same shimmers of eternity." The essay had until this point made no special demand upon our sympathies. It had been about Frost's amused detachment from avant-garde poetics and from theories of poetry in general. But all at once his convictions change, with the result that, for my part, I find myself listening quite willingly to talk about minds uncurling and waving "filaments of subtlety" and about "shimmers of eternity." I am almost persuaded that I understand him. Anyone but a brute fool would.

Somewhere in *Apologia Pro Vita Sua* Cardinal Newman distinguishes between an *argument* and a *plea.* Frost is not making an argument here. There is nothing really to "argue" about a filament of subtlety or about a shimmer of eternity. He is making a plea, and a deep connection exists between his satisfied review of the experiments in poetry he let pass by and this meditation on the "fear of Man." The escalating ambitions of the writing in this passage must not obscure that he is still talking about poetry and its audience. He suggests a theory of "correspondence" in art; it is the correspondence of the artist to his community. Recall what he says in the 1931 interview already quoted: "That is where the extreme modernists are defeating themselves. They do not care whether their communication is intelligible to others." Frost's theory of "correspondence" is his answer to extreme modernism. I take it to be, among other things, a plea for the decision he made to write as he did ("intelligibly") for the kind of American audience he chose ("all sorts and kinds"); and it is also, by logical extension, a plea for the singular kind of "popular," *re*-patriated poetic career he had undertaken. By contrast, the "unintelligible" art of his contemporaries—or so it seemed to Frost—was really an art trying to become autonomous from traditional constituencies. Frost's remarks on modernism in the 1931 interview strikingly anticipate Kenneth Burke's argument in "The Calling of the Tune," an essay collected in *The Philosophy of Literary Form* (1941): "The complete autonomy of art could but mean its dissociation from other aspects of the social collectivity. Complete freedom to develop one's means of communication ends as an impairment of communicability (the dilemma of work done in the Joyce-Stein-*transition* school)" (221).

Burke offers a particularly useful context in which to read Frost's introduction to *King Jasper.* He writes in *Permanence and Change* (1935), his second book of critical theory: "The more homogenous a society's ways of living and doing and thinking are, the more homogenous will be the labels [for describing them], hence the greater likelihood that artists will use these labels to their purposes." But on the other hand, as Burke continues: "When Mrs. Emily Post sold many hundred thousand copies of her book between the New Era years of 1925 and 1929, you can confidently look in your literature for a corresponding 'problem of style'" (51). That is, in times of social *heterogeneity* and disorder, such as marked the years 1925 to 1929, the cultural "labels" Burke speaks of may no longer be taken for granted. They must be made explicit. Indeed, they must be studied. Emily Post sells thousands of copies of her *Etiquette* and writers begin casting about for solutions to the problems of a fragmented communicative medium—for ways either to reestablish old constituencies or to establish new ones in their place. In short, you have a "problem of style." As Burke sums it up: "Insofar as the structure of these labels is impaired, their serviceability for communicative purposes is correspondingly impaired. . . . Change, heterogeneity of occupation, and instability of expectation have a radical bearing upon the range, quality, and duration of such linkages. Add geographical shifts, breakdown of former social stratifications, cultural mergers, introduction of 'new matter'—and you have so many further factors to affect the poetic medium adversely" (52). This is, in effect, an explanation of literary modernism—a much more evenhanded one than Mencken sets out in "The New Poetry Movement." In the passage just quoted, Burke is probably thinking of Eliot's well-known remarks in "The Metaphysical Poets" (1921): "We can only say that it appears likely that poets in our civilization, as it exists at present, must be *difficult.* Our civilization comprehends great variety and complexity, and this must produce various and complex results. The poet must become more and more comprehensive, more allusive, more indirect, in order to force, to dislocate if necessary, language into his meaning" (*Selected Essays* 65).

Eliot probably did not associate his project with Emily Post's, as Burke apparently would have. In "The Metaphysical Poets" he seems quite unprepared, in fact, to acknowledge that his is only one of several possible solutions to the problem. His analysis is normative. Burke, however, identifies at least three ways to address this modernist problem of communication. They describe, it seems to me, the various paths charted by Pound, Eliot, and Frost:

> Some poets met the problem by observing once more the old linkages under glass. They recalled the ancient Mediterranean lore. Like Anatole France, with a mixture of melancholy and irony, they "scribbled in the margins of books." Others wrote for the elect, a vague quantity *X* of a public who disliked the entire trend of events, and wished to have their dislike confirmed by an aggressive symbolization of better worlds. Closely connected with these were the writers who hearkened unto themselves, to catch the linkages that grew inescapably out of their own individual lives, hoping that there would be enough overlap upon other lives to establish a bond. (53)

Burke does not say which poets he has in mind in each case. But I would place Pound, especially his earlier work, in the first of these categories; I am thinking of his poetry in the style of medieval Provence, for example, and of his general fascination with historical analogy. The *Cantos* are surely a scribbling in the margins of old books, whether by Confucius, Jefferson, or Martin Van Buren. Pound's remarkable cultural and historical ventriloquism—as in the poems modeled on Villon or as in "Near Perigord," "Pierre Vidal Old," and "La Fraisne" or as in the Chinese translations and "The Sea Farer"—may well symbolize his specifically American experience of vocational alienation; in this way the historical and cultural dislocations of his poetry naturally complement the stylistic and formalistic innovations he advanced in the 1910s. Mencken succinctly remarks in *Prejudices: First Series:* "Ezra Pound? The American in headlong flight from America—to England, to Italy, to the Middle Ages, to ancient Greece, to Cathay and points East" (90). And Edmund Wilson noticed in a 1922 review that Pound seemed "cursed" with a "frantic desire to flee as far from Idaho as possible" and "to prove to Main Street that he has extirpated it from his soul" (*Shores of Light* 45). Of course, Burke's second category is broad enough to include both Eliot and the proletarian writers of the 1930s, who chose to symbolize, respectively, the better worlds of Anglo-Catholicism and of a socialist utopia. Their audiences were equally elect. Obviously, I would associate Frost with Burke's third class of writers. His solution to the conjoined problems of stylistic and social disintegrations, as expressed in the introduction to *King Jasper,* is in fact startlingly close to the terms of Burke's analysis: "It has been said that recognition in art is all. Better say correspondence is all. Mind must convince mind that it can uncurl and wave the same filaments of subtlety, soul convince soul that it can give off the same shimmers of eternity. At no point would anyone but a brute fool want to break off this correspondence." Frost sought to catch the "linkages," as Burke says, that grew inescapably out of his individual life in the hope "that there would be enough overlap upon other lives to establish a bond."

Frost usually is not thought of as sanctioning much talk about the problem of social chaos, as if that might finally be abolished. He had little patience for claims such as Eliot's in "*Ulysses,* Order, and Myth" that the twentieth century is somehow to be distinguished for its "anarchy" and "futility." Even so, it is useful to remember that Frost's introduction to *King Jasper* was published, like *Permanence and Change,* in 1935; the two texts have in common a background of considerable social disintegrations—the Great Depression, fascism and Nazism in Europe, proletarian agitations in any number of countries, the Spanish Civil War. The matter must be handled with a light touch, but the humor of Frost's introduction should not obscure its deep linkages to this larger context of social distress. A remarkable gravity authorizes his distinction between the two possibilities for poetic development: the cultivation of "difference" and the cultivation of "correspondence." In the case of the first, the risks run high enough to include "insanity" and isolation—being "cut off" from people. And the metaphors of infancy and growth applied to the second lend it something of a natural prestige, just as Pound's metaphors of slavery and sacrifice in "The Rest" indirectly lend his own "liberated" poetics the prestige of martyrdom. Quietly and indirectly Frost's own peculiar development as an *intelligible* American poet becomes typical of human development generally: "We began in infancy by establishing correspondence of eyes with eyes. We recognized that they were the same feature and we could do the same things with them. We went on to the visible motion of the lips—smile answered smile; then cautiously, by trial and error, to compare the invisible muscles of the mouth and throat. They were the same and could make the same sounds. We were still together. So far, so good. From here on the wonder grows." The poetry of correspondence, as against the poetry of anxiously cultivated difference, is but a natural outgrowth of these early, salutary phases; such is Frost's argument. And it is interesting to find a parallel argument in Brooks's 1941 attack on high modernist art, discussed briefly above. In describing the merit of what he calls "primary" art—art that expresses "the collective life of the people" rather than the sensibility of a mere "coterie"—Brooks almost becomes mystical: "Primary literature somehow follows the biological grain," he suggests, rather in the way that the poetry of "correspondence" does. "It favors," Brooks continues, "what psychologists call the 'life-drive'; it is a force of regeneration that in some way conduces to race survival" (qtd. in Macdonald, *Memoirs* 213).

But that is the later Brooks speaking, the Brooks who had, it seems, come round to Frost's way of thinking about these matters. For the moment I want to turn again to the Brooks of the 1910s and 1920s, and indeed to his coterie at *The Freeman.* In his "Reviewer's Notebook" column in *The Freeman* for September 13, 1922, Albert Jay Nock quotes Harriet Martineau, who is herself echoing Alexis de Tocqueville: "In the United States 'what is called public opinion has set up a despotism such as exists nowhere else . . . irresistible in its power to quell thought, repress action and silence conviction; bringing the timid perpetually under the unworthy fear of man'" (22). It is not the least of Frost's accomplishments in the introduction to *King Jasper* to have redeemed the "fear of Man." He achieves a transvaluation of American "extreme modernist" values. For him, everything—poet and poem are no exception—has "two compulsions, an inner and an outer, a spiritual and a social, an individual and a racial." He is speaking in the letter to his daughter Lesley, in which he has particular reference to the critic Herbert Read. But he might just as well be answering Brooks, who wrote, in his contribution to *Civilization in the United States:* "If our literature is to grow, it can only be through the development of a sense of 'free will' on the part of our writers themselves. . . . It is in the nature of the artist to live, not in the world of which he is an effect, but in the world of which he is the cause, the world of his own creation" (195). With what ambivalence must Frost have read Brooks's sentences, as almost surely he did; for as he sees it, the great challenge to artists is to live at once in the world of which they are the "cause" *and* the world of which they are the "effect." Artists must remain at once "insiders" and "outsiders," as R. P. Blackmur would say; they must always remain as responsive to the "promptings from without" as they are to the "promptings from within."

In his contribution to *Civilization in the United States,* Brooks sounds very much like Emerson, a writer for whom, in 1922, he nevertheless had little affection: "Build, therefore, your own world," Emerson writes. "As fast as you conform your life to the pure idea in your mind, that will unfold its great proportions" (*Essays* 48). Brooks is perhaps even closer to the Emersonianism of Henry James Sr. in *Moralism and Christianity:* "He alone is the artist, whatever be his manifest vocation, whose action obeys his own internal taste or attraction, uncontrolled either by necessity or duty" (qtd. in Poirer, *World Elsewhere* 23). But while Brooks might well have taken his cue from the elder James, Frost followed his son William—the writer Brooks blamed for the "fatuity," as he put it, of American writing in the 1910s. James writes in *Pragmatism* (1906): "Between the coercion of the sensible order and those of the ideal order, our mind is . . . wedged tightly. Our ideas must agree with realities . . . under penalty of endless inconsistency and frustration" (578). James describes the situation more than commends it. Frost, in effect, gives the same idea a normative and much more *social* turn: the "coercions" of reality—and *social* reality is very much in point here—are beneficial, something we ought positively to value. The "fear of Man" and the "harsher discipline from without" hold an almost redemptive power in his poetics, for they are the forces that socialize the artist, temper his eccentricity, and consolidate his "correspondence" with others. In a sense, Frost saw the writing of poetry as one means to overcome what he felt to be the threat of extreme isolation and subjectivity—a threat that troubled him all the more for personal and biographical reasons presently to be discussed.

Richard Poirier writes in *A World Elsewhere* (1966): "The classic American writers try through style temporarily to free the hero (and the reader) from systems, to free them from the pressures of time, biology, economics, and from the social forces which are ultimately the undoing of American heroes and quite often of their creators" (5). In a later book, *Robert Frost: The Work of Knowing* (1977), Poirier essentially excepts Frost from the writers described here, and with that exception I concur. Frost developed a style that could accommodate him to the "social forces" of which he was in some sense an "effect"; he developed a style that could integrate, or establish correspondence between, the imaginative "world" he created and the "real" or "given" world he found himself inhabiting—both as a man and more particularly as a professional poet writing in America in the early decades of the twentieth century. Frost always worked to strike a compromise between the claims of "difference" and of "correspondence." I take quite seriously his remark in a 1936 talk at the Bread Loaf School of English: "I am so made that I accept almost anything that exists, that really is going—I accept going concerns and I expect everyone to do the same" (*Collected Prose* 154). Frost's basic conservatism finds its deepest roots in sentiments such as these.

I have argued in chapter 1 that Frost's writing accommodates potentially intransigent, even countercultural dispositions while at the same time maintaining an altogether sociable surface. Frost seems to be thinking of this aspect of his work when he writes to Louis Untermeyer in 1917: "You get more credit for thinking if you restate formulae or cite cases that fall in easily under formulae, but all the fun is outside saying things that suggest formulae that won't formulate—that almost but don't quite formulate. I should like to be so subtle at this game as to seem to the casual person altogether obvious" (*CPPP* 692). This dubiety—I hesitate to say "duplicity"—held a certain fascination for Frost, and we find it symbolized throughout his work. It reappears, for example, in his dialectic of "conformity" and "formity," which is another way to frame the opposition of "formulaic" to "unformulaic" writing. I find it yet again in his parable of Martin Luther in the introduction to *King Jasper.* Surprised, excited, and a little troubled by his sense of his own difference, Luther represents, for Frost, the struggle between heresy (formity) and congregation (conformity), or between the "unformulaic" and the "formulaic." The same struggle obtains between "going concerns" (formulae) and the innovations or heresies that we are always building into them.

I am reminded, here, of a passage in Sigmund Freud's *Civilization and Its Discontents.* The analogy may at first seem unlikely, but Frost and Freud are, I think, confronting similar questions about human experience and about the motives of creative artists. Freud writes:

> The hermit turns his back on the world and will have no truck with it. But one can do more than that; one can try to re-create the world, to build up in its stead another world in which its most unbearable features are eliminated and replaced by others that are in conformity with one's own wishes. But whoever, in desperate defiance, sets out on this path to happiness will as a rule attain nothing. Reality is too strong for him. He becomes a madman, who for the most part finds no one to help him in carrying through his delusion. (732)

Frost makes a similar point in "The Constant Symbol" when he acknowledges the necessity of our accession to "the harsher discipline from without" or when, in the introduction to *King Jasper,* he warns against the willful and "anxious" cultivation of personal "difference" on the part of creative artists (or religious thinkers). Such remarks are echoed often in Frost's work. One thinks, for example, of his essay "Caveat Poeta": "The conventions have to be locked horns with somewhere," he says (*CPPP* 830). And his acknowledgment of worldly coercions unmistakably recalls the psychology and philosophy of William James, not simply of Freud in *Civilization and Its Discontents.* For when Frost and James welcome rather than attempt to refine away the "crudity," "rawness," and imperfection of the world—to adopt the terms they sometimes use—clearly they reject the alternative that Freud names only to dismiss: "to re-create the world" building up in its stead "another world in which its most unbearable features are eliminated." In its context, the passage from Freud presents an example of the artistic impulse *in extremis;* it follows a discussion of the satisfactions, through fantasy and illusion, that works of art afford. As Freud explains, creative art is in part a process of "making oneself independent of the external world by seeking satisfaction in internal, psychical processes" (732). It is crucial to recall that the "external world," as Freud earlier points out, includes the sphere of social relations, not simply, or perhaps even chiefly, the pressures of what we call Nature. As if in confirmation of Freud's thesis about the motives of the creative artist, Brooks writes, in his contribution to *Civilization in the United States,* in a passage quoted already: "It is in the nature of the artist to live, not in the world of which he is an effect, but in the world of which he is the cause, the world of his own creation." Given Frost's way of thinking about these matters, it is quite as if, over against Brooks, he affirms Freud's "reality principle": a mechanism of socialization whereby the vagaries of the single person are subordinated to the coercions of social realities. "We *must* be preserved from becoming egregious," Frost writes in "The Constant Symbol," and this is, after all, what the "fear of Man" accomplishes as it keeps in check the private and potentially antisocial energies of eccentricity, and finally of insanity itself. In short, Frost's eulogy on the "fear of Man" would impress upon us the truth of Freud's observation: "Whoever, in desperate defiance, sets out on this path [of re-creating the world] . . . will as a rule attain nothing. Reality is too strong for him. He becomes a madman, who for the most part finds no one to help him in carrying through his delusion."

All differences between them allowed, I am pointing to an almost mythological paradigm underlying both Frost's and Freud's work: namely, the mythology of a fundamental antagonism, which drives individuals and large social entities alike, between "inner" desire and "outer" discipline and form or between "difference" and "correspondence"—to borrow terms perhaps more congenial to Frost. (Analogous to this basic antagonism is the Nietzschean antagonism of "Dionysian" and "Apollonian" tendencies, which, largely through Mencken's agency, came to color Brooks's cultural and aesthetic criticism in the 1910s.) We find in Frost none of Freud's gothic imagery of Eros and Ananke, which might, for my purposes here, be renamed the gods of Formity and Conformity. But as a model of socialization and social development, this passage from Frost's essay "The Future of Man" (1959) has curiously Freudian implications, and in fact probably depends on a model related to Freud's description of the psyche, which by the 1950s had achieved preeminence even in popular culture: "The great challenge, the eternal challenge, is that of man's bursting energy and originality to his own governance. His speed and his traffic police. We become an organized society only as we tell off some of our number to be law-givers and law-enforcers, a blend of general and lawyer, to hold fast the line and turn the rest of us loose for scientists, philosophers, and poets to make the break-through, the revolution, if we can for refreshment" (*CPPP* 869). The theme is familiar from the introduction to *King Jasper.* Once again the "fear of Man"—figured here as a fear of law enforcement—keeps eccentricity and willfulness within socially acceptable bounds and functions among us as a kind of generalized superego. At the same time, the periodic eruption of these potentially destructive forces in a "bursting . . . originality"—rising up, so to speak, from a social unconscious—keeps the social contract from becoming too repressive. The poet's role is in this sense egoistic: he balances and reconciles contrary impulses toward conformity (the office of the superego) and toward irrationality and eccentricity (the office of the id). Admittedly, my use of Freud's familiar tripartite description of psychic structure in this connection is unusual. But the analogy helps us see that Frost regarded the writing of poetry as a means for integrating and managing conflicting impulses not only within the poet but within society as a whole, considered as a kind of superagent. He seemed to regard social and individual development as analogous and interlocked: that is to say, both individual and social agents must reconcile anxiously competitive tendencies toward difference and correspondence. In this respect Frost's thinking is in fact very close to Freud's, as when the latter writes in *Civilization and Its Discontents:* "The analogy between the process of civilization and the path of individual development may be extended in an important respect. It can be asserted that the community, too, evolves a super-ego under whose influence cultural development proceeds." This communal superego is the "traffic police" of which Frost rather light-heartedly (but seriously) speaks in "The Future of Man." Freud goes on to explain an "important point of agreement between the cultural and the individual super-ego": "the former, just like the latter, sets up strict ideal demands, disobedience to which is visited with 'fear of conscience'" (769). This "fear of conscience" corresponds to Frost's "fear of Man," which regulates dissent and eccentricity within the social body: "There is such a thing as being too willing to be different," Frost says. And notice that within this broad scheme, poetic form fulfills, for Frost, an essentially repressive function: just as social "correspondence" is a check against dangerous, potentially "insane" tendencies toward difference, form in poetry monitors and keeps in check insubordinate energies within the poet. And we will see below that exercises in poetic form held a specifically *therapeutic* value for Frost, and I speak of therapy in the clinical, even medical sense.

Frost sketches a considerably more congenial picture of "organized society" than does Freud in *Civilization and Its Discontents.* That is to say, Frost places less emphasis on the discontents that follow from our inclinations to govern ourselves. "The Future of Man" balances the more pessimistic account of difference and its effects given earlier in the introduction to *King Jasper.* Here, heretics such as Martin Luther are "refreshing" rather than susceptible to "insanity" and social isolation. Frost's own sympathies shift slightly, as, in the later essay, he ranges poets among the "law-breakers" rather than among the agents of "correspondence"—the agents of Apollo. This is as close as he comes in sympathy to the idea, propounded by Brooks, that the "creative spirit" is essentially "skeptical," radically individualistic, and "disruptive"—in other words, "Dionysian." (Frost remarked late in life: "I'm less and less for systems and system-building in my old age. I'm afraid of too much structure" [qtd. in Rotella 60].) And it is as close as he comes in spirit to Mencken's Nietzschean views, as expressed, for example, in *Prejudices: Sixth Series* (1927), in which Mencken describes the repressive consequences of conformity: "The democrat with a yearning to shine before his fellows must not only repress all the common varieties of natural sin; he must also repress many of the varieties of natural decency. His impulse to tell the truth as he sees it, to speak his mind freely, to be his own man, comes into early and painful collision with the democratic dogma that such things are not nice—that the most worthy and laudable citizen is that one who is most like the rest. In youth, as every one knows, this dogma is frequently challenged, and sometimes with great asperity, but the rebellion, taking one case with another, is not of long duration." He concludes with a charming aphorism: "The campus Nietzsche, at thirty, begins to feel the suction of Rotary" (161). In any case, "The Future of Man" gives full social significance to Frost's central dialectic of "formity" ("bursting . . . originality") and "conformity" ("governance"). And at last, I would call attention more to the consistency than to the differing emphases of "The Future of Man" and the introduction to *King Jasper.* In both essays Frost attends to the capacity of poetry—or more precisely to the capacity of the general human desires and dispositions that poetry embodies—either to promote or to undermine social integration. And on balance, the entire course of his "conformist" career—and, following Frost's lead, I do not use the word pejoratively—suggests that his sympathies essentially lie more with the promotion of correspondence and sociality, more with the Apollonians than with the Dionysians.

The better to bring these points home, I turn to Frost's well-known poem "Mending Wall," which perfectly exhibits the balance he sought between dispositions of conformity and formity. The speaker of that poem allies himself with the insubordinate energies of spring, which yearly destroy the wall separating his property from his neighbor's: "Spring is the mischief in me," he says (*CPPP* 39).[12] This alliance at first has the effect of setting the speaker against the basic conservatism of his neighbor beyond the hill, who as everybody knows never "goes behind his father's saying": "Good fences make good neighbors." But the association of the speaker with insubordinate natural forces should not be permitted to obscure an important fact, which has been often enough noticed: *he,* not the neighbor, initiates the yearly spring repair of the wall; moreover, it is again he, not the neighbor, who goes behind hunters who destroy the wall in other seasons and makes repairs. So if the speaker is allied with the vernal mischief of spring and its insubordinations, he is nevertheless also set against them in his efforts to make the stones of the wall balance and remain in place: "Stay where you are until our backs are turned!" he wryly says to the stones. Here, in fact, the speaker is rather like those of Frost's earlier poems "Rose Pogonias" and "October," each of whom, in imagination at least, attempts to arrest the naturally entropic and destructive forces of nature in the hope of achieving a momentary stay against confusion. In "Rose Pogonias," for example, we read:

We raised a simple prayer
    Before we left the spot,

That in the general mowing
    That place might be forgot;
Or if not all so favored,
    Obtain such grace of hours,
That none should mow the grass there
    While so confused with flowers.
(*CPPP* 23)

And in "October":

O hushed October morning mild,
Begin the hours of this day slow.
Make the day seem to us less brief.
Hearts not averse to being beguiled,
Beguile us in the way you know.
Release one leaf at break of day;
At noon release another leaf;
One from our trees, one far away.
Retard the sun with gentle mist;
Enchant the land with amethyst.
Slow, slow!
(*CPPP* 35)

The happy irony of "Mending Wall" is this: the speaker in this case allies himself *with* the destructive energies of nature, not against them as in "Rose Pogonias" and "October"; but at the same time he ritually initiates the wall-building exercise that so inefficiently resists and contains those same energies. The speaker of "Mending Wall" is obviously of two minds: at once wall-builder and wall-destroyer, at once abettor and antagonist of seasonal entropies. I would point out further that his impatience with his neighbor's aphoristic turn of mind is significantly (and playfully) qualified by the admonitory aphorism he himself devises *and twice repeats,* clearly delighted at having thought of it himself: "Something there is that doesn't love a wall," he says in a tone that by the poem's end *almost* acquires an air of finger-wagging, country pedantry. The difference is that, unlike his benighted neighbor, the speaker of the poem does indeed go behind his own favored aphorism to play both sides of the fence. In short, the two opposed men in the poem fairly shape up into one, and his name is Robert Frost.

At last, then, we have alternative aphorisms about walls and fences, and the truth of the matter resides in the "gap" between them that this famously mischievous poem opens up. In this way "Mending Wall" at once acknowledges the limitations of walls (and aphorisms) and also their seductions and value. As has often been pointed out, this dual theme is embodied even in the movement of the blank verse lines of "Mending Wall," which subtly play both within and against the metrical and structural impositions of the iambic pentameter line. When his speaker has in view the energies that disturb walls and boundaries, Frost's prosody vagrantly resists the regularities of his metrical contract:

> Something there is that doesn't love a wall,
> That sends the frozen-ground-swell under it
> And spills the upper boulders in the sun
> And makes gaps even two can pass abreast.
> (39)

Enjambment and metrical variations—trochaic feet for iambic ones, spondaic and pyrrhic substitutions, and so on—contribute subtly to the theme of these lines. It is exactly as Pope would have it. How better to describe a disordered wall than in lines themselves disordered? At such times Frost's blank verse recalls "Tintern Abbey," in which Wordsworth describes those "hedgerows hardly hedgerows" in eloquently unruly lines. In any case, here—as at a number of moments in "Mending Wall"—metrical and rhythmical patterns work in a kind of loosely running counterpoint characterized more by "formity" than by "conformity," as Frost might say. By contrast, when Frost imagines the reconstruction of the wall as the two men labor, the rhythm and meter of his lines coincide quite exactly:

> I let my neighbor know beyond the hill;
> And on a day we meet to walk the line
> And set the wall between us once again.
> We keep the wall between us as we go.
> (39)

Here, end-stopped lines are the rule: grammatical and rhetorical units more or less confine themselves to their prescribed ten-syllable boundaries. And there is little or no rhythmical variation against the basic iambic grid, which reasserts itself in these lines rather as the wall itself is "reasserted." Other such examples of Frost's metrical dexterity in this poem might be given, but these two suffice to suggest how tightly integrated in "Mending Wall" are form and theme.

In sum, the speaker of the poem exhibits, both in his manner and in his actions, a certain flexibility. He unsettles walls that he also always repairs; he is at once Apollonian and Dionysian. Once again—as in the introduction to *King Jasper* and "The Future of Man"—Frost's conservative and rebellious tendencies are perfectly balanced, just as the "intransigent" and "accommodating" tendencies of the speaker of "Good Hours" are metrically and thematically balanced, as I indicate in chapter 1. We might also regard "Mending Wall" in light of what Frost says in his 1934 letter to his daughter Lesley about the doctrine of Inner Form. The "neighbor beyond the hill" is all on the side of conformity, the speaker of the poem (at least by his own account) all on the side of formity. Frost himself—and here we should perhaps distinguish him from his speaker—stands at the dialectical intersection of these two opposed terms, for as he says in "The Constant Symbol" about the "discipline[s]" from "within" and from "without": "He who knows not both knows neither"—a matter I will return to at greater length in chapter 3.

We may say generally, then, that Frost honors his contract with the "superego," but not at the cost of exacerbating its repressions. His "speed" and his "traffic police" remain in constant and indecisive engagement. We can therefore discern in his poetry and prose a specifically modernist (even perhaps Freudian) parable about the necessity of balancing the imperatives of sociality and discipline against the imperatives of difference and insubordination. And as Richard Poirier has pointed out, a crucial theme in such poems as "The Witch of Coös" and "Home Burial" is how the confinements of a "home"—often symbolized in Frost's writing by the lesser confinements of poetic form—can, when unrelieved by expressions of extravagance, induce frustrations that shade off even into insanity: the constrictions of form must be relieved by extravagance, extravagance must be controlled and managed by form.[13] Clearly, the alternative positions Frost takes in "The Future of Man" and in the introduction to *King Jasper* correspond to the two poles of this dialectic—to the dangers of excessive conformity and to the dangers of excessive extravagance. The subject of the next section of this chapter is Frost's argument for the psychologically therapeutic benefit of exercises in form—of exercises in keeping things in order or of merely keeping things *in*. It is all there is to satisfaction, he said; and it is everybody's sanity to feel it.

"Everybody's Sanity"

In 1939, Frost was awarded the Gold Medal of the National Institute of Arts and Letters, of which he had been a member for a number of years. He delivered a brief acceptance speech, copying it out onto a sheet of paper at the ceremony itself. The speech was later published in the institute's *Bulletin* and reads, in part:

> "Have you ever thought about rewards," I was asked lately in a tone of fear for me that I might not have thought at my age. I don't know what I was supposed to think unless it was that the greatest reward of all was self esteem. Saints, like John Bunyan, are all right in jail if they are sure of their truth and sincerity. But, so, also, are many criminals. The great trouble is to be sure. A stuffed shirt is the opposite of a criminal. He cares not what he thinks of himself so long as the world continues to think well of him. The sensible and healthy live somewhere between self-approval and the approval of society. They make their adjustment without too much talk of compromise.
>
> Still, an artist, however well he may fare within and without, must often feel he has to rely too heavily on self-appraisal for comfort. For twenty years the world neglected him; then for twenty years it entreated him kindly. He has to take the responsibility of deciding when the world was wrong. He can't help wishing there was some third more disinterested party such as God or Time to give absolute judgement. (*CPPP* 779)

By now, the parable of Frost's own career latent in these paragraphs should be plain. He is writing in 1939, twenty years after he had achieved recognition, but forty years after he had begun trying to get it. If in 1913 Frost started making "adjustment[s]" to the "approval of society" without "too much talk of compromise"—and in the first chapter we have seen what this entailed—he could not forbear making them without at least some talk of the health and sanity those adjustments may be taken to symbolize. In this undertaking, Frost is of course very far from Mencken, who writes in *Prejudices: Sixth Series* (1927): "To-day the yearning to get into Heaven is in abeyance, at least among the vast majority of humankind, and so the ancient struggle takes a new form. In the main, it is a struggle of man with society—a conflict between his desire to be respected and his impulse to follow his own bent. Society usually wins," he ruefully concludes (160). In a 1921 review essay of Everett Dean Martin's *The Behavior of Crowds: A Psychological Study,* Mencken isolates several fundamental facts about herd behavior, or more generally about any quest for social approbation: "The first of these facts is that an individual, when he joins a crowd, whether of life-long Democrats, Methodists or professors, sacrifices his private judgment in order to partake of the power and security that membership gives him." Another signal fact is that the crowd's "primary motive is almost always fear, or, as Mr. Martin puts it, hate. This fear, of course, is seldom plainly stated; it is almost always concealed beneath a profession of altruism" (*Smart Set Criticism* 154). Mencken's radical libertarianism is firmly grounded in this Nietzschean analysis of social psychology.

By contrast, Frost's apologia for "conformity" depends upon a sharply different valuation of the subordination of "private judgment" to social approval, as his remarks in the introduction to *King Jasper* and in the 1939 Gold Medal speech suggest. "Conformity" to the sensibility of a community was, for him, a necessary check against individual vagaries, as we have seen already. So, the fear of which Mencken speaks so derisively—the fear that forms the basis of any social body's integrity—becomes something to be valued positively in Frost's philosophy. The "fear of Man" becomes a force for sanity, continuity, and sympathy—at least in large part—not a force for the craven suppression of social difference. Himself no Coriolanus, and indeed rather suspicious of Coriolanian truculence, Frost offers us a way to regard the struggle of a person with society of which Mencken speaks in an altogether more eulogistic light: "Saints, like John Bunyan, are all right in jail if they are sure of their truth and sincerity. But, so, also, are many criminals," he adds, lodging a necessary caution. "The great trouble is to be sure. . . . The sensible and healthy live somewhere between self-approval and the approval of society." These remarks, along with the introduction to *King Jasper,* constitute an important, if oblique, response to the Nietzschean individualism current among certain American writers in the modernist era, and for that matter among American writers generally. Twain consistently vilifies the quest for social approval, finding in it, as he says in his essay "Corn Pone Opinions," only "the natural instinct to passively yield to that vague something recognized as authority" and "the human instinct to train with the multitude and have its approval" (509). Frost locates danger more in excess of self-approval and in the "anxious" desire to be "different." There is at last no basic conflict in his thinking between the claims of self and the claims of society and this distinguishes him sharply from the tradition in American writing of which Twain, in "Corn Pone Opinions" and the first two-thirds of *Huckleberry Finn,* offers so clear an example and of which Mencken is perhaps the most perfect exponent in Frost's own generation.

Frost's strategy in the Gold Medal speech is the same one used in the considerably more subtle parable he tells in the introduction to *King Jasper.* The Gold Medal is taken not merely as a sign that he had consolidated the favor of a particular constituency—the National Institute of Arts and Letters and those whose tastes it represented—though that is what he had done. It is tentatively taken as a sign of "health" and "sensibleness." Contrast Frost's position in these essays with Pound's in the "Mr. Nixon" section of *Hugh Selwyn Mauberley,* in which he alludes to Robert Browning's poem "Bishop Blougram":

> Likewise a friend of Blougram's once advised me:
> Don't kick against the pricks,
> Accept opinion. The "Nineties" tried your game
> And died, there's nothing in it.
>
> (192)

By holding this attitude up for ridicule Pound advances the case that artists should not trouble themselves about "rewards," and certainly not about rewards of the respectably institutional sort Frost has in mind in the 1939 speech. We have Pound's word to this effect in "Tenzone": "I beg you, my friendly critics, / Do not set about to procure me an audience. / I mate with my free kind upon the crags" (*Personae* 83). Pound is rather like Dickinson, alone in her Amherst garret:

> Publication—is the Auction
> Of the Mind of Man—
> Poverty—be justifying
> For so foul a thing
> Possibly—but We—would rather
> From Our Garret go
> White—Unto the White Creator—
> Than invest—Our Snow.
>
> (348)

This aristocratic strain in American poetry exhibits a familiar contempt for commerce and the bourgeois marketplace. By contrast, in such poems as "Christmas Trees" and in his 1958 statement accepting a consultancy at the Library of Congress, Frost writes in favor of what he calls "the trial by market everything must come to"—even poetry (*CPPP* 845). Much more than mere "poverty," he needed to believe, "justified" bringing his poems to market. He writes in favor of socializing his "difference," of making it correspond even to the rigors of the American literary marketplace. Bear in mind his remarkable contention in a 1915 letter to Louis Untermeyer, in which he indirectly criticizes Pound's elitist ideals, as set forth, for example, in "Tenzone": "I think a book ought to sell. Nothing is quite honest that is not commercial" (*Frost to Untermeyer* 8–9). By contrast Pound always castigates any situation in which "the beautiful" is "decreed in the market place," as he says in *Hugh Selwyn Mauberley* (187). He did not give a damn about securing "the affections of Americans," no more so, apparently, than did Dickinson, whose anti-Jacksonian Whig politics nicely complement Pound's antidemocratic convictions.[14] Pound regarded with suspicion any modern poet who achieved a democratic sort of constituency on terms more or less set by the literary marketplace. This line of thought is at least as old as Tocqueville, who writes in *Democracy in America:* "Aristocracies produce a few great pictures, democracies a multitude of little ones. The one makes statues of bronze, the other of plaster" (468). Pound's way of framing the matter in *Mauberley* quite neatly echoes Tocqueville:

> The "age demanded" chiefly a mould in plaster,
> Made with no loss of time,
> A prose kinema, not, not assuredly, alabaster
> Or the "sculpture" of rhyme.
>
> (186)

"There is one qualifying fact always to bear in mind," Frost wrote to his friend John Bartlett in 1913, in a letter already quoted. "There is a kind of success called 'of esteem' and it butters no parsnips. It means success with the critical few who are supposed to know. But really to arrive where I can stand on my legs as a poet and nothing else I must get outside that circle to the general reader who buys books in their thousands." Frost carefully admonishes Bartlett lest his friend regard his motives for "reaching out" (as he puts it) as strictly monetary: "I *believe* in doing it—dont you doubt me there." Van Wyck Brooks (like Pound) found this way of thinking about the literary marketplace abhorrent, at least in the early phases of his career. In a passage that brings to mind any number of remarks by Mencken, Brooks writes in "The Literary Life": "In the philosophy of American publishing, popularity has been regarded not only as a practical advantage but as a virtue as well. Thanks to the peculiar character of our democracy, our publishers have been able to persuade themselves that a book which fails to appeal to the ordinary citizen cannot be good on other grounds" (188). Given the atmosphere of debate that such sentiments as these created, Frost's apologia for the "general reader who buys books in their thousands"—his aspiration to fit "into the nature of Americans"—must necessarily have been attended by a certain air of defensiveness, a certain air of self-consciousness. And if he accepts the National Institute's reward in the higher sense he speaks of in his 1939 address, he also suggests that he has an *interest* in so accepting it, and indeed that its members have an interest in agreeing with him: "For twenty years the world neglected him; then for twenty years it entreated him kindly. He has to take the responsibility of deciding when the world was wrong. He can't help wishing there was some third more *disinterested* party such as God or Time to give absolute judgement." Frost's speech is informed by a skepticism rather more complicated than the obvious one he dismisses in his opening remark—that rewards, whether of institutions or of the marketplace, really should not concern an artist. As in the introduction to *King Jasper*, he transfigures the particular balance he struck between "self-approval" and the "approval of society" into a symbol of sanity and health. But at the same time he is well aware of his own participation in that transfiguration; he brings up deliberately enough the question of motives and interests, even if he does so quietly, and this is characteristic of him. In effect, he has brought into the speech, as a kind of secondary concern, the *act* of assigning meaning to rewards, and by extension the *act* of assigning meaning to his own career. That is why his remarks about his career or about poetics seldom strike me as "rationalizations," in the unflattering sense of that term. There is a tentativeness about the metaphors he uses, as if he were simply trying to offer one valuable way of describing rewards or the proper relation of poet to reader, not as if he were really trying to settle the point. In these matters he almost always lacks the assurance of Pound and Dickinson.

There is in Frost's best writing a sense always of his participation in the creation of value and meaning, rather than in the mere discovery of it. I would describe it impressionistically. It is almost as if we hear him listening to himself explain the meaning of his achievements in poetry, just as he listens to himself explain the meaning of birdsong and its attendant mythology in "Never Again Would Birds' Song Be the Same." Call it an effort to reconcile his own beliefs—his own interests, wishes, hopes—with what he feels is just. Or to put it less ambitiously, it is an effort to reconcile his eloquence with what he feels permitted, simply, to say. I recognize in this another transposition of his constant symbol: the "figure of the will braving alien entanglements" (*CPPP* 787), where "will" names an entire field of significance usually parceled out in such words as "belief," "interest," or "desire."

For these reasons, the personal motives I trace out in his criticism should not be allowed to undermine it. I take it for granted, following Burke, that such "strategic" motives as these underlie most descriptive enterprises, whether in poetics, philosophy, or whatever. A description of poetry, no less than a description of the class structure of a society or of the operation of the "free" market, permits and sanctions some actions, while discouraging and stigmatizing others. And it is to be valued for the *kind* of actions it does make possible, though those actions are obviously bound to include ones taken or preferred by its author. As I understand it, this is, at bottom, the argument of pragmatism, as when, in the introduction to *Objectivity, Relativism, and Truth,* Richard Rorty characterizes his position as "one which does not view knowledge as a matter of getting reality right, but rather as a matter of acquiring habits of action for coping with reality" (1). Rorty has much in common with both Burke and Frost, though he never mentions them. And the Gold Medal speech certainly reflects Frost's deeper affiliations with pragmatism. The "correspondence" in poetry, in all art, that he speaks of in the introduction to *King Jasper* is by no means the correspondence of the artwork to the world. Works of art can make no pretense at fitting "into the nature of the Universe," as he says later in the Gold Medal speech; they are not a matter of "getting reality right." They may fit, if they fit into the nature of anything, only into the "nature" of people—into the "nature" of the community, which is, as Frost understood, really a matter of *culture:* "I should be sorry to concede the artist has no . . . recourse to tests of certainty at all," Frost writes. "His hope must be that his work will prove to have fitted into the nature of people" (*CPPP* 780). The test is social rather than objective or scientific.

This seems a simple point but it registers nothing less than Frost's qualification of at least two ways of thinking about art: as a mirror of the world and as a means to penetrate and disable inherited modes of consciousness so as (in Emerson's well-known phrase) to enjoy "an original relation to the universe" (*Essays* 7). For Frost, art is chiefly a means of *consolidating* fellowship, not a means of escaping its consequences. In this he stands opposed not only to Emerson but also to Pound and Charles Olson, who are quite close to Emerson in certain respects. Richard Rorty's distinction between "solidarity" and "objectivity" usefully describes the difference I am getting at here. He writes in *Objectivity, Relativism, and Truth:* "There are two principal ways in which reflective human beings try, by placing their lives in a larger context, to give sense to those lives. The first is by telling a story of their contribution to a community. . . . The second is to describe themselves as standing in immediate relation to a nonhuman reality. I shall say that stories of the former kind exemplify the desire for solidarity, and that stories of the latter kind exemplify the desire for objectivity" (21). I would add one qualification to these definitions. The desire for "objectivity" may manifest itself also reactively, as the effort merely to escape as many of the effects of human fellowship as possible, even without the hope of actually establishing an "immediate" relation to some "nonhuman reality." Bacon's casting out of the "Idols of the Mind" is in this sense "objectivist." So is Emerson's desire to see beyond the many "terministic screens," to use Kenneth Burke's phrase, of our cultural inheritances—whether those screens are philosophical, literary, political, or theological. Here, also, I would place Pound's early, somewhat more practical efforts in Imagism to disable his aesthetic inheritances of poetic form; poetic form *mediates* the "direct treatment" of the thing which he thought the poet must always try to achieve. Frank Lentricchia usefully argues in *Modernist Quartet* that the doctrine of the image, as developed by Pound and T. E. Hulme, is essentially anticommunitarian: perception, as the modernists view it, is always radically individualistic, radically *particular* and subjective. Pound was, in this phase of his career, one of what Lentricchia calls "the new and insistent cultural voices on behalf of the aesthetic fragment and the private pleasures of the percept, set against the tradition of reason" (42).

The Emersonian implications of Pound's approach are brought out very clearly in Charles Olson's essay "Projective Verse," which essentially marks the terminus of Pound's Imagist aesthetics. It is fitting for my purposes that Olson christens his poetics "objectism": "Objectism is the getting rid of the lyrical interference of the ego, of the 'subject' and his soul, that peculiar presumption by which western man has interposed himself between what he is as a creature of nature (with certain instructions to carry out) and those other creations of nature which we may, with no derogation, call objects" (24). Much might be said about these curious sentences. But in brief, they amount to nothing less than a call to abolish in poetry the very *idea* of the "human"—"that peculiar presumption," in Olson's words. It is an ambition Frost never shared. As I have tried to show, his poetics grew in direct reaction against the several currents that would receive their ultimate statement in "Projective Verse." Olson's desire, in Rorty's terms, is to tell a story of our relation to what may lie beyond the "presumptions" of the human—beyond the interference of the subject and her soul. Frost's desire is to tell such stories of his affiliation to a community as we find in the introduction to *King Jasper* and in the Gold Medal speech, whether he speaks of "correspondence" or of fitting "into the nature" of people. In *Modernist Quartet* Lentricchia points out that, in thinking about the currents that would soon issue in modernism, the Harvard philosopher Josiah Royce had come to understand that "socially isolating *perception* was the ground of agreement [between philosophers and poets alike], and that imagism and Bergsonism were its key contemporary cultural signs, and he wondered aloud what would become of us if, in cultivating the modern, we ceased to care about what connects us" (42–43). In response, Royce developed a counterphilosophy of community that sought a completion of private aspirations in social cooperation; Eliot studied under Royce at Harvard and was much affected by his ideas, as Lentricchia demonstrates. I am suggesting that in surveying the developments of "extreme" modernism—which he believed tended to break off communication—Frost had arrived at something like his own Roycean communitarian poetics, in which the chaotic energies of radical individualism are subordinated to the ideals of community and correspondence.

In this regard, Frost is considerably closer to Hawthorne than to Emerson. In saying this I have particularly in mind Sacvan Bercovitch's study *The Office of "The Scarlet Letter"* (1991). The central problems of Hawthorne's novel are quite plain: Why does Hester Prynne, of her own accord, ultimately forfeit her inclination toward radical individualism and rebellion? After long residence in Europe with a daughter and family who love her, why does she resume the punitive "scarlet letter" in Massachusetts Colony? Or to frame the matter in terms more congenial to Frost: Why does she give up her "anxiety" to cultivate her own heterodox "difference" and accede instead to "the fear of Man"—to the fear that she shall be "cut off" from people? Why does she accede to the claims of community that this fear represents? As Bercovitch shows, her gesture embodies the paradox of compulsory consent that lies at the heart of the Puritan penal code in the novel. Hester is compelled to wear the letter but in an important sense she also volunteers to wear it. It is as Frost says in a 1934 letter to his daughter Lesley: "I want to be good, but that is not enough the state says I have got to be good." The sentence concerns a perfectly Hawthornian paradox of free will and law, whereby we consent to be compelled. In so volunteering, Hester herself becomes able, to an extent, to define the meaning of the letter she wears; she comes partly into possession of it. At the novel's end we understand that its significance is a thing arrived at by tacit contract, so to speak, between Hester and the Puritan patriarchy: neither party to this contract controls the meaning of the letter entirely, but neither is excluded from controlling it. This is the compromise of which Bercovitch ultimately speaks, by means of which the interests both of dissent and of community are preserved. In this way, as Bercovitch shows, the letter comes generally to represent the management of dissent within community and of consent within the regime of law—liberal ideals in which Hawthorne, never either a radical or an autocrat, invested much value, and which were of special concern to Americans of his convictions in the compromise year of 1850 when *The Scarlet Letter* was published. We can therefore regard the moral-political problem of the novel as quintessentially liberal and American: What is the proper relation of center to margin in the national compact—the proper relation of "difference" to community and of liberty to law? Or, how can the interests of radical individualism and of unity both be served?

The introduction to *King Jasper* suggests that Frost shared Hawthorne's liberal faith in consensus and compromise, as well as his antipathy to radical individualism, absolutism, and conflict: "There is such a thing as being too willing to be different. And what shall we say to people who are not only willing but anxious? What assurance have they that their difference is not insane, eccentric, abortive, unintelligible?" This constitutes a defense of orthodoxy, as the skeptical allusion to Martin Luther's heresies earlier in the same passage quite literally suggests. In light of these remarks, consider Hawthorne's description of Pearl, a daughter born of sin: "Her nature appeared to possess depth, too, as well as variety; but—or else Hester's fears deceived her—*it lacked reference and adaptation to the world into which she was born.* The child could not be made amenable to rules; in giving her existence, a great law had been broken; and the result was a being, whose elements were perhaps beautiful and brilliant, but all in disorder; or with *an order peculiar to themselves,* amidst which the point of variety and arrangement was difficult or impossible to be discovered" (195; my emphasis). To lack "reference and adaptation," in the sense given the words here, is to remain unsocialized. *The Scarlet Letter* ultimately argues that we must to some extent subordinate ourselves to social authorities and restraints; we must "correspond" or fit "into the nature" of people. Hawthorne would affirm Frost's injunction in the 1939 Gold Medal speech that we strike a balance between "social approval" and "self approval" because such a balance keeps us oriented with regard to the people among whom we live. For to live by an order entirely peculiar to one's self is to live by no order at all and to court criminality, martyrdom, or psychosis (as the case may be); such is the idea Frost and Hawthorne seem to advance, in any event. It requires the conviction either of a saint or a criminal to live contentedly under such conditions of isolation; the "great trouble" is to be sure which, as Frost memorably puts it. (Hawthorne and Frost are very far from the Emersonian, even Nietzschean individualism of Emily Dickinson, for whom, in "Much Madness is Divinest Sense," "sanity" designates a condition of social conformity that is thoroughly unrespectable.)

Frost's and Hawthorne's communitarianism (if such it may be called) is fundamentally cautious and conservative—perhaps even pessimistic. More particularly, Frost's attitude toward the radical leftists of the 1930s closely follows Hawthorne's response to the feminist and abolitionist radicals of his own day. Frost remained, I believe, temperamentally incapable of acting from certainty in political matters, and for that reason he valued strategies of what he terms in the introduction to *King Jasper* "grief" and "patience," as against "grievances" and "impatience." The result is a politics of resignation and gradualism that is basically conservative in emphasis, very much in Hawthorne's manner. I am thinking of the following passage from Frost's introduction:

> Grievances are a form of impatience. Griefs are a form of patience. We may be required by law to throw away patience as we have been required to surrender gold; since by throwing away patience and joining the impatient in one last rush on the citadel of evil, the hope is we may end the need of patience. There will be nothing left to be patient about. The day of perfection waits on unanimous social action. Two or three more good national elections should do the business. It has been similarly urged on us to give up courage, make cowardice a virtue, and see if that won't end war, and the need of courage. Desert religion for science, clean out the holes and corners of the residual unknown, and there will be no more need of religion. (Religion is merely consolation for what we don't know.) But suppose there was some mistake; and the evil stood siege, the war didn't end, and something remained unknowable. Our having disarmed would make our case worse than it had ever been before. Nothing in the latest advices from Wall Street, the League of Nations, or the Vatican inclines me to give up my holdings in patient grief. (*CPPP* 743)

The skepticism is comprehensive: political, economic, and scientific "perfection" are essentially impossible ideals, for which reason, Frost suggests, they are also dangerous ideals to hold. The bleak irrationalism of his position—which maintains that something shall always remain "unknowable" and that "evil" is an organic feature of our lives—essentially marks his difference from the radicals of the 1930s, whose often utopian hopes ultimately derived from Enlightenment Reason, as manifested, for example, in historical materialism with its progressive model of social change. This is what gives point to Frost's oddly indirect defense of religion, which, given its acceptance of an organic principle of evil, stands alike opposed to Marxist and Enlightenment ways of thinking about humankind. Frost takes for granted that evil is not socially produced and therefore not susceptible to human remedy. In closing the introduction to *King Jasper,* he writes apropos of Robinson's poetry: "There is solid satisfaction in a sadness that is not just a fishing for ministration and consolation. Give us immedicable woes—woes that nothing can be done for—woes flat and final" (*CPPP* 747–48). This is a prescription for resignation, for "grief" (as Frost terms it) and "patience"; and it is inimical to social and political reform. Recall the profound resignation of Frost's sonnet "Acceptance," which drew criticism from the influential Marxist critic Newton Arvin for its conservative implications: "Now let the night be dark for all of me," the sonnet concludes. "Let the night be too dark for me to see / Into the future. Let what will be be" (*CPPP* 228).

In the wake of World War II, American intellectuals moved somewhat closer to Frost's pessimistic, irrationalist position as they tried to understand the Nazi genocide, the development of nuclear weapons by the United States and the USSR, and the advent of the cold war. Lionel Trilling would eventually commend Frost as a great poet of darkness, terror, and human limitation, as a peculiarly *modern* poet in this regard, and the endorsement made cultural sense in the context of the 1950s when it was delivered. By then, many American intellectuals had abandoned the progressivist ideals that had earlier sustained them. For the first time since the mid-1910s Frost oddly found himself in alliance, culturally, with certain elite intellectuals in New York City. In a 1951 review of Hannah Arendt's *The Origins of Totalitarianism* published in *The New Leader,* Dwight Macdonald argued that "irrational irruptions of . . . anti-humanity" in the midtwentieth century had rendered the "rational-utilitarian way of looking at life obsolete." He further suggested that the twin horrors of Nazism and Stalinism had destroyed a "progressive-materialistic world view that went back to the Encyclopedists of the enlightenment" (qtd. in Wreszin 253–54). In *The Root Is Man* (1946), Macdonald further described how he had arrived at a new "radical" politics that repudiated Marxian progressivism. "The Radical," he wrote, "is more aware [than the Progressive] of the dual nature of man; he sees evil as well as good at the base of human nature; he is skeptical about the ability of science to explain things beyond a certain point; he is aware of the tragic element in human fate not only today but in any conceivable kind of society" (39). In 1935 a radical intellectual speaking of the inevitability of "tragedy" in "any conceivable kind of society" would have been accused of "mystification." That is essentially the reception Frost's political writings met with on the far Left in the 1930s. After World War II, however, the tragic skepticism expressed in the introduction to *King Jasper* and in poems such as "Acceptance," "Design," "The Flood," "November," and "The Rabbit Hunter" seemed to make sense (though this circumstance still did not place Frost's work at the center of interest in an intellectual climate yet governed by the pious, forthright pessimism of *The Waste Land*).

The same qualities in Frost's work that Lionel Trilling admired in 1954, then, had disqualified him in the eyes of left intellectuals of the 1930s, when his way of thinking about these matters was distinctly unfashionable. He struck most radicals as defeatist and defeated. In a review of Frost's 1936 volume *A Further Range*, the Marxist critic Newton Arvin, writing in the *Partisan Review*, relegated the poet to a "minor" strain in New England literature: "The New England of nasalized negations, monosyllabic uncertainties, and non-commital rejoinders; the New England of abandoned farms and disappointed expectations, of walls that need mending and minds that need invigoration, of skepticism and resignation and retreat." Over against this strain Arvin set a "major" strain that he called "the true essence of the New England spirit." Animated by such men as John Brown, Wendell Phillips, George Ripley, Emerson, and Roger Baldwin, this tradition is characterized by "militancy, positiveness, conviction, struggle" (27–28). Arvin carefully excepts Hawthorne from this optimistic major strain, and indeed Frost's remarks in the introduction to *King Jasper*—which Arvin had unfavorably reviewed the previous year—recall the conservative pessimism of Hawthorne in *The Life of Franklin Pierce* (1852). Hawthorne has in view particularly the Garrisonian abolitionists, who worked in what Arvin would call the "major strain" of New England culture: "There is no instance, in all history, of the human will and intellect having perfected any great moral reform by methods which it adapted to that end; but the progress of the world, at every step, leaves some evil or wrong on the path behind it, which the wisest of mankind, of their own set purpose, could never have found the way to rectify" (113–14). The idea rejected here—that moral progress is confidently to be achieved through institutional channels—likewise strikes Frost as quaintly preposterous: "Two or three more good national elections should do the business," he writes, dispensing in this case with Roosevelt and the entire New Deal.

"I had it from one of the youngest lately," Frost writes in the *King Jasper* introduction: "'Whereas we once thought literature should be without content, we now know it should be charged full of propaganda.' Wrong twice, I told him. Wrong twice and of theory prepense. But he returned to his position after a moment out for reassembly: 'Surely art can be considered good only as it prompts to action.' How soon,

I asked him. But there is danger of undue levity in teasing the young. . . . We must be very tender of our dreamers. They may seem like picketers or members of the committee on rules for the moment. We shan't mind what they seem, if only they produce real poems" (*CPPP* 742–43). The young dreamer Frost speaks of here might well be the subject of his poem "The Lost Follower," first collected in *A Witness Tree.* This lyric and the two that succeed it—"November" and "The Rabbit Hunter"—argue eloquently for a poetics of resignation and grief. Here, with a sympathy not felt in the introduction to *King Jasper,* Frost makes the Hawthornian point that suffering and evil are as natural to our world as the killing seasons of autumn and winter. The idea in these poems seems to be that a certain amount of misery, even of an "economic" sort, always proves intractable and is less a *social* phenomenon subject to our interventions than a kind of epiphenomenon of the natural world itself. It is an irrational, deeply skeptical position. As Richard Poirier has pointed out, Frost often "talks as if history not only partakes of nature but is identical with it." And he continues on the same page: "Frost did not have the historical vision which would allow him to see that perhaps even what he calls 'grief' rather than 'grievance' is not necessarily an inevitable result of the nature of life" (233).

"The Lost Follower" considers the case of a young poet who left the pure calling of lyric for the impure poetry of grievance and social struggle:

> As I have known them passionate and fine
> The gold for which they leave the golden line
> Of lyric is a golden light divine,
> Never the gold of darkness from a mine.
>
> The spirit plays us strange religious pranks
> To whatsoever god we owe the thanks.
> No one has ever failed the poet ranks
> To link a chain of money-metal banks.
>
> The loss to song, the danger of defection
> Is always in the opposite direction.
> Some turn in sheer, in Shelleyan dejection
> To try if one more popular election
>
> Will give us by short cut the final stage
> That poetry with all its golden rage
> For beauty on the illuminated page
> Has failed to bring—I mean the Golden Age.
>
> And if this may not be (and nothing's sure),
> At least to live ungolden with the poor,

Enduring what the ungolden must endure.
This has been poetry's great anti-lure.

The muse mourns one who went to his retreat
Long since in some abysmal city street,
The bride who shared the crust he broke to eat
As grave as he about the world's defeat.

With such it has proved dangerous as friend
Even in a playful moment to contend
That the millennium to which you bend
In longing is not at a progress-end

By grace of state-manipulated pelf,
Or politics of Ghibelline or Guelph,
But right beside you book-like on a shelf,
Or even better god-like in yourself.

He trusts my love too well to deign reply.
But there is in the sadness of his eye,
Something about a kingdom in the sky
(As yet unbrought to earth) he means to try.
(*CPPP* 325)

Form is very much a part of the meaning of this poem. A quiet chiasmas (gold-golden-golden-gold) binds together the first quatrain. Delicate enjambments in lines two, fourteen, twenty-seven, and thirty-five make us feel the agreeable and supple pressure of line against sentence. Frequent effects of consonance and assonance, together with tight quartet rhymes, enforce the feeling, very impressive in this poem, of sonic unity. In short, we cannot read "The Lost Follower" without feeling its *design.* This artificiality—the manifestly *designed* quality of the poem—is very much in point, for part of Frost's argument is that the promise of a Golden Age can exist only *in art,* never in society. That promise is simply *unreal.* To make this point is to argue against reformers—all those who, like the left intellectuals and writers of the 1930s, dream of the Golden Mountains, to borrow Malcolm Cowley's phrase in the title of his book about the period. We make the world beautiful and perfect *in art,* not in life, Frost suggests. "State-manipulated pelf" is of little avail. The phrase refers to the New Deal and more generally to any effort to redistribute wealth to counteract the unjust effects of the market. This poem ultimately claims that socialist visions of utopia are generically related to *literary* visions of it: so much for the "scientific," progressive pretensions of the American Communists of the 1930s. If the Golden Age can exist only "book-like on a shelf," then political action and poetry really do not belong together. "The Lost Follower" concerns not merely the career of a single poet but the career of American poetry itself in the 1930s. Frost's almost invincible poignance in the poem was bound to strike some readers as patronizing and complacent.

"November" deftly extends Frost's argument for a poetics and politics of resignation. Here, the governing metaphor of seasonal change essentially *naturalizes* destruction and waste: contrary to the beliefs of the young rebel poet of "The Lost Follower," this poem contends, suffering and misfortune are irremediable and therefore lie beyond the reach of state planners:

> We saw leaves go to glory,
> Then almost migratory
> Go part way down the lane,
> And then to end the story
> Get beaten down and pasted
> In one wild day of rain.
> We heard "Tis over' roaring.
> A year of leaves was wasted.
> Oh, we make a boast of storing,
> Of saving and of keeping,
> But only by ignoring
> The waste of moments sleeping,
> The waste of pleasure weeping,
> By denying and ignoring
> The waste of nations warring.
> (*CPPP* 326)

Together, "The Lost Follower" and "November" illustrate Frost's point in the introduction to *King Jasper* that poetry should confine itself to "melancholy." I suggested that the lyricism of "The Lost Follower" contributes to its meaning; the same may be said of "November," which works in the lyrical mode of *A Boy's Will.* These poems sound the "music" of the "golden line of lyric" that we hear, for example, in Francis Turner Palgrave's *Golden Treasury*—a wistful, late Victorian sort of anthology that finds poetry very far indeed from the social struggles of the 1930s. The last seven lines of "November" suggest that nothing we "keep" is ever really preserved, no matter what our efforts, from the inexorable tendency toward decay symbolized by the season of fall. It is a *fallen* world not subject to any but a "divine" redemption—and that, one gathers, is *not* forthcoming. The "world's defeat"—as Frost puts it in "The Lost Follower"—is irrevocable. And yet it is somehow "treason" to the "heart of man," these poems maintain with "Reluctance," meekly to give in to dissolution. In fact, poetry is itself a response to decay, however imperfect a stay against confusion it may be. Poetry is where we may find if not the Golden Age then at least something *like* it. The only grace sustaining this world is the grace of lyrics such as the ones before us here: one way to "ignore" all the "waste," one way strategically to endure it, is to tell ourselves beautiful lies about the keeping of time in art. And the last lines of "November" open up still further implications. In "A Prayer in Spring" and "Putting in the Seed," human procreative energies are allied with the larger, natural creative energies of spring. "November" completes this idea by associating our destructive energies—"the waste of nations warring"—with the destructive energies of fall and winter. Human "nature" forms a part of these larger natural processes of desolation. There is a little winter, a little of the killing season, in all of us—that is what these poems suggest. Suffering—even when *socially* derived as in war—is simply intractable. Our woes are "immedicable," as Frost puts it in the introduction to *King Jasper*.

"The Rabbit Hunter" continues the work of naturalizing human destructiveness:

> Careless and still
> The hunter lurks
> With gun depressed,
> facing alone
> The alder swamps
> Ghastly snow-white.
> And his hound works
> In the offing there
> Like one possessed,
> And yelps with delight
> And sings and romps,
> Bringing him on
> The shadowy hare
> For him to rend
> And deal a death
> That he nor it
> (Nor I) have wit
> To comprehend.
>
> (*CPPP* 327)

Here, winter is itself a part of the hunter's mood. Or perhaps it is more accurate to say that the hunter's mood forms a part of winter. The phrase "ghastly snow-white" attaches equally to the hunter and to the bleak swamps, grimly merging them into a single thought, into a unit. The hound works, we are told, as "one possessed"; he is subject to a greater will. But the hunter is no better off than his hound: he lacks wit to "comprehend" his own actions and from the outset is "careless." The latter word, as used here, does not mean "clumsy" or "imprudent"; it means *bereft of deliberation.* This hunter merely executes some larger, more "comprehensive" will that things should die; and like his hound, he is agency, not agent. This makes it seem as if even *human* violence were beyond our management, as if our destructions were subsidiary functions of some larger natural force. All of this gives the funereal theme of "November" a still more sinister twist, as if finally to put to rest the hopes of dreamers like the young poet spoken of in "The Lost Follower": it develops in the penultimate line of "The Rabbit Hunter" that the speaker/poet is *himself* no better able than the hunter or the hound to "comprehend" what happens here and no better able to manage it—at least not *outside* the lyric line of poetry.

It is worth considering further Frost's place as a social thinker in the American literary tradition, and to this end I return to *The Scarlet Letter.* Hester Prynne exists within a society that cannot adequately accommodate her abiding sense of personal and moral "difference"—and it is, after all, a difference that she "anxiously" cultivates, to borrow Frost's term. Hawthorne is at pains, several times in the novel, to portray Hester as intransigently (if nonetheless magnificently) proud. And yet as every reader knows, after long suffering and much stubbornness, Hester decides to accept the terms of the Puritans' condemnation of her. She *voluntarily* takes up the scarlet letter once again. In so doing she gains a marginal but important status: she finds an accredited outlet for her aspirations—a social place within the Massachusetts Colony, a way to negotiate her sense of personal difference with the Puritans, who eventually come to her for counsel as to a sage. That this negotiation and compromise of difference should be accomplished is the purpose of her return to the colony and of her resumption of a letter that, according to the law, she in fact need no longer wear. In this way the novel symbolizes perfectly the liberal, consensus ideals of its author, as Sacvan Bercovitch describes them.

Huck Finn is another figure whose dawning sense of his own difference forces him to the margins of his community and, as does Hester, he essentially accepts the terms in which that community would condemn him. When at last he decides to assist Jim, Huck consigns himself to Hell, earnestly believing that he is wicked—that his community's slave-holding morality is the right one, even if he cannot abide by it. Of course, Twain does not ask us to *admire* Huck for accepting this morality. We are meant deeply to regret it, which marks Twain's difference from his New England predecessor. Hawthorne does in fact expect us to commend Hester for relaxing her intransigence to accept the harsh letter of Puritan law. Huck's acquiescence to his own "letter" or badge of guilt—to his supposedly "criminal" status as an accomplice to a fugitive slave—symbolizes not a healthy, liberal negotiation of opposed values of dissent and community. It symbolizes instead the extent to which the social contract has already damaged the heart and mind of a young boy whose native instincts are profoundly humane. As a novel *Huckleberry Finn* seems no longer to believe in the liberal possibility of compromise and consensus that sustains *The Scarlet Letter.* Any return on Huck's part to take up his shame as an abolitionist in the community from which he came would be disastrous; no reader can avoid feeling that this is so. "Community" in this novel—as in Twain's essay "The United States of Lyncherdom"—has become a kind of disease, a moral contagion from which it is all but impossible to escape infection. For this reason, *Huckleberry Finn* is bleaker than *The Scarlet Letter.* Twain's pessimism is everywhere felt, despite his (perhaps disingenuous) effort, in the last section of the novel, to return to the comic mode of *Tom Sawyer*—an aesthetic problem that has engaged interpreters of Twain for decades. The real complement to *Huckleberry Finn* is not *Tom Sawyer* but the profoundly bitter "The United States of Lyncherdom." And as this association suggests, the novel's proper historical context is less the antebellum South than post-Reconstruction America, a place where—as Twain points out in "Lyncherdom"—terrorism was rampant and civility all but a sham. American civilization, Twain argues, is a kind of virus incontinently carried abroad by Christian missionaries who would do better to minister to men and women sitting in darkness in Missouri rather than China. In *Huckleberry Finn,* the ideals of self-realization and of community are irreconcilably at odds; no compromise, in the liberal sense of that term, is possible between the claims of difference and correspondence. And accession to the "fear of Man" is, in Twain's work generally, little better than capitulation—the "selling" of one's self "down the river" morally. It is much better to be "insane" under conditions such as these, as Dickinson—to recur once more to her famous lyric—notoriously suggested:

> Much madness is Divinest Sense
> To a Discerning Eye

> Much sense the starkest madness—
> Tis the majority in this as all prevail.
> (209)

It is an out-of-the-way irony of American literary history that when Frost reaffirms a Hawthornian, liberal ideal of compromise in the introduction to *King Jasper,* he authorizes that affirmation with an allusion to Mark Twain's "ordeal"—an allusion, that is, to Van Wyck Brooks's study *The Ordeal of Mark Twain.* But Frost's allusion may actually be more perceptive than ironic, for at bottom Twain *did,* it seems, desire to remain "charming" and "bearable," despite the darkness of the rebellious message "occluded" by his humor. *Huckleberry Finn* suggests that its author was himself incapable of sustaining the rebellion against civility, gentility, and community that his adolescent hero, Huck, manages at last to sustain only by "lighting out for the territory" (rather than for the genteel East and the *Atlantic Monthly,* where his author ended up). The novel famously concludes with Huck's intransigent declaration that he will never again submit to "*sivilization.*" But as has often been suggested, it is to civility of a sort—specifically, a noticeably charming and bearable humor—that Twain has already acceded when he brings Tom Sawyer back into the story and, through a series of insufferably baroque pranks and implausible twists of plot, reduces Huck's agency in the novel to degree zero: Huck becomes merely incidental to the embarrassing minstrel show that Tom—and Twain too, it must be conceded—stages at Jim's expense. Brooks's argument in *The Ordeal* is that this is an example of Twain's "conformist" humor getting the better of his higher, more radical "formist" ideals (to use Frost's terms). The "approval of society" is supposed merely to *balance* "self approval" but often *overwhelms* it instead. The claims of correspondence may finally outweigh those of rebellion and difference, which is precisely what happened in Mark Twain's ordeal—or so Brooks had argued. And this is, I am suggesting, the nature also of Frost's ordeal: his sympathies finally lie more with "correspondence" than with the "anxious" cultivation of "difference," and he would remain, as a writer, eminently charming and bearable, even at the cost, as his most sympathetic readers have sometimes felt, of selling out to "the trial by market everything must come to," or of working into his later work, beginning in the 1920s, a little Tom Sawyerish fooling of his own. In this respect, Frost is as close to Twain as to Hawthorne. Like Twain himself, Frost can be considerably more puckish than Huckish. Both writers seemed to have found cause to distrust, at least in certain moods, the more heterodox impulses in their constitutions. Mencken perceptively writes, apropos of Twain's timidity in bringing his iconoclastic collection *What Is Man?* (1905) into print: "Mark knew his countrymen. He knew their intense suspicion of ideas, their blind hatred of heterodoxy, their bitter way of dealing with dissenters. He knew how, their pruderies outraged, they would turn upon even the gaudiest hero and roll him in the mud. And knowing, he was afraid. He 'dreaded the disapproval of the people around him,'" Mencken concludes, quoting a phrase from Twain's preface to *What Is Man?* And then: "But part of that dread, I suspect, was peculiarly internal. In brief, Mark himself was also an American, and he shared the national horror of the unorthodox. His own speculations always half appalled him" (*Chrestomathy* 487–88). The "fear of Man," as Frost eulogizes it, is but another expression of this national horror of the unorthodox.

Richard Poirier rightly points out that Frost "resists the transcendentalist willingness to disentangle the self from ties of 'home' and from any responsibility to domesticate whatever might be encountered while one is 'extra-vagant'" (*Robert Frost* 144). "Extra-vagance" names the insubordinate, chaotic energies Frost warily considers in the introduction to *King Jasper,* "domestication" names the reduction of these to cultural and social authorities. Frost ultimately appeals to the claims of community and against the claims of egregiousness and heterodoxy—even against, to a degree, what Brooks called "that extreme form of individuality, the creative spirit."[15] To some, this has seemed narrow-minded on his part. No doubt Frost's exasperation with the prestige of Pound and Eliot is partly associated with the moral arguments he made for correspondence in poetry, as when he forgets, for example, that their poetry does not break off communication *as such;* it breaks off communication simply with one *kind* of audience, while establishing it with another. The poetics even of "extreme" modernists forged alliances. And there is always the temptation to ask whether Frost's ideas about the "fear of Man," and its associated prosody, may not be elaborate, often very persuasive excuses for keeping in check such political and artistic differences as he vaguely hints at in the introduction to *King Jasper.* It is "a question to be asked," as impious, insubordinate Falstaff said to the Prince, very much in fear that his own "difference" would soon seem eccentric, abortive, insane, and that he might be cut off from men. It may be that Frost (like Prince Hal or Mark Twain) found it in him to deny the insubordinate and chaotic energies that animated his play at its best. There would be more force in this objection had not Frost at times emphasized, as in "The Future of Man," the subversiveness of art. In any event, there is much to be regretted in Falstaff, and the situation may be put in terms more charitable to Frost and to Henry V, who also has his advocates. Frank Lentricchia writes: "Frost . . . teaches us that the dreaded antifictive—the real thing—is often to be preferred to what we make in the imagination, because the fictive 'world elsewhere' may be a place of madness" (*Landscapes* xii). As Frost's 1939 Gold Medal speech suggests, the saint and the psychotic are alike confident in their convictions. A broader court of appeal than the simple, separate personality must be engaged, and this is the value of the "harsher discipline from without."

In an engaging chapter on *Pride and Prejudice,* Tony Tanner describes a "major problem" in the Anglo-American literary tradition: "namely that of the relationship and adjustment between individual energy and social forms. If one were to make a single binary reduction about literature one could say that there are works which stress the existence of, and need for, boundaries; and works which concentrate on everything within the individual—from the sexual to the imaginative and the religious—which conspires to negate or transcend boundaries" (43). Frost remained deeply interested in this problem, and, as I have been suggesting throughout the present chapter, he comes down for the most part with Austen on the side of boundaries. (His remarks in "The Future of Man" qualify this fact somewhat.) Tanner continues by offering a useful account of the romantic alternative to neoclassical emphases on "boundary" and "place." He refers to Locke's evident comfort with the idea that human thought is bounded by a horizon: "Blake took the word 'horizon,' transformed it into 'Urizen' and made that figure the evil symbol of all that restricted and restrained man. He thus stood the Enlightenment on its head, and if it was at the cost of his sanity, then, like the Romantics, he preferred to enjoy the visionary intensities of his 'madness' rather than subscribe to the accepted notions of mental health" (45). Tanner's remarks help us see how Frost's introduction to *King Jasper* places him on the neoclassical side of this argument as a latter-day revisionist of certain forms of literary romanticism (as I will propose in chapter 3). With these ideas in view we may begin more completely to answer the questions implicit in the foregoing pages: Why was Frost reluctant *fully* to trust the insubordinate faculty of imagination? With what disturbing tendencies, specifically, had it come to be associated in his mind? And why had it acquired these associations?

We have already seen how the contours of Frost's "conformist" poetics—in his special sense of the term—mirror the contours of his career. There is, I think, an even deeper and more intimately personal ground than that for his defense of form and correspondence. When he speaks of insanity, as in the introduction to *King Jasper,* or of sanity, as in his "'Letter' to the *Amherst Student*" and elsewhere, he is not just speaking academically. "Difference" may indeed shade off imperceptibly into insanity, as it did in the lives of Frost's sister Jeanie and of his son Carol. Both suffered paranoid delusions that left the one in an asylum and the other a suicide. As a child Frost himself used to imagine that he heard voices and would bury his head among pillows to blot them out. Lawrance Thompson reports a conversation he had with Frost in August 1940:

> Speaking of his early life, he talked about how he had been frightened as a child by "voices" which he heard in his imagination as clearly as he could have heard them if he had been listening to someone talking beside him. He was frightened by the voices and yet did not say anything to anyone about them. He would draw up his feet into his chair and sit there listening until they stopped. Later, he had the same experience in another form; a sound of voices that repeated everything he said, almost as though with a slightly different inflexion which mocked his own thoughts. ("Notes on Conversations")

This reads like an account of a mild childhood psychosis, and yet it is probably much more commonplace than that. It describes the young Frost's fear of losing control of his own imagination, as his stream of thought became increasingly disorderly and insubordinate—a fear that can, at times, exacerbate itself. Significantly, this experience later came to be associated in Frost's mind with the composition of poetry. He offered the following explanations in the same 1940 conversation with Thompson:

> In speaking of his own writing, he said that when he started out with a poem he heard the words; that it all tied back to his own experience in "voices," a kind of auto-suggestion. As a child he used to hear voices. A voice outside himself, so clear that it frightened him. . . . Later, those same voices seemed connected with his writing. At its best, poetry was for him a gathering together of past experience, past emotion, past thought, in such a vivid fashion that the words spoke themselves in a voice, and his business was merely to record the words uttered by the voice. He said that he never saw the truth of the thought or the idea when he began; that he never saw the end of a poem when he began, but before he had progressed very far he could feel it or half realize the idea that was being symbolized by the experience he was recording in the poem.

The writing of poetry is linked, in this report of Frost's remarks, with the earlier "frightening" apparition of voices, which had arisen as if from psychosis. The motivation for poetry—its imperative voice, so to speak—is imagined as a force speaking from outside the poet himself. And yet the writing of the poem is what internalizes and therefore *personalizes* this initially disturbing, *alien* voice. The writing of poetry gives over to the poet possession of what had originally dispossessed and frightened him. In this way, the composition of poetry is an exercise in self-control—a reclaiming of a self-integrity that is threatened when the insubordinate inspiration for poetry takes hold of the poet. Frost's remarks suggest that the composition of poetry, an activity at times motivated by disturbing and alien voices, is actually a means to harness and to reassert control over those voices. In phrases that are perhaps apposite here, Frost writes in "Poetry and School," a collection of aphorisms published in the *Atlantic Monthly* in 1951: "Practice of an art is more salutary than talk about it. There is nothing more composing than composition" (*CPPP* 808).

In chapter 3 I will discuss at some length the idea that writing may be a means to shore up or recover a threatened self-integrity. For the moment, I am more immediately concerned with the related idea that composition held a specifically *therapeutic* value for Frost, a value specifically associated with poetic form and informed by his experience of insanity in his family. There is fairly good evidence that Frost feared insanity was in his family blood, as indeed it seems to have been. A moving letter from his sister Jeanie, written to him in 1925 from the State Hospital for the Insane at Augusta, Maine, places the onset of her own disorder in her infancy: "I am very peculiar and did not start right. If I ever was well and natural it was before I can remember. I hate to have anyone understand how I feel in a way. To the mind of anyone who could understand the condition of my mind, there could not be any worse horror. . . . Few people realize how entirely this depression cuts me off from things so that only for occasional moments I might as well be stone deaf and blind" (*Selected Letters* 319). Reading this letter, one begins to understand what Frost may have meant when he spoke, in the introduction to *King Jasper*, of "the fear that men won't understand us and we shall be cut off from them." His remarks certainly have familial and biographical coordinates.

Frost's daughter Irma suffered a pattern of paranoia and depression much like the one that crippled Jeanie Frost, and when her condition deteriorated he turned to his friend Merrill Moore, the poet and psychiatrist. Frost's memorial essay on Moore, published in the *Harvard Med-*

ical Alumni Bulletin in 1958, singles out for praise a treatment he had devised for the mentally ill: "On a visit to Sanibel Island he had the bright idea of shovelling up from the beach with his own hands a ton or two of sea shells and shipping them North for his patients to sort out. I wish you could hear the disc recording of his speech about the therapeutic value of this exercise in beauty" (*CPPP* 842–43). Frost's approval of the "therapeutic value of this exercise in beauty" is ratified by a number of his remarks on the satisfactions of exercises in form and order, not simply by his decision to place Irma Frost under Moore's care. One thinks particularly of the following passage from his 1935 "'Letter' to *The Amherst Student*":

> When in doubt there is always form for us to go on with. Anyone who has achieved the least form to be sure of it, is lost to the larger excruciations. I think it must stroke faith the right way. The artist, the poet might be expected to be the most aware of such assurance. But it is really everybody's sanity to feel it and live by it. Fortunately, too, no forms are more engrossing, gratifying, comforting, staying than those lesser ones we throw off, like vortex rings of smoke, all our individual enterprise and needing nobody's cooperation; a basket, a letter, a garden, a room, an idea, a picture, a poem. (*CPPP* 740)

And in an appearance on "Meet the Press" in 1956, Frost said: "I think the thing that confuses the mind is a loss of a sense of form, and if you lose the sense of form, the doctor can restore it by teaching you how to make a horse shoe or a basket or something like that, or to blow smoke rings or anything to restore your sense of form, and as long as so many of us, nearly all of us have a chance to make a little rounding out of something . . . that is what keeps the sanity and that is what keeps and saves us from the sense of confusion" (*Interviews* 160). It was in this sense that literature became, for him, "equipment for living," to borrow a useful phrase from Kenneth Burke. And if, as I have suggested, Frost's defense of form and correspondence in poetry arose out of his efforts symbolically to master the particular confusions of his own career and family life, there is also in his poetics a sense in which form *as such* is therapy for difficulties and confusion in general.

At times, Frost seems to argue that exercises in form are perhaps *the* characteristic human and humanizing activity. An enigmatic passage in his "'Letter' to *The Amherst Student*" suggests that there is an almost evolutionary imperative behind our attraction to form: "We people are thrust forward out of the suggestions of form in the rolling clouds of nature. In us nature reaches its height of form and through us exceeds itself" (*CPPP* 740). The air of mystery in these sentences calls to mind George Santayana's account of poetic form and measure in *Interpretations of Poetry and Religion* (1900), a book with which Frost was almost certainly acquainted:

> Although a poem be not made by counting syllables upon the fingers, yet "numbers" is the most poetical synonym we have for verse, and "measure" the most significant equivalent for beauty, for goodness, and perhaps even for truth. Those early and profound philosophers, the followers of Pythagoras, saw the essence of all things in number, and it was by weight, measure, and number, as we read in the Bible, that the Creator first brought Nature out of the void. Every human architect must do likewise with his edifice; he must mould his bricks or hew his stones into symmetrical solids and lay them over one another in regular strata, like a poet's lines. (151)

In his own way, Frost echoed these sentiments often, and for him "measure" (a term he favored) always signifies tact, grace, control, and form; it signifies even sanity itself, as Frost's tribute to Merrill Moore suggests. In this way, exercises in "measure" and "numbers" acquire a moral significance for Frost. The writing of poetry symbolizes general human experiences of control and self-management; the *mores* of versification become the *morality* of a deeply philosophical poetics.

I suggested that Frost's remarks in the "'Letter' to *The Amherst Student*" attribute a natural, even *evolutionary* imperative to our exercises in form and art. Frost expresses the same idea beautifully in a lyric titled "The Aim Was Song," collected first in *New Hampshire* (1923):

> Before man came to blow it right
> The wind once blew itself untaught,
> And did its loudest day and night
> In any rough place where it caught.
>
> Man came to tell it what was wrong:
> It hadn't found the place to blow;
> It blew too hard—the aim was song.
> And listen—how it ought to go!
>
> He took a little in his mouth,
> And held it long enough for north
> To be converted into south,
> And then by measure blew it forth.
>
> By measure. It was word and note,
> The wind the wind was meant to be—

> A little through the lips and throat.
> The aim was song—the wind could see.
> (*CPPP* 207)

Through us nature "exceeds itself" in form, Frost says, and this lyric brings us to the place where nature evolves into culture, where chaos resolves itself through human agency into something "created" and orderly. The wind is articulated or "measured" out in speech, and not only into speech, but "song"—poetry. In "The Ax Helve" Frost's speaker similarly suggests that an artisan crafting a wooden helve merely "expresses" the native curves of its grain (*CPPP* 175). Together these poems imply that form is latent in nature until we bring it out and further suggest that form somehow *aspires* to be brought out. Art is not necessarily opposed to nature. It may *complete* a "nature" from which it genetically derives.

This is an old topic in English literature. In *The Winter's Tale,* the King of Bohemia debates the point with Perdita in a sort of philosophical set piece. Perdita grows only "natural" flowers in her garden, disdaining the "streaked gillyvors" that horticulturalists impiously make by processes of grafting. People call these flowers "nature's bastards," she says, and of that kind her "rustic garden's barren": "For I have heard it said / There is an art which in their piedness shares / With great creating nature." To this position, the King makes the classic reply:

> Say there be;
> Yet nature is made better by no mean
> But nature makes that mean: so, over that art,
> Which you say adds to nature, is an art
> That nature makes. . . . This is an art
> Which does not mend nature, change it rather, but
> The art itself is nature.
> (4.4.82–96)

In exactly this way Frost imagines in "The Aim Was Song" an art that nature makes—an art that is itself somehow genetically natural. Our human additions of "word and note" to the wind only realize what all along had been its latent "aim," its aspiration, just as (to take another example) the song of birds awaited completion in the added "oversound" of human song in "Never Again Would Birds' Song Be the Same": "And to do that to birds was why she came," Frost's speaker says of Eve (*CPPP* 308).

Frost is best remembered, and rightly so, for poems suggesting that the forms we impose on natural settings are fragile, ephemeral, and inherently insecure: the natural world, so-called, almost always reclaims the orders, domestic and otherwise, that we establish on it, as is clear from "The Birthplace," "Directive," "Storm Fear," "Ghost House," and a host of other poems. But Frost also liked, if only rarely, to tell the alternative story of "The Aim Was Song." The latter poem argues that form, measure, and order are not conditions enforced temporarily upon a chaotic, inhuman, and indifferent nature. "Form" and "measure"—and through them the making of poetry—symbolize instead gestures that *affiliate* us with the deeper rhythms and aspirations of a "nature" with which ideally, these poems suggest, we are in harmony and which find completion only through our efforts. It is in this sense that "form" and "measure" in poetry symbolize the very "nature" from which insanity, as Frost conceives it, alienates us. Poetry is a kind of second nature, human creativity a cousin to the creative forces of nature itself. This idea is most eloquently delivered in poems such as "A Prayer in Spring" and "Putting in the Seed." The former, collected first in *A Boy's Will,* begins by gracefully describing the resurgent energies of spring and concludes with the following lines:

> For this is love and nothing else is love,
> The which it is reserved for God above
> To sanctify to what far ends He will,
> But which it only needs that we fulfill.
> (*CPPP* 22)

This way of thinking involves a particularly Lucretian naturalism. The idea is that the affections that draw and bind us together—those we express sexually, for example—are in fact continuous with the larger forces even of magnetism and gravity. Nature is everywhere alive with "affection," as the Chaucerian season of spring reminds us. Spring *is* love, Frost says, and means it quite literally: in making love (the poem argues) we "fulfill" the larger ends of God *in nature.* Sexually creative performances are therefore essentially a part of nature; they are nature realizing itself in and through us.[16] "The Aim Was Song" and the "'Letter' to *The Amherst Student*" offer a complementary mythology of harmony between the conventionally opposed realms of the natural on the one hand and of the cultural and the human on the other: poetic creation and sexual creation alike—and in Frost they may be taken as reciprocal processes—realize and fulfill the elementally creative aspiration of nature. "We people are thrust forward out of the suggestions of form in the rolling clouds of nature," Frost writes. "In us nature reaches its height of form and through us exceeds itself."

Frost's attachment to the twin ideals of order and of a "natural" sexuality present certain problems. "A Prayer in Spring" is a poem of marriage, and its liturgical qualities sanctify heterosexual love by rendering it "natural." The logic of this thinking implies but does not say that forms of sexual insubordination are essentially barren and exist apart from nature, just as the insubordinations of anxious personal difference (to recur to Frost's introduction to *King Jasper*) can issue in an unwholesome detachment from community—in eccentricity or even in insanity. There is often something *normative* about Frost's language—normative in the psychological, sexual, and moral senses, as well as in the aesthetic. This only reminds us of what must always be borne in mind. There may be an "anxious" cultivation of order and correspondence just as there may be of difference and extravagance. If we sometimes sense this anxiety in Frost's writing, it is due to the insecurities that he felt were working against his own embattled patterns of "correspondence"—against his own efforts to achieve a "stay against confusion." His emphasis on correspondence and order must be explained with reference to a deeply felt experience of what he vaguely calls "confusion." The fact that Frost lived so long in the neighborhood of insanity perhaps accounts for the compensating prominence, in his scheme, of order, conformity, and "nature," as well as for those occasions on which these terms are given what may strike us as an overcompensating preeminence.

Kenneth Burke writes in *Language as Symbolic Action* (1966): "If man is characteristically the symbol-using animal, then he should take pleasure in the use of his powers as a symbolizer, just as a bird presumably likes to fly or a fish to swim. Thus, on some occasions, in connection with aesthetic activities, we humans might like to exercise our prowess with symbol systems, just because that's the kind of animal we are. I would view the poetic motive in that light" (29). Of course, there is no reason why the poetry of "extreme modernism" might not accommodate these motives as well as Frost's alternative poetry of "conformity" and "correspondence," though Frost sometimes seems unwilling to acknowledge the fact. That is finally no worse than Eliot's insistence that something about our age obligates poets to write poetry pretty much as Eliot himself chose to write it. Neither man could afford Burke's detachment in surveying the various strategies of the modernists. In Frost's case this is perhaps not so hard to understand if we bear in mind what I have suggested about his writings on poetry.

Though they amount to a description of the motives and satisfactions of form broad enough to embrace poetic strategies other than his own, they issue also from apologetic motives of a personal and strictly contingent nature. His poetics and poetry can offer just about anyone "equipment for living"; but this equipment was designed for the particular (and often extraordinary) difficulties of living Frost's own life.

Frost was, at last, a writer in whom biography—or, as he would say, "diary"—philosophy, and aesthetics blended perfectly. That is why the question of how his poetics is a kind of "apology" for his temperament and career must be handled with delicacy. In his "official" biography of Frost, Lawrance Thompson often takes the poetics as an apology in the very worst sense. Much of what Frost says about style, or about the strategies of other poets, seems to him mere obfuscation and jealousy. He is unable to see how the marriage of philosophy to diary may be something more respectable than a shotgun wedding.

3 *Believing in Robert Frost*

We are sure, that, though we know not how, necessity does comport with liberty, the individual with the world, my polarity with the spirit of the times.
—Ralph Waldo Emerson, "Fate"

When we understand necessity, as Spinoza knew, we are free because we assent.
—T. S. Eliot, "The Perfect Critic"

H. L. MENCKEN ARGUED, following Nietzsche, that any social code valuing humility—always *disingenuously* valuing it, in his view—and valuing the subordination of personal desire to social or moral imperatives is essentially authoritarian, and also probably Christian, in character. T. S. Eliot's work presents an interesting example of this, from his early assertion that the poet must surrender herself to the larger imperatives of tradition and suffer a "continual extinction of personality," to his later writings in favor of an orthodox Christian society. In certain of his critical writings Eliot revives the classicist's preference for tradition over novelty, for order over anarchy, for the general over the particular, and for the office over the person. Each of these things accorded perfectly with his Anglo-Catholicism. An impersonal theory of poetry also formed a crucial part of Eliot's response to the kind of romanticism Nietzsche and Mencken had advocated—a romanticism that set liberty above all things, despised conformity, was inimical to tradition, detested humility, exalted personality and style above form and temperance, and placed Dionysus over Apollo. In chapter 2 we saw how Frost speaks eulogistically of "conformity" and of the necessity of setting "social approval" against "self approval." We saw also that he speaks in favor of what he calls the "fear of Man" and against "heretics" such as Luther and John Bunyan. In so doing Frost rejects, with Eliot, both extreme romanticism and extreme libertarianism. That much, in any event, Frost has in common with Eliot, as I will explain in the first part of this chapter. We find in Frost—at least at first look—little of the romantic or modernist revaluation of morality that animates Mencken's and Pound's work in the 1910s, as should by now be clear. This is why Frost must to an extent always be understood as a contrarian figure in the context of the modernist avant-garde, as this was represented by Pound. And he has typically been understood in exactly this way.

But once this is said there remains to be taken into account the possibility that Frost's poetics of conformity and of the "fear of Man"—call it his poetics of *humility*—yields ultimately to a version of the romantic doctrine of Inner Form (to adopt his phrase for it). There remains to be considered, that is, the remarkable force of personality in his poetics—the force of *self*-discipline working against the "harsher discipline[s] from without" and of *difference* working against conformity and "correspondence." The latter values achieve a high place in Frost's poetics, as he "believes into existence," as he would have said, a powerful self never completely stated and contained. This movement in Frost's philosophy from "conformity" to "formity" (or *self*-discipline) is the subject of the remainder of this study. The first section of this chapter considers the related issues of motive and personality in poetry and touches on certain parallels between Frost's thinking and Eliot's. Here, I investigate the sense in which Frost, too, advanced an "impersonal" theory of poetry. In the second section I consider the more general theoretical problems of "authority" and "the author" to show how Frost's poetics transcends his central dialectic of "conformity" and "formity" to move toward a romantic theory of *self-realizing* poetry. The familiar question Frost can help us with is whether, and to what extent, there is a controlling "intelligence" identical to the author of a poem, or of any other utterance, and whether this intelligence, whatever its constitution, may be so defined as to hold total responsibility for the possibilities of meaning in that utterance. It is a question of whether "the category of intention," as Jacques Derrida writes in "Signature Event Context," is "able to govern the entire scene and system of utterance" (18). In Derrida's view it cannot, and to this idea Frost offers a kind of provisional assent. In fact, Frost's analysis of the conditions of authorship anticipates later insights of Derrida and Michel Foucault and also affirms the theories of his pragmatist contemporaries Burke and John Dewey (though it really would be no less accurate to say that Frost looks back to Emerson). The great distinction of Frost's poetics, however, lies in his ambivalent aspiration to transcend conditions of authorship that can alienate the writer from himself. The result is a complicated skepticism, a skepticism not simply of the possibilities for self-expression and personality in language—which we think of, for example, in connection with Derrida's and Foucault's arguments—but also of linguistic skepticism itself. Frost's circumscriptions of the poet's integrity are always also *affirmations* of it—a final ambivalence that his poetics refuses to resolve.

The Motives of Poetry

In 1934 Frost's daughter Lesley Frost Francis delivered a lecture on the New Movement poetry of the mid-1910s. Apparently at her request Frost wrote her a long letter, quoted already in other connections, sketching his own history of the movement and summarizing the aesthetic doctrine of the Movement poets and their successors. He refers to the poet and critic Herbert Read, author of *Form in Modern Poetry* (1932), to whom, as we have seen already, he attributes "the doctrine of Inner Form": adherence exclusively to "the form the subject [of the poem] itself takes if left to itself without any considerations of outer form. Everything else," Frost goes on to explain, "is to have two compulsions, an inner and an outer, a spiritual and a social, an individual and a racial. . . . Everything but poetry according to the Pound-Eliot-Richards-Reed school of art." Over against this position Frost asserts his own, arguing that *everything,* even a poem, has "not only formity but conformity": "I want to be good, but that is not enough the state says I have got to be good" (*CPPP* 735). These remarks succinctly frame Frost's interest in the general question of motivation, not simply in Herbert Read and his "school." And in the pages that follow I consider his contribution to the theory of motive and personality in poetry. As I am concerned with it here, a theory of personality in poetry addresses the question of who or what chiefly *motivates* a work of literary art. Is the controlling discipline (or "compulsion") in a poem the "inner voice" of the writer, her will to expression? Is it the impersonal agencies either of language, form, society, or tradition? Or is it rather a mixture of personal and impersonal motives? If the latter, then what *sort* of mixture? In considering Frost's answers to these questions we confront some of the most important matters addressed in his essays and letters on poetics. Thinking about his theories of personality in poetry also helps us place his work more clearly within the context of his modernist contemporaries. The dismissive force of his reference later in the letter to Lesley to the "Pound-Eliot-Richards-Reed" school of art, for example, should not be allowed to obscure what I take to be the deeper sympathy between certain aspects of Frost's thought and Eliot's.

The letter to Lesley Frost is certainly succinct in its expression: "I want to be good, but that is not enough the state says I have got to be good"—a very simple statement of a very complex problem. With characteristic concision and informality Frost suggests how difficult it is to know where external "compulsion" ends and where "inner" desire begins. As I take it, the idea is that, at least until the state withers away, we simply cannot speak of pure acts of "goodness": there is always an incalculable element of coercion, whether by force or by incentive, since we always act within a texture of constraints and goads ranging from convention to legal imperatives. In view of this Frost describes a dialectic of necessity and freedom: everything has "two compulsions, an inner and an outer, a spiritual and a social, an individual and a racial. . . . Everything has not only formity but conformity."

Kenneth Burke's remarks on a related problem of motivation are illuminating. He is discussing, in *A Grammar of Motives,* what he calls the "paradox of purity" or of "the absolute":

> The paradox may be implicit in any term for *collective* motivation, such as a concept of class, nation, the "general will," and the like. Technically it becomes a "pure" motive when matched against some individual locus of motivation. And it may thus be the *negation* of an individual motive. Yet despite this position as dialectical antithesis of the individual motive, the collective motive may be treated as the source or principle from which the individual motive is familially . . . derived in a "like begets like" manner. (37)

The question is whether "collective," external motives exist in antithesis to individual motives or whether the former "parent" the latter. Frost confronts the paradox implicit in "collective motivation" quite plainly: "I want to be good, but that is not enough the state says I have got to be good." Is his virtue enforced by a "collective" will working against his own "inner" form? Or does his inner desire to "be good" itself derive from his engagement in a collective social enterprise? Collective motives—what Frost would call motives of "conformity"—may be described genetically: they exist in harmony with individual motives as their originating principle. Or they may be described contextually: they work in antithesis to personal motives—what Frost would call the motives of "formity."

Later in the *Grammar* Burke makes a suggestion that helps bring out the broader implications of Frost's remarks to his daughter. Burke asks whether or not, strictly speaking, "action" is compatible with "motivation": "If we quizzically scrutinize the expression, 'the motivating of an act,' we note that it implicitly contains . . . [a] paradox. . . . Grammatically, if a construction is active, it is not passive; and if it is passive, it is not active. But to consider an *act* in terms of its *grounds* is to consider it in terms of what it is not, namely, in terms of motives that, in acting upon the active, would make it a passive" (40). Frost asks a similar question in his letter. Does the motivation to conform exercised on us by social forces actually rob individual actors of their agency? Is it possible, again strictly speaking, to perform a "good" action if virtue is enforced? Inner and outer motivation may negate rather than complement one another. In the "Afterword" to an edition of *Limited Inc* (1988) Jacques Derrida makes much the same point: "A decision can only come into being in a space that exceeds the calculable program that would destroy all responsibility by transforming it into a programmable effect of determinate causes. There can be no moral or political responsibility without this trial and this passage by way of the undecidable" (116). Where Derrida writes "moral responsibility" I read "selfhood" or "agency" since that is really what we are talking about: agency and selfhood are what *exceed* calculation and prediction from without. At bottom Frost, Derrida, and Burke address the same basic set of questions: What is the meaning of "agency"? Is it personal? Impersonal? Is it masterable? What are its conditions?

That true agency exists only beyond the limits of law seemed quite evident to Frost. Here, "law" can refer to previous dispositions of the self—a kind of gravitational, constraining inertia—as well as to forces imposed from without. Frost seems to be thinking of this when he offers in his notebooks what must strike some as an odd definition of "sincerity": "There is such a thing as sincerity. It is hard to define but it is probably nothing but your highest liveliness escaping from a succession of dead selves" (40). "Sincerity" is not an expression of the deep heart's core. It consists instead in an experience of transition *out* of previous self-definitions, not in an affirmation or further elaboration of them. To Frost this held true for corporate agency and "sincerity" as well, as when he writes in an unpublished version of his essay "The Future of Man" (1959), in a passage quoted already in another connection: "The great challenge, the eternal challenge, is that of man's bursting energy and originality to his own governance. His speed and his traffic police. We become an organized society only as we tell off some of our number to be law-givers and law-enforcers, a blend of general and lawyer, to hold fast the line and turn the rest of us loose for scientists, philosophers, and poets to make the break-through, the revolution, if we can for refreshment" (*CPPP* 869). This is to say, with Derrida, that true agency—bursting energy, originality, refreshment—exists only on the margins of definition and governance in a "passage by way of the undecidable." Pure formity must be defined against even *self-conformity.* And making the "break-through" means rising, even as an "organized society," to our "highest liveliness escaping from a succession of dead selves." Or to return to Frost's 1934 letter: There is nothing especially "personal" about good behavior if the state simply compels you so to behave. A "cloistered virtue"—to borrow Milton's phrase in *Areopagitica*—may be derivative or enforced, depending on how you look at it. But in neither case is it properly *intrinsic* to the agent, who is, as Derrida says, merely a "programmable effect of determinate causes."

Another complexity of the problem is that all actions imply further actions, no matter what, or how pure, their originating motivation may have been. All our actions therefore carry within them the seeds of necessity, as Emerson recognizes in "Goethe": "A certain partiality, a headiness, and loss of balance, is the tax which all action must pay. Act, if you like,—but you do it at your peril. Men's actions are too strong for them. Show me a man who has acted, and who has not been the victim and slave of his actions" (*Essays* 749). Frost understood the point well, though he usually seems less troubled by it than Emerson. In the talk at Dartmouth College that served as the basis for his essay "The Constant Symbol," Frost remarks: "I always test the other man. I suspect him of having gotten lost in his steadily deepening commitments. Everybody does this. . . . We are all always testing each other's sincerity. I do it when I read poetry. I do it when I watch the president of the United States as he gets deeper and deeper into commitments. I watch every marriage that way. . . . In this unfolding of the kept or lost intentions within the deepening commitments is the root and basis of all good writing" (qtd. in Tallmer 3). Two aspects of this passage are especially important: the potentially antithetical relationship it establishes between "sincerity" and "commitments" and its paradoxical idea that "intention" is a thing at once "unfolded" (or revealed) *and* "kept." As I see it the paradox holds in suspension two very different ideas: (1) that intentions are the grounds or cause of our actions and (2) that intentions are the products of our actions. Jonathan Culler usefully expresses the point in *On Deconstruction* (1982): "When questioned about the implications of an utterance I may quite routinely include in my intention implications that had never previously occurred to me. My intention is the sum of further explanations I might give when questioned on any point and is thus less an origin than a product, less a delimited context than an open set of discursive possibilities" (127–28). This is essentially what "The Constant Symbol" is about: namely, how the manifold commitments in which we engage in speaking, in writing a poem, or most generally in acting, produce an intention that we cannot with fidelity say we ever fully or originally possessed. We might describe our actions more accurately as the *revelation* than as the *expression* of purpose.

We can see how intention is revealed rather than expressed, Frost suggests, by considering the progress of a career or of a life or simply by considering the progress of a poem, which is a symbol for each of these larger progressions. "Take the President in the White House," he writes in "The Constant Symbol":

> A study of the succession of his intention might have to go clear back to when as a young politician, youthfully step-careless, he made choice between the two parties of our system. He may have stood for a moment wishing he knew of a third party nearer the ideal; but only for a moment, since he was practical. And in fact he may have been so little impressed with the importance of his choice that he left his first commitment to be made for him by his friends and relatives. It was only a small commitment anyway, like a kiss. He can scarcely remember how much credit he deserved personally for the decision it took. Calculation is usually no part in the first step in any walk. And behold him now a statesman so multifariously closed in on with obligations and answerabilities that sometimes he loses his august temper. He might as well have got himself into a sestina royal. (*CPPP* 787)

There is an element of satire here. This "youthfully step-careless" politician probably serves purposes not his own, even if he is not aware of it. The mind of the president is not the same thing as the Presidential Mind, which in Frost's account is more a social than an individual concern. The situation requires that we use the word "sincerity," for example, a little loosely, since the agent in this particular economy of motives is larger than a single man: "Behold him now a statesman so multifariously closed in on with obligations and answerabilities that sometimes he loses his august temper."

But Frost hardly wants to suggest that purely self-derived motivation becomes meaningless only when we describe the progress of "step-careless" politicians. His satire has a complicated irony, some of it directed at himself as a writer: after all, the president "might as well have got himself into a sestina royal." Later in "The Constant Symbol" Frost raises similarly skeptical questions about Shakespeare's integrity: "What's the use in pretending he was a freer agent [in writing his sonnets] than he had any ambition to be" (*CPPP* 789)? Much of the irony of Frost's portrait of "the President in the White House" and of the poet turns upon the word "temper," which derives from the Latin word *temperare:* "to regulate" or "to govern." Frost's use of the word in this connection ironically suggests that no pure regulation or integrity of purpose is ever really there to be lost: we must speak, not of intention, but of a "succession" or evolution of intention. And Frost indicates that we may in fact deserve very little "personal" credit for the "succession" that brought us to our present position of power. All our actions are intemperate.

These considerations lead us down "The Road Not Taken," a meditation that apparently concerns "step-carefulness" but really concerns "step-care*less*ness." The ironies of this poem have been often enough remarked. Not least among them is the contrast of the title with the better-remembered phrase of the poem's penultimate line: "the [road] less travelled by" (*CPPP* 103). Which road, after all, is the road "not taken"? Is it the one the speaker takes, which, according to his last description of it, is "less travelled"—that is to say, not taken *by others?* Or does the title refer to the supposedly better-traveled road that the speaker himself fails to take? Precisely *who* is *not* doing the taking? This initial ambiguity sets in play equivocations that extend throughout the poem. Of course, the broadest irony in the poem derives from the fact that the speaker merely *asserts* that the road he takes is "less travelled": the second and third stanzas make clear that "the passing there" had worn these two paths "really about the same" and that "*both* that morning *equally* lay / In leaves no step had trodden black." Strong medial caesurae in the poem's first ten lines comically emphasize the "either-or" deliberations in which the speaker is engaged, and which have, apparently, no real consequence: nothing issues from them. Only in the last stanza is any noticeable difference between the two roads established, and that difference is established by fiat: the speaker simply declares that the road he took was less travelled. There is nothing to decide between them. There is no *meaningful* "choice" to make, or rather no more choice than is meaningfully apparent to the "step-careless" politician of Frost's parable of decision in "The Constant Symbol."

Comical as "The Road Not Taken" may be, there is serious matter in it, as my reading of "The Constant Symbol" is meant to suggest. "Step-care*less*ness" has its consequences; choices—even when they are undertaken so lightly as to seem unworthy of the name "choice"—are always more momentous, and very often more providential, than we suppose. There may be, one morning in a yellow wood, no difference between two roads—say, the Democratic and the Republican parties. But "way leads on to way," as Frost's speaker says, and pretty soon you find yourself in the White House. As I argue throughout this chapter, this is the *indifference* that Frost wants us to see: "youthful step-carelessness" really *is* a form of "step-care*ful*ness." But it is only by setting out, by working our way well into the wood, that we begin to understand the meaning of the choices we make and the *character* of the self that is making them; in fact, only then can we properly understand our actions *as choices.* The speaker vacillates in the first three stanzas of "The Road Not Taken," but his vacillations, viewed in deeper perspective, seem, and in fact really are, "decisive." We are too much in the middle of things, Frost seems to be saying, ever to understand when we *are* truly "acting" and "deciding" and when we are merely reacting and temporizing. Our paths unfold themselves to us as we go. We realize our destination only when we arrive at it, though all along we were driven toward it by purposes we may rightly claim, in retrospect, as our own. Frost works from Emerson's recognition in "Experience":

> Where do we find ourselves? In a series of which we do not know the extremes, and believe that it has none. We wake and find ourselves on a stair; there are stairs below us, which we seem to have ascended; there are stairs above us, many a one, which go upward and out of sight. But the Genius which, according to the old belief, stands at the door by which we enter, and gives us the lethe to drink, that we may tell no tales, mixed the cup too strongly, and we cannot shake off the lethargy now at noonday. . . . If any of us knew what we were doing, or where we are going, then when we think we best know! We do not know today whether we are busy or idle. In times when we thought ourselves indolent, we have afterwards discovered, that much was accomplished, and much was begun in us. (*Essays* 471)

Frost's is an Emersonian philosophy in which indecisiveness and decision feel very much alike—a philosophy in which *acting* and *being acted upon* form indistinguishable aspects of a single experience. There is obviously a contradiction in "The Road Not Taken" between the speaker's assertion of difference in the last stanza and his indifferent account of the roads in the first three stanzas. But it is a contradiction more profitably described—in light of Frost's other investigations of questions about choice, decision, and action—as a *paradox*. He lets us see, as I point out above, that every action is in some degree intemperate, incalculable, "step-careless." The speaker of "The Road Not Taken," like the politician described in "The Constant Symbol," is therefore a figure for us all. This complicates the irony of the poem, saving it from platitude on the one hand (the M. Scott Peck reading) and from sarcasm on the other (the biographical reading of the poem merely as a joke about Edward Thomas). I disagree with Frank Lentricchia's suggestion in *Modernist Quartet* that "The Road Not Taken" shows how "our life-shaping choices are irrational, that we are fundamentally out of control" (75). The author of "The Trial by Existence" would never contend that we are fundamentally out of control—or at least not do so in earnest.

A certain intemperancy of action, then, is associated with the dialectic of "formity" and "conformity" featured throughout Frost's work. To appreciate the range of his concern with this dialectic, we need only consider two works that at first glance seem to have little in common, though these superficial differences reveal a deeper coherence: his tendency to range all phases of our experience—no matter how apparently diverse—within the same dialectic of inner and outer motivation, or "formity" and "conformity." I am thinking of his sonnet "The Silken Tent" and of his brief, unpublished essay on the subject of "divine right":

> She is as in a field a silken tent
> At midday when a sunny summer breeze
> Has dried the dew and all its ropes relent,
> So that in guys it gently sways at ease,
> And its supporting central cedar pole,
> That is its pinnacle to heavenward
> And signifies the sureness of the soul,
> Seems to owe naught to any single cord,
> But strictly held by none, is loosely bound
> By countless silken ties of love and thought
> To everything on earth the compass round,
> And only by one's going slightly taut
> In the capriciousness of summer air
> Is of the slightest bondage made aware.
> (*CPPP* 302)

> We were talking about the Divine Right of a king or of anyone else who rules. A principle like that may vary in strength but even in a Democracy it never dies out. It is his right first of all to consult the

> highest in himself. His first answerability must be to the highest in himself, however close a second his answerability may be to his subjects and constituents. He needs the consent of the governed. But he is no sort of leader unless his pride is in providing them with something definite to consent to. Or dissent from! A ruler is distinguished by the proportions in which the two answerabilities are blended in his nature. (*Collected Prose* 195)

"The Silken Tent" strikingly illustrates its idea of freedom-in-bondage by the way Frost sets the single, finely modulated sentence that composes it so comfortably into the strictly answered form of a Shakespearean sonnet. Hardly a single "bond" of meter, rhyme, or stanza goes unfulfilled, though in the sonnet form these "silken ties" are especially arresting. Moreover, a careful reading shows that effects of assonance and consonance "bind" together an uncommon (for Frost) number of syllables in the poem with various silken "ties" of sound. And yet in reading "The Silken Tent" we are really never "of the slightest *bondage* made aware." Necessities of "bondage"—whether we mean meter, rhyme, assonance, consonance, or "argument"—never seem to govern the happy way in which the poem finds its words. We never feel as if its course is being unduly "managed" or "disciplined." As but one example of the sonnet's graces, take its seventh line, the midpoint or center of the fourteen-line poem: "And signifies the sureness of the soul." Three alliterated words carry and focus the force of the line: first, a verb of three syllables; second, an abstract noun of two syllables; and third, a monosyllabic noun linked by a rhyme as "conceptual" as it is "sonic" to its deputy in the poem—the "central cedar pole" of line five. I have mentioned that the rhyme scheme of the sonnet is Shakespearean. This is so, and yet its argumentative development is rather more Petrarchan than Shakespearean. The first eight lines impress upon us chiefly a feeling for the tent's free reign: it "seems to owe naught to any single cord." And a gently managed turn occurs with the ninth line, a turn delicately punctuated by an alliterative "b" four times repeated and by the logical term "but": "But strictly held by none is loosely bound / By countless silken ties." The last six lines develop this idea of bondage and thereby balance the subject of lines one to eight. Frost's sonnet is itself loosely bound to Petrarchan and Shakespearean traditions, owing its rhyme scheme to the latter, its logical structure to the former, and its theme—praise of a woman's loveliness—to both. Considered purely as a performance, "The Silken Tent" consummately expresses what Frost calls, in the little essay on "divine right," the blending of answerabilities: the answerability to aspirations of the self (or to the "heaven"-turned "central cedar pole" of this fourteen-line sentence) and the answerability to contractual obligations (whether to voters or to the "obligations" of poetic form and tradition). As regards the general question of motivation, the difference between these two works is simply one of emphasis. "The Silken Tent" gives more weight to commitments, the "countless silken ties" of Frost's second answerability; the remarks on divine right give slightly more weight to the first, the "highest" in the self.

Even so, the boundary between the two answerabilities is not definitive: one cannot always tell when the essential motive of his action is the "highest in himself" and when it is the desires of what might be called his "constituents." It is by now a familiar difficulty: "I want to be good, but that is not enough the state says I have got to be good." The term "constituents" is a felicitous (if somewhat inevitable) choice in Frost's brief essay. To an unknowable extent the disciplines from without *constitute* the discipline of the self. It is not possible exactly to know when one is an actor and when one is merely an executive, and in this undecidability lies the mystery of freedom in Frost's work. In this he follows Emerson in "Fate": "We are sure, that, though we know not how, necessity does comport with liberty" (*Essays* 943). Sidney Cox writes in *A Swinger of Birches:* "I recall the relaxed irony in Frost's voice when I divulged in 1924 that I was learning to accept the inevitable. 'If you could tell what *is* inevitable,' he said" (46).

In short, a possibility of indifference and exchange between "external" and "internal" motivation—between necessity and freedom—is always implied in the very distinctions Frost draws to separate them. Think in terms of his metaphor in "The Constant Symbol": "the figure of the will braving alien entanglements," where the "will" is intrinsic and the "entanglements" extrinsic or "alien." This entanglement does not begin at a determinate moment, as an intervention into pure self-realizing motivation. Instead, the entanglement of will reaches back even to its origin—which is, I take it, the inevitable corollary of Frost's remark about "the state" in the letter to his daughter. John Dewey makes a similar point in *Art as Experience:* "Erroneous views of the nature of the act of expression almost all have their source in the notion that an emotion is complete in itself within, only when uttered having impact upon external material. But, in fact, an emotion is *to* or *from* or *about* something objective, whether in fact or in idea. An emotion is implicated in a situation, the issue of which is in suspense and in which the self that is moved in the emotion is vitally concerned." All emotion, he concludes, must be understood as "an interpenetration of self with objective conditions" (72–73). Read "desire" and "will" where Dewey speaks of "emotion" and "entanglements" where he speaks of "interpenetration" and the analogy to Frost becomes clear. It should be understood, then, that I use the terms "extrinsic" and "intrinsic" with no undue insistence on their rigor.

In his 1934 letter to his daughter, Frost misrepresents the case in linking together Eliot, Pound, and Read as equal advocates of "inner" as against "outer" form. There is much to be said for Frost's and Eliot's similar advocacy of submission to "outer" forms and disciplines. Eliot admiringly quotes Middleton Murry in "The Function of Criticism": "'Catholicism,' [Murry] says, 'stands for the principle of unquestioned spiritual authority outside the individual; that is also the principle of Classicism in literature.' Within the orbit within which Mr. Murry's discussion moves, this seems to me an unimpeachable definition. . . . Those of us who find ourselves supporting what Mr. Murry calls Classicism believe that men cannot get on without giving allegiance to something outside themselves" (*Selected Essays* 15). This "something" corresponds to Frost's second "answerability." That he places it second and Eliot places it first is not without importance. But for the moment I simply emphasize the value each assigns to "authority outside the individual"—or to what Frost recognizes as the "social" motive to "conform." Later in "The Function of Criticism" Eliot parodies the advocates of the "Inner Voice" in terms that further suggest his affiliation with Frost and that anticipate Frost's own parody of the doctrine of Inner Form in the 1934 letter to his daughter. The English, Eliot objects, "are not, in fact, concerned with literary *perfection* at all—the search for perfection is a sign of pettiness, for it shows that the writer has admitted the existence of an unquestioned spiritual authority outside himself, to which he has attempted to *conform*. . . . Thus speaks the Inner Voice" (*Selected Essays* 17–18). When speaking in character, Eliot essentially agrees with Frost: "Everything has not only formity"—the *self*-disciplined Inner Voice—"but conformity." Doubtless he would also have approved Frost's remarks in a manuscript draft of "The Constant Symbol": "Poems together maintain the constant symbol of the confluence of the flow of the spirit of one person with the flow of the spirit of the race. The figure of confluence without compromise. Like walking into an escalator and walking with it. Like entering into the traffic to pass and be passed."[1] This figure of the blending of the two answerabilities would have appealed to the author of "Tradition and the

Individual Talent." In this respect at least, Frost's and Eliot's projects are one. Both value the reconciliation of innovation—of originality, difference, and idiosyncrasy—with tradition and community. The idea is fundamental to Frost's poetics, whether in "The Constant Symbol," as noted here, or in "The Future of Man," where it is given a new turn. There, the idea is that society itself works almost organically to resolve and manage the contrary forces of, on the one hand, stability and continuity, and, on the other, of "bursting originality" and extravagance.

We begin, here, to see how Frost's scattered writings on form and personality register his participation in a critical debate very much current in the period between the wars: the debate over the constitution and the relative merits of "classicism" and "romanticism." While in England just before World War I, Frost had discussed poetics with T. E. Hulme, the man who in many ways set the terms of the debate; he watched Eliot closely of course, and later Herbert Read, whose monograph *Form in Modern Poetry* is chiefly concerned with Romanticism and classicism in relation to personality in poetry. Romanticism and classicism, as Eliot describes them in "The Function of Criticism," define the two poles (so to speak) in a ratio of *poet* to *poetry:* Romanticism emphasizes the motives of the poet, classicism the motives of poetry itself. Romanticism values inner authority as against outer authority, expression and sincerity as against composition; classicism values a subjection of the inner voice to the outer authorities of form. The one emphasizes the personality of the writer, her distinction; the other emphasizes the scene of writing itself, here broadly understood as consisting in the forms of language and poetry and also of the tradition—each of which acts as a check against the eccentricities, even the desires, of the poet. This is why Eliot, affirming the classicist position, suggests that the Romantic is "not in fact interested in art" and why in the same paragraph he quotes with approval Middleton Murry's adage: "The principle of classical leadership is that obeisance is made to the office or to the tradition, never to the man" (*Selected Essays* 18).

Today Frost is not often thought of in connection with the classicism here described. But his consistent emphasis on the "harsher discipline from without" (as he puts it in "The Constant Symbol") developed quite naturally in this climate of debate, as did his arguments against expressive theories of poetry. His classicism was evident enough to his contemporaries. In a perceptive early study of Frost published in 1927 Gorham Munson argues that "the purest classical poet of America today is Robert Frost" (100). As he sees it this "should explain why Frost declares that he has written several books against the world in general. For since Rousseau romanticism has been in the ascendancy. A new conception of nature as impulse and temperament has supplanted the old nature as a strict model, a 'return to nature' has come to mean 'letting one's self go.' For imitation has been substituted the self-expression of the spontaneous original genius" (109). There is a sense in which Frost's aphorism in "The Constant Symbol" is impeccably classical, in Eliot's sense of the term: "Strongly spent is synonymous with kept." I would cite also the complex (and strangely Eliotic) idea of "salvation in surrender" underpinning these lines from "The Gift Outright," which essentially transpose the aphorism of "The Constant Symbol" into a new key:

> Something we were withholding made us weak
> Until we found out that it was ourselves
> We were withholding from our land of living,
> And forthwith found salvation in surrender.
> (*CPPP* 316)

Recognition of the value due external motivation—the discipline from without—marks only the first phase of this classicism. There remains a complementary idea that the "inner voice" of the poet is transformed and redeemed by the impersonal motives of poetry and language: in a sense, self-surrender is self-realization, self-*salvation.* In a moment of insight that seems to me very like some of Frost's own, Eliot writes in "Shakespeare and the Stoicism of Seneca": "Shakespeare, too, was occupied with the struggle—which alone constitutes life for a poet—to transmute his personal and private agonies into something rich and strange, something universal and impersonal" (*Selected Essays* 117). Compare this statement to Frost's admonition in an April 1932 letter to Sidney Cox:

> A subject has to be held clear outside of me with struts and as it were set up for an object. A subject must be an object. . . . It would seem soft for instance to look in my life for the sentiments in the Death of the Hired Man. There is nothing in it believe me. . . . The objective idea is all I ever cared about. . . . Art and wisdom with the body heat out of it. You speak of Shirley. He is two or three great poems—one very great. He projected, he got, them out of his system and I will not carry them back in to his system. . . . To be too subjective with what an artist has managed to make objective is to come on him presumptuously and render ungraceful what he in pain of his life had faith he had made graceful. (*CPPP* 729)

There is a suggestion here of catharsis: "He projected, he got, them out of his system." The transformation of "subject" to "object" carries this suggestion even more clearly in Eliot's "Three Voices of Poetry." The poet, Eliot argues, "is oppressed by a burden which he must bring to birth in order to obtain relief. Or, to change the figure, he is haunted by a demon. . . . and the words, the poem he makes, are a kind of form of exorcism of this demon" (107). Common to these passages is the idea that the poet's personal motives and necessities are transformed, perhaps even exhausted, in the act of writing; in a word, they are made objective. Dewey makes a similar point in *Art as Experience:* "With respect to the physical materials that enter into the formation of a work of art, everyone knows that they undergo change. Marble must be chipped; pigments must be laid on canvas; words must be put together. It is not generally recognized that a similar transformation takes place on the side of 'inner' materials, images, observations, memories and emotions. They are also progressively re-formed; they, too, must be administered" (81). The "inner" and "outer" materials of the artist are therefore alike in kind, at least with regard to how they are treated: as objects to be transformed.

In a September 1929 letter to Cox, Frost writes: "There is no greater fallacy going than that art is expression—an undertaking to tell all to the last scrapings of the brain pan" (*CPPP* 714). I want now to investigate in detail some of the specific conditions of authorship that justify Frost's dismissal of this "fallacy."

The incompatibility of pure expression and composition issues first of all from the transformation, described by both Eliot and Frost, of the subjective into the objective—the operation of "extrinsic" impersonal motives upon "intrinsic" personal ones. The idea that the "inner" materials of the artist are "re-formed" by the "outer" materials in which he works helps us understand the implications of the reading of "Stopping by Woods on a Snowy Evening" given by Frost himself in "The Constant Symbol." Much commentary on "Stopping by Woods" has suggested that the poem expresses a complicated desire for self-annihilation. The idea is well handled by Richard Poirier in *Robert Frost: The Work of Knowing:* "The recognition of the power of nature, especially of snow, to obliterate the limits and boundaries of things and of his own being is, in large part, a function here of some furtive impulse toward extinction, an impulse no more predominate in Frost than in nature" (181). Frank Lentricchia makes a similar point about Frost's winter landscapes in general and quotes an especially apposite passage from Gaston Bachelard's *The Poetics of Space:* "In the outside world, snow covers all tracks, blurs the road, muffles every sound, conceals all colors. As a result of this universal whiteness, we feel a form of cosmic negation in action" (qtd. in Lentricchia, *Landscapes* 31).

During Frost's own lifetime, however, the matter was often handled much less sensitively. Indeed, critics sometimes set his teeth on edge with intimations about personal themes in the poem, as if it expressed a wish quite literally for suicide or marked some especially dark passage in the poet's life. Louis Mertins quotes him in conversation (and similar remarks may be found in transcripts of a number of Frost's public readings):

> I suppose people think I lie awake nights worrying about what people like [John] Ciardi of the *Saturday Review* write and publish about me [in 1958]. . . . Now Ciardi is a nice fellow—one of those bold, brassy fellows who go ahead and say all sorts of things. He makes my "Stopping By Woods" out a death poem. Well, it would be like this if it were. I'd say, "This is all very lovely, but I must be getting on to heaven." There'd be no absurdity in that. That's all right, but it's hardly a death poem. Just as if I should say here tonight, "This is all very well, but I must be getting on to Phoenix, Arizona, to lecture there." (Mertins 371)

As does Eliot, Frost often couples suggestions of private sorrows and griefs with statements about their irrelevance. William Pritchard describes the practice well in pointing out how Frost typically "[holds] back any particular reference to his private sorrows while bidding us to respond to the voice of a man who has been acquainted with grief" (230). It is worth bearing in mind that, later in the conversation with Mertins, Frost says: "If you feel it, let's just exchange glances and not say anything about it. There are a lot of things between best friends that're never said, and if you—if they're brought out, right out, too baldly, something's lost" (371–72). To similar effect, he writes in a letter to Sidney Cox: "Poetry . . . is a measured amount of all we could say an we would. We shall be judged finally by the delicacy of our feeling for when to stop short. The right people know, and we artists should know better than they know" (*CPPP* 714). I think of Eliot in "Tradition and the Individual Talent": "Poetry is not a turning loose of emotion, but an escape from emotion; it is not the expression of personality, but an escape from personality. But, of course, only those who have personality and emotions know what it means to want to escape from these things" (*Selected Essays* 10–11). He has in mind exactly the sort of readers and writers Frost acknowledges here: "The right people know, and we artists should know better than they know." In any event, Frost's subtle caveat to Mertins is probably meant equally to validate Ciardi's suggestion about "Stopping by Woods" and to lay a polite injunction against it.

But his turning aside of Ciardi's reading is more than an example of tact. He speaks out of fidelity to his belief that the emotions that give rise to a poem are in some way alienated by it in the result, and his alternative reading of "Stopping by Woods" is worth dwelling on as a roundabout contribution to the theory of personality and motive in poetry. Frost directs our attention not to the poem's theme or content but to its form: the interlocking pattern of rhyme among the stanzas. He once remarked to an audience at Bread Loaf, again discouraging biographical or thematic readings of the poem: "If I were reading it for someone else, I'd begin to wonder what he's up to. See. Not what he means but what he's up to" (Cook 81). The emphasis is on the performance of the writer and on the act of writing. Following are the poem and Frost's brief comments on it in "The Constant Symbol":

> Whose woods these are I think I know.
> His house is in the village though;
> He will not see me stopping here
> To watch his woods fill up with snow.
>
> My little horse must think it queer
> To stop without a farmhouse near
> Between the woods and frozen lake
> The coldest evening of the year.
>
> He gives his harness bells a shake
> To ask if there is some mistake.
> The only other sound's the sweep
> Of easy wind and downy flake.
>
> The woods are lovely, dark and deep,
> But I have promises to keep,
> And miles to go before I sleep,
> And miles to go before I sleep.
>
> (*CPPP* 207)

> There's an indulgent smile I get for the recklessness of the unnecessary commitment I made when I came to the first line in the second stanza of a poem in this book called "Stopping By Woods On a Snowy Evening." I was riding too high to care what trouble I incurred. And it was all right so long as I didn't suffer deflection. (*CPPP* 788)

In emphasizing the lyric's form Frost really only defers the question of theme or content. It is not that the poem does not have a theme, or one worth a reader's consideration; the form simply *is* the theme. If this seems surprising, it is only because Frost's emphasis makes for so complete a reversal in mood. The mood of the poem at this second level of form-as-theme is anything but suggestive of self-annihilation: "I was riding too high to care what trouble I incurred." This is the kind of transformation Poirier has in mind when he remarks in *The Performing Self* (1971), quoting an interview with Frost originally published in the *Paris Review* in 1960: "If [a] poem expresses grief, it also expresses—as an *act,* as a composition, a performance, a 'making,'—the opposite of grief; it shows or expresses 'what a *hell* of a good time I had writing it'" (892). I would point out further that Frost's reading, appearing as it does in "The Constant Symbol," lends the last two lines of "Stopping by Woods" added resonance: "promises" are still the concern, though in "The Constant Symbol" he speaks of them as "commitments" to poetic form. Viewed in these terms "Stopping by Woods" dramatizes the artist's negotiation of the responsibilities of his craft. What may seem to most readers hardly a metapoetical lyric actually speaks to the central concern of the poet *as* a poet when the form of the poem is taken as its theme.

The question immediately presents itself, however, of a possible disjunction between form and theme, even as they seem to work in tandem. The "unnecessary commitment" that exhilarated Frost—the rhyme scheme—does in fact "suffer deflection" in the last stanza: here there are four matched end rhymes, not three. Promises are broken, not kept, as Frost relinquishes the pattern he carried through the first three stanzas. Of course, as John Ciardi points out in the *Saturday Review* article alluded to above, this relinquishment is really built into the design itself: the only way *not* to break the pattern would have been to rhyme the penultimate line of the poem with the first, thereby creating a symmetrical, circular rhyme scheme. Frost chose not to keep this particular promise, with the result that the progress of the poem illustrates one form of the lassitude that it apparently *resigns* itself to being a stay against—to put the matter somewhat paradoxically.[2] Paradox is only fitting, however, in acknowledging the mixture of motives animating the poem: motives, on the one hand, of self-relinquishment in what Poirier calls Frost's "recognition of the power of nature . . . to obliterate the limits and boundaries of things and of his own being"; and motives, on the other hand, of self-assertion and exhilaration in what Frost calls the experience of "riding . . . high." Frost's remark about Robinson's poetry in the introduction to *King Jasper* seems to apply rather well to "Stopping by Woods": "So sad and at the same time so happy in achievement" (*CPPP* 747).

A slighter example of dark emotion redeemed by poetic form and thereby brought to happy achievement is Frost's little poem "Beyond Words":

> That row of icicles along the gutter
> Feels like my armory of hate;
> And you, you . . . you, you utter. . .
> You wait!
>
> (*CPPP* 356)

If the hatred truly were "beyond words" it could not have found expression, let alone expression in a poem. Here, form has "disciplined" the hatred to which the lines allude into the obviously very different mood and feeling that we get from reading the poem itself. The playful rhyme of "gutter" to "utter" has the peculiar subsidiary grace of suggesting the guttural tone in which the poem thinks of itself as being uttered. In his "'Letter' to *The Amherst Student*" Frost says that, so long as we have form to go on, we are "lost to the larger excruciations" (*CPPP* 740). "Beyond Words" helps us see what he means. Resources of rhythm and rhyme transform darker, chaotic emotions into the lighter, altogether more manageable one of what Frost liked to call "play." In "Beyond Words" this "play" is also felt in the tension between the iambic rhythms that underlie the lines and the more agitated rhythms of the spoken phrases. The only true "materialist," Frost explains in "Education by Poetry," is the person who gets "lost in his material" without a guiding metaphor to throw it into shape (*CPPP* 724). Here, a metaphor comparing icicles along a gutter to an "armory of hate," together with the sonic equation of "gutter" to "utter," essentially tame a troubling experience. "Beyond Words" offers an example of how hatred can find a profitable, even redemptive outlet—just as an urge toward self-relinquishment may find its outlet in "Stopping by Woods on a Snowy Evening."

Another implication of Frost's reading of "Stopping by Woods" is that any distinction between form and theme must remain provisional. Relative to readings of "Stopping by Woods" as a poem concerned with possibilities of self-annihilation, Frost's own reading seems rather too exclusively fixed upon form and doubtless has struck many readers as evasive. But in the context of the essay in which his reading of the poem appears, "The Constant Symbol," that reading is quite thematic in its concerns, not at all formalistic—as should presently become clear. And in the larger work comprising both the poem and his commentary on it, Frost is in fact interested in destabilizing the oppositions of theme to form and of content to form.

Three terms concern us: content, theme, form. In approaching some poems it is necessary first to describe the content. Reading Wallace Stevens's poem "The Emperor of Ice Cream," for example, we may say that it describes a funeral—a statement about content. (By contrast, nothing could be plainer than the content of most of Frost's lyrics, especially "Stopping by Woods.") In any event a critic needs some intelligible ground against which to work in speaking of the theme, or if you prefer, the "concern" of the poem—what it aims to draw our attention to as readers of poetry. What the poem "has in mind" is not to be confused with what it "has in view," though the two categories often overlap. "The Emperor of Ice Cream" may or may not have a funereal theme; "Stopping by Woods" may or may not be "thinking" of a man in a sleigh. Form is still another matter, and to address it a critic usually has to define and stabilize for purposes of investigation some notion of theme to work against. Which yields these three (somewhat unstable) concepts: what a poem describes—its content; what it has in mind—its theme; and how it holds together—its form.

Whatever a critic's terminology, it is perhaps inevitable that she rely on each of these concepts. I am suggesting that Frost's critical theory and practice show how they are exchangeable: each term must be considered for its place in a kind of escalation of significance in which theme, form, and content change places. This is, it seems to me, the meaning of Frost's definition in "The Constant Symbol": "Every poem is an epitome of the great predicament; a figure of the will braving alien entanglements" (*CPPP* 787). Here is a theme which is not one: that is to say, a theme which stands in no comfortable opposition either to content or form. "Figure" works in three senses here: in the sense of metaphor; in the sense of "subject" or "theme," as when we say that a painting is *of* a human *figure;* and in the sense of "pattern" or form. The "figure" or pattern a poem makes may "pose" and become either the content or the theme of a particular poem; that is, a poem may either have that pattern "in view" or "in mind." In Frost's reading of "Stopping by Woods," for example, the figure *that* poem makes, its rhyme and stanza scheme, becomes its "figure" or theme. But it is not enough to say that a poem is a "figure"—whether we mean metaphor or theme—of the will braving alien entanglements: it is also an *example* of it, not merely a representation, and this directs our attention to the act of description in a poem rather than to the things it describes. More precisely, it extends the category of "things described" (the content) to include also the act of description. Considered in this light the content of every poem "written regular" (as Frost says) is this "figure of the will braving alien entanglements." His reading plainly undermines the distinction between form and content: the container becomes the thing contained—which brings us to the very heart of the matter.

This exchange and merger of container and contained—of outside and inside, form and content—is central to Frost's understanding of motive. When he writes to Lesley Frost: "I want to be good, but that is not enough the state says I have got to be good," the observation quite naturally occurs to him in connection with a discussion of form in poetry. This suggests the broader implications of the fact that outer motivations become indistinguishable from the inner motivations of the agent—whether he is a poet writing a poem or a citizen simply endeavoring to be good. It is as impossible to define the essential motive of "Stopping by Woods"—intrinsic? extrinsic? personal? formal?—as it would be to define the essential motive of the desire to be virtuous. In both cases the motive is the *product,* not the antecedent, of engagements with alien entanglements—that is, with the coercive motives, however benign, of form and state.

Since this points to the indissociability of external and internal motivations it naturally bears closely on the question of personality in poetry. To say that a poet "expresses" himself is to assign priority to intrinsic motives as against extrinsic ones and to elevate autobiographical impulses above the act of composition. Furthermore, in putting content above form, expressive theories of poetry necessarily assume a stable opposition of message to vehicle, in which the former remains uncontaminated by the latter. Thinking of poetry in terms of expression inevitably engages the battery of assumptions Derrida skeptically describes in "Signature Event Context": "If men write it is: (1) because they have to communicate; (2) because what they have to communicate is their 'thought,' their 'ideas,' their representations. Thought, as representation, precedes and governs communication, which transports the 'idea,' the signified content" (4). In Frost's Derridean-Burkean grammar the sentence must always read: a poem *is* expressed, which captures the mixture of external and internal motives he finds in himself and in writing. No pure governing intention precedes a poem to be embodied in it. We must speak instead of a "succession" of intention.

This idea of a "successive intention" seems to motivate most of Frost's accounts of the writing experience and suggests another respect in which composition is impersonal. Poems, in his descriptions, have motives of their own to which the motives of the poet become merely incidental or catalytic. He remarks in "Before the Beginning and after the End of a Poem," a talk delivered at the Winter Institute of the University of Miami in 1931: "The subject should emerge as the poem is written. One should not know what to name a poem until he is at least two-thirds through it. . . . The person who knows the name of his poem or the end of his poem before he writes it ought not to write it. And yet, the thing should emerge as if it had all the enthusiasm of the name, and of the object's being foreknown. When does a person know what he means by a poem? When he draws near the end" (8). In the lecture delivered at Dartmouth College that formed the basis of "The Constant Symbol," Frost phrases the idea more succinctly: "A poem is the having of an idea—not an idea put into verse" (qtd. in Tallmer 3). And he writes to similar effect in "Poetry and School": "Almost everyone should almost have experienced the fact that a poem is an idea caught fresh in the act of dawning" (*CPPP* 807). Surely Frost would have agreed with Dewey's remarks in *Art as Experience:* "Even the Almighty took seven days to create the heaven and the earth, and, if the record were complete, we should also learn that it was only at the end of the period that he was aware of just what He set out to do with the raw materials of chaos that confronted Him" (71).

There is a tendency in each of Frost's descriptions to reduce or qualify the agency of the poet, whose actions in part become catalytic and responsive. It is here that he comes closest to the specific emphases of Eliot's impersonal theory of poetry. Consider this passage from "The Figure a Poem Makes" (1939): "I tell how there may be a better wildness of logic than of inconsequence. But the logic is backward, in retrospect, after the act. It must be more felt than seen ahead like prophecy. It must be a revelation, or a series of revelations, as much for the poet as for the reader. For it to be that there must have been the greatest freedom of the material to move about in it and to establish relations in it regardless of time and space" (*CPPP* 777). There is an impersonal quality in the very movement of these sentences, a carefully modulated vagueness that seems quite faithful to the implication that Frost might know as little about the outcome here as we do. Once again he describes the dawning of an idea in poetry: "It must be a revelation." As he does elsewhere in the same essay, Frost leans heavily on the impersonal pronoun "it," a word made all the more strange in this passage because its antecedent seems to remain fluid. Initially "it" refers to "the logic." But in the last sentence the pronoun fairly comes unmoored: "For it [the logic] to be that [a revelation] there must have been the greatest freedom of the material to move about in it [the revelation? the logic? the poem itself?] and to establish relations in it regardless of time and space."

The difficulty is that he is describing the *medium* in which poetry composes itself. That medium, whatever its qualities, is at least not to be reduced merely to the personality or desire of the writer: there are impersonal exigencies of language, "material," and form to be considered. When Frost curiously speaks of the "freedom of the material to move about in it," I understand him to mean: to move about *in the poem,* in the writing, not simply in the poet. It is exactly as if the poet were a catalyst, a filament of platinum, to recur to Eliot's analogy in "Tradition and the Individual Talent" (*Selected Essays* 7); or as if the poet were merely the "fine instrument for transformations" that Eliot finds in Shakespeare (*Selected Essays* 119). I am also reminded of Eliot's difficult point in "Tradition and the Individual Talent": "The poet has, not a 'personality' to express, but a particular medium, which is only a medium and not a personality, in which impressions and experiences combine in peculiar and unexpected ways" (*Selected Essays* 9). Frost seems to have in view something like this "medium": an "it" in which the "materials" of the poem (images? memories? language itself?) move about and recombine.

Recall Dewey's observation in the passage quoted already: A "transformation takes place on the side of 'inner' materials. . . . They are also progressively re-formed; they, too, must be administered. This modification is the building up of a truly expressive act." In acknowledging this "administrative" complement, Frost sharply distinguishes his own poetics from the poetics of pure expression and personality. For him, the "truly expressive act" is never a mere "undertaking to tell all to the last scrapings of the brain pan." For him as for Dewey, the "truly expressive act" combines and administers disciplines both from within and from without. It marks the confluence of his "two answerabilities," a confluence of the desires and personality of the poet with impersonal forces and commitments.

In "The Poet's Next of Kin in College," Frost makes the point concisely by analogy to the rodeo: "The great pleasure in writing poetry is in having been carried off. It is as if you stood astride of the subject that lay on the ground, and they cut the cord, and the subject gets up under you and you ride it. You adjust yourself to the motion of the thing itself. That is the poem" (*CPPP* 771). The athleticism of this analogy is discernible in Frost's description in "The Constant Symbol" of his own experience in "Stopping by Woods on a Snowy Evening": "I was riding too high to care what trouble I incurred." And in "The Poet's Next of Kin" Frost is already implicitly concerned with what he would later call the "constant symbol" of poetry. The rodeo artist gives form to the unpredictable and forceful motions of the horse; he expresses them and is in a sense also expressed by them. Frost admires his performance, it seems proper to say, as the constant symbol of an artist at once controlling and being controlled by his "subject." The answerabilities to "formity" and to "conformity" merge, becoming all but indistinguishable, as in "The Silken Tent." Inner desire and outer coercion form two aspects of a single experience. Every poem constantly symbolizes this convergence of necessity and freedom, of the impersonal and the personal. And this is why, according to Frost, motives personal to the poet can never be said to exhaust, or even substantially to define, the motives of the writing itself: "The subject gets up under you and you ride it. You adjust yourself to the motion of the thing itself. That is the poem."

Believing in Robert Frost

A discussion of impersonality in poetry cannot accomplish much without engaging more general problems of literary "authority," about which Frost is quite illuminating. He has much to contribute to contemporary debates over the meaning and constitution of "authorship," though in this respect his work has for the most part been overlooked. In the balance of this chapter, I examine certain similarities among writings by Frost, Derrida, and Michel Foucault that bear variously on the matter of "authorship." It is useful to set Frost's remarks on the subject in the context of more contemporary debates to show that his concerns are really perennial. Moreover, Foucault's work can help us see how, in thinking about his own writing, Frost often relies in an intriguing fashion on what has come to be called the "author-function." But as the latter observation suggests, my purpose here is ultimately to investigate the path by which Frost diverges from the kind of thinking we associate with Derrida and Foucault. It is along this divergence that Frost's more important affiliations with Burke, Dewey, and Emerson become evident. One final remark is necessary before I proceed. Because I am writing more about a concept in Frost's writings ("authorship") than about a single work, and because Frost nowhere considers this concept at great length, I will be drawing together a number of passages from lectures, essays, letters, and poems in an effort to arrive at a composite sense of his thinking about authorship.

In an unpublished talk at Kenyon College in 1950, Frost says:

> All through the years I've been confronted with the idea . . . whether I say more than I know myself. A poet builds better than he knows.

> You might say there may be an exactness in the statement but there may be an inexactness in the implication and people can run off in different directions with the implication. . . . I'm always re-examining a phrase in somebody's poetry with this idea. . . . And then I hear people speak of teen-agers. That comes to me from various quarters, teen-agers. And I think, did the person who gave them that name know what he was saying? Shall I assume that he didn't? Got to be careful about what you assume people don't know. Matthew Arnold uses the word *teen.* He speaks of using our nerves with bliss and teen.[3] . . . It means with grief and pain. They're pain-agers. Maybe. Maybe that's in it, I don't know. . . . That question's always there and then there's two words if I may bring them out. Two words in Latin that I've turned over in my mind for years with this question in mind, "Did Catullus know what he was saying when he said that?" And I said that to a Latinist a little while ago and he said, "You may pretty safely say he did." He believed in Catullus, but I rather think Catullus hadn't thought it all out. He said two words, *mens animi,* and . . . I've seen translations of it this way, poetic translations—look out for them. It said "the thoughts of the heart." *Mens*—mind, and *animus*—the spirit, see. . . . And it was very arresting to me so I went back to see it again, why I'd been arrested by it—*mens animi.* And I suppose that's what we've been talking about today. The order—*mens* is the order—*mens,* the order of my wildness . . . see that's the way I translate enterprise of the spirit . . . that's the *animus,* that's the enterprise, that's the spirit that breaks the form.[4]

These remarks raise a number of questions. Are we to "believe" in Catullus as Frost's "Latinist" does? Is Catullus responsible for the meaning Frost secures from his poem? Can we even determine the boundaries of his "intelligence," the point beyond which Catullus forfeits responsibility for the meanings of his poem to some other agency? We might assign responsibility to Frost's own genius as a reader, though that seems unsatisfactory—a mere inversion of the figure of the author. After all, Frost's point is that it is impossible to *know* whether he (or any reader) is responsible in these terms or not, and the uncertainty is precisely what interests him. Frost's remarks suggest that the aim of literary theory is to investigate the *extent* of a writer's "authority," not the false dilemma of whether "authority" is either total or totally absent.[5] The more engaging question posed in Frost's Kenyon College speech is whether an author can "mean" something of which he is unaware—whether he "say[s] more than [he] knows [himself]." In what sense does a poet build "better than he knows?"—to use the phrase Frost borrows from Emerson's poem "The Problem."[6] There are, of course, unconscious agencies of the self that constitute forms of authority. But if the poet builds better than he knows, should our attentions properly be devoted to the building rather than to the builder, as the New Critics seemed to maintain? At what point exactly, and for what reasons, does *the builder* become irrelevant? For his part, Frost suggests that we should be wary of dismissing the categories of intention and authorship altogether: "Got to be careful about what you assume people don't know."

Appeals to sincerity, intention, and especially to "authorship" almost inevitably involve arguments from fitness to design, which is what Frost points out with regard to Catullus's *mens animi.* The phrase is susceptible of the meaning he assigns it; that is, it is fit to accommodate an idea of "the spirit that breaks the form." But does this fitness warrant attribution of design? To think that it does is essentially to "believe" Catullus into existence, as Frost's Latinist does—not Catullus the historical figure but "Catullus" the "author" of a particular "work." Close reading of the sort Frost valued—and the Kenyon College lecture offers one example of it—necessarily calls "authorship" into question. Especially in its careful attentions to tone of voice, and to the figurative values of language, this kind of reading discloses possibilities of meaning and irony, as well as possible incoherences and fractures in meaning, that always promise a diminishment of authorial presence, at least insofar as "authorship" implies integrity of intention and unity and coherence in the work itself. (And as Foucault points out, "the author is the principle of thrift in the proliferation of meaning" [159].) This instability of authority is what leads Frost to raise questions about Catullus. The more "fit" a poem or any other utterance is to sustain complexity of meaning, the more anxious becomes the question of "design." The difficulty is only compounded when, as with Catullus, a chasm of historical and linguistic distance must imaginatively be bridged. And yet, it may be that linguistic and historical distances of this order differ more in degree than in kind from the distances we must bridge in reading any poem.

As the Kenyon College speech suggests, Frost would have us raise the following questions: Did the poet reach the same conclusions about his poem that we have reached in reading it closely? *Could* he possibly have reached the same conclusions? How did *we* go about reaching them? In considering these and cognate problems, Frost ultimately confronts the same questions Foucault addresses in his well-known essay "What Is an Author?" The "author-function," Foucault argues,

> does not develop spontaneously as the attribution of a discourse to an individual. It is, rather, the result of a complex operation which con-

> structs a certain rational being that we call an "author." Critics doubtless try to give this intelligible being a realistic status, by discerning, in the individual, a "deep" motive, a "creative" power, or a "design," the milieu in which writing originates. Nevertheless, these aspects of an individual which we designate as making him an author are only a projection, in more or less psychologizing terms, of the operations that we force texts to undergo, the connections that we make, the traits that we establish as pertinent, the continuities that we recognize, or the exclusions that we practice. (150)

Frost's Latinist simply constructs "a certain rational being" called "Catullus," and, in his name, licenses a specific range of meanings to the poem. Working from philological, historical, and interpretive evidence to which Frost's anecdote gives us no access, he has "forced" Catullus's poem to "undergo" a particular set of "operations," setting up "exclusions" determining what the phrase "*mens animi*" could and could not have meant to Catullus. That is to say, Frost's Latinist performs an action described by Roland Barthes in "The Death of the Author," the landmark 1968 essay that more or less set the terms of subsequent debate in these matters and to which Foucault's essay in particular is a response: "To give a text an Author is to impose a limit on the text, to furnish it with a final signified, to close the writing" (147). In his engagements with Catullus's poem, Frost himself remains more or less open and agnostic: he is not quite sure how to manage the proliferating possibilities of meaning in the poem. He asks—as in the sonnet "Design," which treats a related philosophical theme—*if* design govern in a thing so small: "I rather think Catullus hadn't thought it all out." Of course, neither Frost's rather vague version of Catullus nor the Latinist's rather more clarified version is unequivocally "present" in the poem. Catullus's consciousness, intention, and design—traditional attributes of "authorship" according to Foucault's analysis—are instead the "psychologizing" *projection* of readers more rather than less inclined to faith as they engage the words associated with him. And yet as Frost seems to acknowledge—and here he is to be distinguished from Foucault—the fact that it is an enterprise in faith does not *necessarily* make it an enterprise in fiction: "Got to be careful about what you assume people don't know."

Frost's skepticism about Catullus's authority calls to mind his 1946 essay "The Constant Symbol." As we have seen, his sketch therein of a presidential career leads us to speak of intention almost in a corporate sense, or at the very least as a volatile factor (a "succession") in the total equation of an act or utterance. In all of this I am reminded of

Jacques Derrida's description, in *Limited Inc,* of how difficult it is to name the "author" of John Searle's contentious *Reply* to his own essay "Signature Event Context." He writes:

> Why did I say "société plus or moins anonyme," "a more or less anonymous company or corporation"? The expression "three + n authors" [which Derrida had earlier used] seems to me to be more rigorous for the reasons I have already stated, involving the difficulty I encounter in naming the definite origin, the true person, responsible for the *Reply:* not only because of the debts [to other writers] acknowledged by John R. Searle [in a note] *before even* beginning to reply, but because of the entire, more or less anonymous tradition of a code, a heritage, a reservoir of arguments to which both he and I are indebted. How is this more or less anonymous company to be named? In order to avoid the ponderousness of the scientific expression "three + n authors," I decide here and from this moment on to give the presumed and collective author of the *Reply* the French name "Société à responsibilité limitée"—literally, "Society with Limited Responsibility" (or Limited Liability)—which is normally abbreviated to *Sarl.* (36)

With the same satirical aims, Derrida essentially (and ingeniously) says of Searle what Frost says of the "President in the White House": "behold him now . . . so multifariously closed in on with obligations and answerabilities that sometimes he loses his august temper." His *individuality*—his *personality*—has become somewhat difficult to locate. And in Frost's calculus, motive and meaning are best accounted for in terms of Derrida's "limited corporation," wherein the intelligence of a poem (or of a career) is too dynamic and too social a function to be situated exclusively in the personality and desires of its assigned author.

We speak of the "integrity" of someone's actions or ideas, but, as Frost's and Derrida's analyses suggest, we seldom have a clear sense of what that integrity consists of or in. Probably not in the personality: "commitments" vitiate that, as action comes to consist more in a constellation of what Frost calls "answerabilities" than in a single personality. We are all partners in "a more or less anonymous company or corporation" of such "answerabilities." If our subject is a writer, the imperatives of convention and tradition vitiate her personality still further, whether it is the tradition of philosophy, in Derrida's and "Sarl's" case, or of poetry. These imperatives led Eliot to speak, in "Tradition and the Individual Talent," of the poet's "surrender" to forces more valuable than her own personality (*Selected Essays* 6), and Frost himself points out, in the introduction to *The Arts Anthology of Dartmouth Verse,* that the poet "has to begin as a cloud of all the other poets he ever read. That can't be helped" (*CPPP* 709).[7] This is simply to make the Emersonian point that "authorship" may be a "diffuse" phenomenon, more a matter of the "condensation" in the poet of other, already extant factors than of the origination of a new and altogether personal one. Frost goes on to argue, in the Dartmouth anthology introduction, that only by extraordinary effort of will can a poet understand and overcome the influence of other poets into his work; only by extraordinary force can he *individualize* his writing. And "The Constant Symbol" makes clear that Frost fully understood how "transindividual" motives specific to language and to literary form undermine the integrity and "freedom" of the writer yet again, until the condition of authorship is precisely what he describes in a talk at Dartmouth College that served as the basis for "The Constant Symbol": an "unfolding" of "kept or lost intentions" within "deepening commitments" or "answerabilities" (qtd. in Tallmer 3). As he points out in the passage quoted above: the "intemperate" president in the White House might just "as well have got himself into a sestina royal"—a poetic form characterized by manifold and peculiarly strict "answerabilities." Frost certainly understood that writing is as much the experience of self-expenditure as of self-assertion. Derrida succinctly expresses the difficulty in "Signature Event Context" when he speaks of the "*relative* specificity of effects of consciousness" in language (19; my emphasis); he has in view the same impure ratio of "kept" to "lost" intention within deepening commitments to language and form that interests Frost in "The Constant Symbol" and elsewhere. Among the corollaries of this view is the impersonalist conception of authorship associated with post-structuralist thought, a conception that, I am suggesting, Frost also entertained.

But this brings us to the point at which Frost importantly differs from Derrida, as also from Foucault. Perhaps the most intriguing and ambitious aspect of his poetics is his aspiration to transcend the difficult conditions of authorship I have just described: he "believes" himself into existence as the "author," rather than merely the writer, of his own works. This is precisely why comparison to Foucault and Derrida is in this case profitable. In short—to adapt Foucault's words in "What Is an Author?"—we are now in a position to see how Frost ultimately lends *his own* "authorship" a "realistic status" by tentatively discerning in himself "a 'deep' motive, a 'creative' power, or a 'design.'" This follows from a suggestion in Frost's early poem "The Trial by Existence" that "life has for us on the wrack / Nothing" but what we "somehow" chose (*CPPP* 30). He imagines a kind of authorship in which the intention of the poet "somehow" governs the entire scene of his poem. This marks a specifically "tragic" dignification of authorship, in which the force of individual personality significantly reappears, and in the balance of this chapter I pursue an analogy between Frost's account of the "figure a poem makes" in the essay of that title and Kenneth Burke's analysis of "the dialectic of tragedy" in *A Grammar of Motives* (1945). As I indicate in the introduction to this study, I use the term "tragedy" in a conventional sense: the "tragic" hero (or heroine) undergoes an ordeal that somehow follows from his own initial action—from his *intrinsic* motives. This ordeal seems to him unjust, arbitrary, and alien. Lear claims in the midst of his own ordeal: "I am a man more sinned against than sinning." But the tragic resolution involves the hero's recognition that his misfortunes are not arbitrary, but mark instead the inevitable unfolding of his own character. Character and fate are at last seen as complements, not opponents—as I suggest in the introduction. A corresponding movement in Frost's poetics shows that what he calls "formity" (intrinsic, *personal* discipline and motivation) and "conformity" (the extrinsic, *impersonal* "discipline[s] from without") are really two opposed aspects of a single experience. In a word, Frost imagines a final transcendence of his own central, dialectical "ordeal" of "formity" and "conformity"—a matter to which I will return in concluding this study. On Frost's account, as the poet writes he loses his "august temper," just as does the protagonist of a tragedy; but Frost's poetics also holds out the promise, if only as a kind of supreme fiction, of the poet's recovering his "temper" and self-integrity in an affirmation of authorial power and integrity not imagined by Foucault or Derrida in the essays we have been considering.

In the section of *A Grammar of Motives* titled "The Dialectic of Tragedy" Burke speaks of "extrinsic" and "intrinsic" motivations. According to him there occurs in tragedy first a transposition and then a merger of extrinsic and intrinsic motivations. The tragic act, issuing from the intrinsic motives and force of the hero, brings out and organizes the extrinsic forces that oppose him; and yet, these two forces are alike in kind insofar as they work in bitter but compensatory fashion to bring about the resolution of the tragic struggle. The extrinsic forces act upon the hero until he learns "to take the oppositional motives into account . . . [and so] widens his terminology accordingly," finally arriving at a "higher order of understanding" wherein his original act is seen in light of what ensued (40). His action now appears potentially to have contained the suffering that seemed merely unjust as he underwent it. We realize that action and passion (doing and suffering) are really two aspects of the same experience.

This pattern mirrors, on a larger scale, the "figure" a poem makes in Frost's poetics. I begin by expressing the relation schematically, though as we proceed the pattern of this "figure" will become clearer and more fully ramified. The poem "assumes direction," as Frost says in "The Figure a Poem Makes," with "the first line laid down" (*CPPP* 776). This initial act organizes its opposition as the grammatical and formal commitments implicit in it immediately begin to close in upon both poet and poem, as Frost explains in "The Constant Symbol" (*CPPP* 789). The initial act, then, has both generative and limiting properties. Or as Burke explains: "When an act is performed, it entails new sufferances, which in turn entail new insights. Our act itself alters the conditions of action, as 'one thing leads to another' in an order that would not have occurred had we not acted" (69). The act itself becomes a part of the scene of action and therefore a component of what now "opposes" continued action. If the poet or tragic hero is to succeed he must accept and "pitch into" these "commitments" and oppositions without getting "lost" in them, to borrow Frost's terms in "The Constant Symbol" (*CPPP* 786); he must salvage his integrity. If he does, he arrives at something like Burke's "higher order of understanding"—what Frost, in "The Figure a Poem Makes," calls a "clarification of life" or "wisdom" (*CPPP* 777). The idea is most succinctly expressed by Burke when he says: "The dialectical (agonistic) approach to knowledge"—which I associate with Frost's poetics—"is through the *act* of assertion, whereby one 'suffers' the kind of knowledge that is the reciprocal of his act" (38). Consider John Dewey's remarks on a similar dialectic in *Art as Experience:* "Impulsion from need starts an experience that does not know where it is going; resistance and check bring about the conversion of direct formal action into re-flection; what is turned back upon is the relation of hindering conditions to what the self possesses as working capital in virtue of prior experiences. As the energies thus involved reënforce the original impulsion, this operates more circumspectly with insight into end and method. Such is the outline of every experience that is clothed with meaning" (66). He might well be talking about tragedy or about poetics in general—at least in a debate whose terms are set by Frost.

In Burke's view, tragic resolution brings about a "conversion" or rebirth in the hero. At first it may seem incongruous to link these larger transformations of tragedy to what happens, according to Frost's description, in the little theater of a poem. But in "The Figure a Poem Makes" he does speak with vague ambition of an accession to "wisdom" (*CPPP* 777), which in my view corresponds to what Burke calls a "conversion to a new principle of motivation" (407)—that is, a conversion to a larger frame of reference within which to understand previous actions and beliefs. As Frost sees it, the writing of poetry entails a continual redefinition of the self, a continual redrawing of the circles that mark its limitation; that is what I mean here by "rebirth." Emerson writes in "Circles": "The life of a man is a self-evolving circle, which, from a ring imperceptibly small, rushes on all sides outwards to new and larger circles, and that without end" (*Essays* 404), and this figure seems to motivate an interesting reference to Yeats in a passage from Frost's notebooks reprinted in *Prose Jottings:* "WBY says the artist has a choice of some seven poses. One of them he must assume. Don't believe it children. There is such a thing as sincerity. It is hard to define but it is probably nothing but your highest liveliness escaping from a succession of dead selves. Miraculously. It is the same with illusions. Any belief you sink into when you should be leaving it behind is an illusion" (40). These sentences are hardly transparent but they do suggest a specifically Emersonian experience of self. It is a volatile self, always in a state of transition and revision—what Frost calls a continual escape from "a succession of dead selves." I will recur to this passage later but it is interesting to note here that Frost apparently writes out of the conviction Harold Bloom describes in *Agon:* "We read to usurp, just as the poet writes to usurp. Usurp what? A place, a stance, a fullness, an illusion of identification or possession; something we can call our own or even ourselves" (17). Or as Frost might say: We write in order to escape from a succession of dead selves—a succession of outworn stances or illusions of identity. The implications of this escape or usurpation range rather far, as Burke's remarks on a similar process in *A Grammar of Motives* suggest: "We must recognize that dialectically one may die many times (in fact, each time an assertion leads beyond itself to a new birth) and that tragedy is but a special case of dialectical processes in general. In the Hegelian dialectic, for instance, the series of dyings is presented as a gradual progress toward greater and greater self-realization. For the spirit has its counterpart in objectification; and by seeing himself in terms of objects, 'from them the individual proceeds to the contemplation of his own inner being' (*Philosophy of History*)" (39). This transformation of the subjective into the objective becomes a process of self-realization, a means to a higher self-possession and to a deeper and renewed experience of subjectivity and identity.

Burke's remarks call to mind some curiously Hegelian ideas in Frost. In "The Constant Symbol" Frost speaks of poetry as the "commitment" of "spirit" to "form"—in a word, as the materialization of spirit: "The bard has said in effect, Unto these forms did I commend the spirit"

(*CPPP* 787). This extends a line of thought that appears much earlier in his English notebooks, published posthumously as an appendix to John Evangelist Walsh's *Into My Own: The English Years of Robert Frost.* There, Frost places the "sentence form"—what he elsewhere calls the "sentence sound"—in relation to the sentence proper as soul is related to body: "The sentence form almost seems the soul of a certain set of words. We see inspiration as it takes liberties with the words and yet saves the soul" (220). It is as if Frost were thinking of Donne's description in "The Ecstasy" of the subtle knot that binds spirit to form:

> As our blood labors to beget
> Spirits as like souls as it can,
> Because such fingers need to knit
> That subtle knot which makes us man,
> So must pure lovers' souls descend
> To affections and to faculties
> Which sense may reach and apprehend,
> Else a great prince in prison lies.
> To our bodies turn we then, that so
> Weak men on love revealed may look;
> Love's mysteries in souls do grow,
> But yet the body is the book.

This "subtle knot" goes to the very heart of Frost's poetics, since for him the sentence is itself a fusion of "soul" to "body," while the animating desire of the bard (his spirit) haunts the forms of poetry: the poem is a subtle knot within a subtle knot. Furthermore, the poet writes and publishes because—to adapt Donne's language—he must bring his "soul" down into "faculties which sense may reach and apprehend." As we saw in chapter 2, for Frost, "correspondence" in poetry was all, as he explains in the introduction to *King Jasper:* love must be revealed. And he writes later in "The Constant Symbol": "The ultimate commitment is giving in to it that an outsider may see what we were up to sooner and better than we ourselves" (*CPPP* 787). Among all the commitments to form and to the "harsher discipline[s] from without" that the poet must accede to, Frost places this one to audience as ultimate. This is consistent with his emphasis on the *two* "answerabilities"—to the highest in the self and to one's "constituents": there must ultimately be a "confluence," as he says in the early manuscript of "The Constant Symbol," "of the flow of the spirit of one person with the flow of the spirit of the race."

In Frost's view the archetypical example of humanity's materialization of spirit is the Fall. He considers it an imitation, on the part of human beings, of God's original gesture of creation, the moment when spirit was first bound to matter—when the first "subtle knot" was tied. The figure of "God's descent" into flesh also looks forward to the incarnation of the Word in Christ. Frost writes in "Kitty Hawk," a long philosophical poem published late in his life:

> Pulpiteers will censure
> Our instinctive venture
> Into what they call
> The material
> When we took that fall
> From the apple tree.
> But God's own descent
> Into flesh was meant
> As a demonstration
> That the supreme merit
> Lay in risking spirit
> In substantiation.
> . . . .
> Spirit enters flesh
> And for all it's worth
> Charges into earth
> In birth after birth
> Ever fresh and fresh.
> We may take the view
> That its derring-do
> Thought of in the large
> Was only one mighty charge
> On our human part
> Of the soul's ethereal
> Into the material.
> (*CPPP* 447)

By this account, self-realization—our "instinctive venture" into the material—necessarily involves self-surrender, or something like the series of dyings and rebirths Burke describes in *A Grammar of Motives*. It works through our charge "into earth / In birth after birth," what Frost calls later in the same poem our "design [as Westerners] for living deeper into matter." Or to recur to Burke's summary of Hegel: "Spirit has its counterpart in objectification; and by seeing himself in terms of objects, 'from them the individual proceeds to the contemplation of his inner being.'" Frost points to God's act of creation and to the incarnation of the Word in Christ as authorizing principles for our own "descent" into matter; he seems to have associated the act of divine creation with the act of poetic creation, which differ only in degree. Both tie a "subtle knot" of soul to body; both commit spirit to form; and, to complete the trinity, both mark a fusion of Frost's "two answerabilities." A precise analogy obtains between the commitment of spirit to form and the "figure of the will" (the first answerability) "braving alien entanglements" (the second).

Already in one of Frost's earliest poems, "The Trial by Existence," this pattern of the "substantiation" of spirit is evident. He imagines that the dead ascend to heaven only to discover that their fate is to descend once again into the material—into an "obscuration upon earth." The "more loitering" and cowardly souls in heaven turn "to view once more the sacrifice / Of those who for some good discerned / Will gladly give up paradise" and return to their "trial" on earth (*CPPP* 29). Frost also spoke of the "trial by market everything must come to"—even poems, as we have already seen. I borrow the line from "Christmas Trees," written in 1916 at about the time Frost first became secure in his career as a published poet. The trials by existence and by market are, for him, tightly associated: both "substantiate" spirit in the "alien entanglements," respectively, of matter and of audience. One recalls as well the 1915 letter to Louis Untermeyer quoted in chapter 1. Alluding to his own efforts to establish his work in the literary marketplace, Frost writes: "Do you know, I think that a book ought to sell. Nothing is quite honest that is not commercial" (*Frost to Untermeyer* 8–9). The remark initiates his career-long effort to defend the "materialization" of spirit, in both the economic and the philosophical senses of the word, quite as if he had it in mind to lend new meaning to the Hegelian idea that "spirit has its counterpart in objectification." Poetic "capital" no less than the financial kind is *meant* to be substantiated, spent, invested; such is Frost's idea, in any event. And here we can see the aesthetic, moral, *and* fiscal significance of his often-quoted adage in "The Constant Symbol": "Strongly spent is synonymous with kept" (*CPPP* 786).

Elsewhere in "Kitty Hawk" Frost redeems Western civilization, and by implication capitalism itself, in much the same terms of providential "expenditure":

> Westerners inherit
> A design for living
> Deeper into matter—
> Not without due patter
> Of a great misgiving.
> All the science zest
> To materialize
> By on-penetration

Into earth and skies
(Don't forget the latter
Is but further matter)
Has been West Northwest.
If it were not wise,
Tell me why the East
Seemingly has ceased
From its long stagnation
In mere meditation.
What's all the fuss
To catch up with us?
Can it be to flatter
Us with emulation?
(*CPPP* 446–47)

"Kitty Hawk" belongs to the era of the cold war and ought to be read in connection with a number of poems collected in Frost's last volume, *In the Clearing* (1962), which have to do with questions of nationalism or with the rivalry between the United States and the USSR. And as it happens, the ethnocentric theo-economy of "Kitty Hawk" (as it might be called) has an important antecedent in western European culture. Frost's thinking, here, bears a striking resemblance to John Calvin's as Burke describes it in *Attitudes toward History:* Calvin saw that "the spiritual futurism of 'providence' could be equated with the worldly futurism of 'investment.' . . . [He] found that one could make profits for the glory of God—every trade was a 'vocation'—and if one worried lest, by Calvinist doctrine, he was one predestined by God for damnation, let him attain material prosperity as a visible sign of God's favor" (137).[8] After all, what is "all the fuss to catch up with us" if our design for living deeper into matter is not somehow providential? In "Kitty Hawk" Frost is practicing a kind of cultural-economic evangelism. And in view of this I think Roger Sell overstates the point in suggesting, in an introduction to Frost's play *In an Art Factory,* that Frost had a "horror at the language of commerce" (273). Though Frost was indeed ambivalent about it—as *In an Art Factory* attests—he was no more "horrified" than Emerson.

In "Kitty Hawk" Frost may have in mind Emerson's motto to the essay "Wealth," collected originally in *The Conduct of Life.* Emerson's poem also draws important connections between the creation of the world and the "materialization" of mind in matter:

Well the primal pioneer
Knew the strong task to it assigned

> Patient through Heaven's enormous year
> To build in matter a home for mind.
> (*Essays* 987)

How readily this language of pioneering and homesteading applied to America in the middle nineteenth century is plain enough, and the essay proper makes clear that the specifically American economic ramifications of this venture of mind into matter are the same for Emerson as for Frost: "Every man is a consumer, and ought to be a producer. He fails to make his place good in the world, unless he not only pays his debt, but also adds something to the common wealth. Nor can he do justice to his genius [that is, to his spirit], without making some larger demand on the world than a bare subsistence. He is by constitution expensive, and needs to be rich" (*Essays* 989). Later Emerson defines wealth as the power to "incarnate" our "designs" and to give "form and actuality" to "thought" (993). These passages suggest how much of Emerson there is in "Kitty Hawk," and they provide a kind of philosophical grounding for Frost's occasional contention that poets *ought* to accept the peculiar genius of the American literary marketplace: "Nothing is quite honest that is not commercial."

With such arguments as these Frost countered charges—which he met often enough in avant-garde literary circles—that America was too "materialistic" or that artists ought to purify themselves of the metaphors and standards of capitalism. By way of response, his strategy is to "naturalize" materialism by referring it, a little more whimsically than Emerson does, to God's original example of creation and to his incarnation of the Word in Christ. Frost's metaphors of expenditure and materialism, then, typically embrace the full range of meanings available to them, from the economic to the spiritual. Kenneth Burke usefully remarks in "I, Eye, Ay—Concerning Emerson's Early Essay on 'Nature' and the Machinery of Transcendence": "Both [Emerson and Whitman] approached the conflicts of the century in terms that allowed for a joyous transcendent translation. . . . We might say that Emerson was as idealistically able as Whitman to look upon travelling salesmen and see a band of angels" (189). With none of Whitman's exuberance, and with much more caution even than Emerson, Frost nevertheless fashioned in his poetics a "frame" (as Burke would say) for "accepting" the consumer culture that flourished in America in the postwar years. And in this he was not at all unlike a great many intellectuals to his political left who, having abandoned the radical positions they held in the 1930s, decided to choose the West, as the saying used to go, after the onset of the cold war.

In setting up a frame for accepting the conditions of consumer capitalism, then, Frost closely follows Emerson in "Wealth": "Nature . . . urges [man] to the acquisition of such things as belong to him. Every warehouse and shop-window, every fruit-tree, every thought of every hour, opens a new want to him, which it concerns his power and dignity to gratify. It is of no use to argue the wants down: the philosophers have laid the greatness of man in making his wants few; but will a man content himself with a hut and a handful of dried pease? He is born to be rich" (*Essays* 990–91). And Frost's Emersonian frame of acceptance also served as a way to defeat the attitude of condescension with which his own popularity—his own decision to accept the trial by market everything must come to—was often treated by American intellectuals. The speech accepting the Gold Medal of the National Institute of Arts and Letters in 1939 provides a good example of this. Here, Frost implies—though I note his possible ambivalence in chapter 2—that his having fit "into the nature of Americans" is something like a sign of election, possibly even a sounder sign than John Bunyan had in jail (*CPPP* 779–80). (Frost's remarks in the Gold Medal speech may betray the special Calvinist sense of election Burke describes in *Attitudes toward History.*) In "The Pod of the Milkweed" and "On Extravagance," Frost frames the American capitalist political economy for acceptance by drawing an analogy between the lavish "waste" and "expenditure" of natural fertility and the material "fertility" and luxury of consumer capitalism. He writes in an especially Emersonian passage in "On Extravagance": "I was thinking of the extravagance of the universe. What an *extravagant* universe it is. And the most extravagant thing in it, as far as we know, is man—the most wasteful, spending thing in it—in all his luxuriance" (*CPPP* 902). In short, there is clearly a consistency among the metaphors on which Frost depends in describing the whole range of issues from the philosophical and the theological to the aesthetic and the vocational: his poetics is an effort to harmonize all these things.

Supporting this ambitious effort in harmony is a "tragic frame" of self-redemption through the substantiation of "spirit" in "objective," material conditions—whether we mean the material conditions of the literary marketplace for the poet or, for the scientist, the material conditions of the earth itself. Only by means of "living deeper into matter" can we realize ourselves. This redemptive objectification of spirit is evident in Burke's favored adage in chapter 1 of *A Grammar of Mo-*

tives: "The suffered is the learned" (39). That sentence epitomizes the tragic process, as I am concerned with it here. Dewey's remarks in *Art as Experience* provide a useful gloss on the idea: "Impulsion forever boosted on its forward way would run its course thoughtless, and dead to emotion. For it would not have to give an account of itself in terms of the things it encounters, and hence they would not become significant objects. The only way it can become aware of its nature and its goal *is by obstacles surmounted* and means employed. . . . *Nor without resistance from surroundings* would the self become aware of itself; it would have neither feeling nor interest, neither fear nor hope, neither disappointment nor elation" (65; my emphasis). There is an interesting analogy, here, to Frost's often-repeated censure of free verse: "For my part I should be as satisfied to play tennis with the net down as to write verse with no verse form set to stay me" (*CPPP* 735). There is an analogy also to Frost's remarks about Shakespeare in "The Constant Symbol": "Up to this point [in the sonnet] his discipline has been the self-discipline whereof it is written in so great praise. The harsher discipline from without is now well begun. He who knows not both knows neither" (*CPPP* 789). The "harsher discipline[s] from without" correspond to Dewey's "obstacles," and, as Frost saw it, only through their agency—as I shall presently explain in greater detail—may we truly come to know the *intrinsic* disciplines of the self: "He who knows not both knows neither." The suffered is the learned.

We begin, here, to see the full meaning of Frost's paradox in "The Constant Symbol": "Strongly spent is synonymous with kept." It involves a dialectic whereby an action of expenditure is transformed into its opposite. This pattern of redemptive self-surrender finds expression throughout Frost's writings, as when the speaker of "Directive" asks that we become "lost enough to find [ourselves]" (*CPPP* 341). The early poem "Into My Own" involves a similar vision of self-possession achieved by "stealing away" into a "vastness" of woods that stretch, so the speaker imagines, even "unto the edge of doom" (*CPPP* 15). The *ex*-cursion actually becomes an *in*-cursion into the self: "They would not find me changed from him they knew / Only more sure of all I thought was true." Self-forfeiture earns the poet his deepest convictions, and it is to this salvation that I turn now, the better to make clearer the "tragic" significance of Frost's concern with the "trial by existence," what elsewhere he calls the "risky" "substantiation" of "spirit" in "matter" whereby we realize the true course and power of the soul. And Frost's curiously tentative ideal of self-realization will inevitably lead us to reconsider his thoughts on the nature of "authorship." He writes in "The Constant Symbol": "The mind is a baby giant who, more provident in the cradle than he knows, has hurled his paths in life all round ahead of him like playthings given—data so-called" (*CPPP* 790). The idea that the mind is a "baby *giant,*" and a providential one at that, suggests how his theory of poetry aims to transcend those conditions of writing that potentially alienate the writer from himself—those conditions that undermine the writer's "august temper," thereby diminishing the power of his authorship.

This providential "baby giant"—with the emphasis on "giant," not "baby"—is a paradoxical figure that all but conceals the magnitude of the claims actually being made. Frost writes in "The Trial by Existence":

> 'Tis the essence of life here,
> Though we choose greatly, still to lack
> The lasting memory at all clear,
> That life has for us on the wrack
> Nothing but what we somehow chose;
> Thus are we wholly stripped of pride
> In the pain that has but one close,
> Bearing it crushed and mystified.
> (*CPPP* 30)

The conclusion that "thus are we wholly stripped of pride" is not entirely candid. It is in fact a great extravagance of power to imagine that life holds nothing for us "but what we somehow chose." The end imagined in this last stanza of "Trial by Existence" is a specifically tragic dignification of human agency, not a statement of humility—let alone a claim of victimization. Kenneth Burke explains in *A Grammar of Motives:*

> It is deplorable, but not tragic, simply to be a victim of circumstance, for there is an important distinction between destiny and sheer victimization. Sheer victimization is not an assertion—and it naturally makes not for vision but for frustration. The victimizing circumstances, or accidents, seem arbitrary and exorbitant, even "silly." But at the moment of tragic vision, the fatal accidents are felt to bear fully upon the act, while the act itself is felt to have summed up the character of the agent. Nor is this vision a sense of cosmic persecution; for in seeing the self in terms of the situation which the act has brought about, the agent transcends the self. (39)

A tragic hero recognizes, even if only late in the day, that his suffering follows from his own action—that the oppositional and extrinsic motives working against him are actually intrinsic and derivative of the self. This is Frost's recognition in "The Trial by Existence" and finally in his poetics more generally: life holds nothing for us but what we somehow choose, though we may suffer the consequences of our choices "crushed and mystified," never fully conscious of our deepest resources of power and will. Frost allies himself with the "successful men" Emerson punningly describes in "Power": "All successful men have agreed in one thing,—they were *causationists.* They believed things went not by luck, but by law; that there was not a weak or cracked link in the chain that joins the first and last of things" (*Essays* 971).

It is as if Frost had all along been prepared to assume total responsibility for his destiny—even at the age of eighteen when he began writing what ultimately would become "The Trial by Existence."[9] This assumption of power is providential, as only befits a "baby giant." And in making it, Frost speaks with Nietzsche's Zarathustra: "To re-create all 'it was' into a 'thus I willed it'—that alone should I call redemption" (Bloom, *Agon* 120). I quote this sentence from *Agon,* in which Harold Bloom cites Zarathustra's "thus I willed it" as the definitive example of "poetic will," and Frost's fantasy is, at last, a specifically *authorial* fantasy. In the "tragic" recognition, scaled down to Frost's "figure of the will braving alien entanglements," the extrinsic or "alien" motives of form and language that buffet and redirect the poet's will are seen in a new light: they are *intrinsic* motives, "somehow" willed and chosen by the poet. This "machinery of transcendence" (to borrow Burke's phrase) restores the "august temper" that a poet expends in writing. In short, to return once again to the terms of debate laid down earlier: Frost "believes" himself into existence as the "author" of his "works," just as in "The Trial by Existence" he "believes himself" into responsibility for and into ownership of his own fate.

In the preface to a selection of his poems reprinted in *This Is My Best* (1942), a popular "auto-anthology," Frost writes:

> I have made this selection much as I made the one from my first book, *A Boy's Will,* and my second book, *North of Boston,* looking backward over the accumulation of years to see how many poems I could find towards some one meaning it might seem absurd to have had in advance, but it would be all right to accept from fate after the fact. The interest, the pastime, was to learn if there had been any divinity shaping my ends and I had been building better than I knew. In other words could anything of larger design, even the roughest, any broken or dotted continuity, or any fragment of a figure be discerned among the apparently random lesser designs of the several poems? I had given up convictions when young from despair of learning how they were had. Nevertheless I might not have been without them. They might be

> turned up out of the heap by assortment. And if not convictions, then perhaps native prejudices and inclinations. (*CPPP* 783–84)

With characteristic ambivalence he wavers between ascribing the integrity and design in his work—signal attributes of "authorship"—to three agencies: to fate, to his own retrospective interpretive gestures, or to his "convictions," "native prejudices," and "inclinations." His prose often works by subtle dislocations of a word or meaning, as apparently happens here with "convictions": "I had given up convictions when young from despair of learning how they were had." A conviction is not, in the ordinary way of thinking, something easily acquired or readily abandoned, and Frost's phrasing alerts us to a basic ambiguity in the word. We usually use it to mean a power unfolded from within, something native to us. But it may refer to a power imposed or adopted from without, as in a court of law or in a religious experience: juries and the gods convict us.

Frost borrows Hamlet's remark to Horatio: "There's a divinity that shapes our ends, / Rough hew them how we will" (5.2.10–11). For Frost—as perhaps also for Hamlet, depending on how you read him—this "divinity" is seated in the deeper self that animates the apparently chaotic happenings of his career. "Divinity" may be fatal but it may also be the "divinity" or foresight of the seer: that is to say, it can be either impersonal or personal, a sign either of fate or of power, just as convictions can. "Conviction" and "divinity" express a marriage of inside and outside, a subtle exchange of freedom and law, and this is only fitting. Even when imposed from without and after the fact, a conviction must "rhyme" with the inner life of the convict—with her guilt or her desire, components of personality that often lie beneath her awareness. If Frost convicts himself of having had meanings "in advance" there may well be justice in it. And the merger of inside and outside suggested in his wry invocation of "divinity" recalls the merger of the two "answerabilities" (as he puts it in "The Constant Symbol") to "inner" and "outer" "discipline[s]"—that is to say, answerabilities to what *we* determine and also to what *determines* us. This merger marks a "tragic" recognition of the essential harmony of character and fate.

The specific ambivalence of conviction and divinity is further reflected in the tone of Frost's remarks. There is a deflationary humor in the claim he makes for the integrity of his work. This claim is after all only entertained as a "pastime." Still, Frost hedges his bets. It *might seem* absurd to have had these meanings in advance, but the fact that a belief or a claim to power seems absurd hardly discredits it, as he points out in a brief essay on *The Four Beliefs* (1944): "There are several beliefs that I know more about from having lived with poetry: One is the self-belief, which is a knowledge that you don't want to tell other people about because you cannot prove that you know. You are saying nothing about it till you see" (*Collected Prose* 198). In the preface to *This Is My Best* Frost is entertaining just this cautious possibility of "believing himself" into existence, to adapt a phrase he uses in the conclusion to his 1931 essay "Education by Poetry" (*CPPP* 728). He approaches himself just as he approaches Catullus in the talk discussed above. He is testing the limits of his own "authority," tentatively discerning in his own writing patterns of coherence, unity, and teleology (a movement "*towards* some one meaning"). These are, of course, qualities preeminently associated with literary "works" and literary "authority." Indeed, Frost seems rather more inclined in this case than in the case of Catullus to "believe" in the possibility of authorship—surely a forgivable vanity for a poet, especially a poet as ingratiatingly skeptical in this regard as Frost. Notice as well that, for him, "belief" is a *creative* factor in this equation. In other words, belief *brings about* its object—in this case, the integrated self of literary authority. The *object* of a belief therefore may not be properly said to exist before the *action* of that belief. In this way, for Frost as also for William James, belief is reimagined as a *realizing agency.* He remarks in an interview given in 1961: "The most creative thing in us is to believe a thing in. . . . You believe yourself into existence" (*Interviews* 271). Frost is certainly aware of the paradox latent in this last sentence—namely, the paradox of a self-creating agent. Something transformative happens and yet does not happen to the self over the course of these transactions in belief; the self at once changes and remains unchanged, apart from transformation. Or perhaps it is better to say that, through these transformations, the self comes into its majority, into possession of itself; the self becomes at last the object of its own knowledge. It is by these means that Frost imagines writing less as the *expression* of authority than as an *accession to it.* Bear in mind his remarks in the notebook entry quoted earlier: "There is such a thing as sincerity. It is hard to define but it is probably nothing but your highest liveliness escaping from a succession of dead selves." "Sincerity" is the constant in this equation, over which the "highest liveliness" of self-realization "succeeds" itself; the self is at once expressed and realized, at once *already* "sincerely" anchored in its place and *only now* coming into being. It is to this basic paradox of permanence and change that I want now to turn.

In what sense—and by now the question is familiar—does the poet "build better than he knows"? In what sense can he both "build"—with all that the term suggests of intention, design, and motive—and *not know* what he "builds"? It is as if some component of the self stood apart from the conscious, public self that "designs" and "calculates" in the ordinary, less flattering senses of those words. There is, then, an apparent self-division, and beneath it a deeper self-integrity—a dualism of recognizably Emersonian derivation. Emerson writes in his journal:

> It is the largest part of a man that is not inventoried. He has many enumerable parts: he is social, professional, political, sectarian, literary, and is this or that set and corporation. But after the most exhausting census has been made, there remains as much more which no tongue can tell. And this remainder is that which interests. This is that which the preacher and the poet and the musician speak to. This is that which the strong genius works upon; the region of destiny, of aspiration, of the unknown. Ah, they have a secret persuasion that as little as they pass for in the world, they are immensely rich in expectation and power. Nobody has ever yet dispossessed this adhesive self to arrive at any glimpse or guess of the awful Life that lurks under it.

These broad Emersonian tones are rarely to be found in Frost's prose and poetry. But the "adhesive" (or merely apparent) self and the "awful Life" lurking beneath it form the paradigm out of which "The Trial by Existence" was written. And the "remainder" Emerson speaks of is what the writing of poetry puts Frost in touch with in himself: the "divinity" shaping his ends, the "meaning it might seem absurd to have had in advance"—in a word, his "conviction." Writing and reading his own poetry become an accession to agency—a paradoxical "discovery" of convictions, designs, prejudices, and inclinations that he did not know he held. He is, in a sense, transformed by writing, and yet these transformations only recall him to his origins. And it is precisely at this point of origin that Frost experimentally discerns in his own work the "deep motives" and "creative power" that have, in Foucault's account, constituted the traditional ideals of "authorship." With regard to his own writing, Frost is exercising the "author-function": he marks his poetry off as having certain integrities, certain patterns of coherence and direction that are characteristic of "authoritative" literary works. In short, he is discovering the "design" in his own writing, and consequently also its *designer,* with the odd twist that in this case the designer has all along been himself.

Frost engages in a similar exercise in "The Figure a Poem Makes." "For me," he writes, "the initial delight [in writing poetry] is in the surprise of remembering something I did not know I knew. I am in a place, in a situation, as if I had materialized from cloud or risen out of the ground. There is a glad recognition of the long lost and the rest follows. Step by step the wonder of unexpected supply keeps growing" (*CPPP* 777). It is in this sense that writing "tempers" the poet or consigns to him a deeper sense of integrity than he had possessed before he wrote. And when Frost speaks of "remembering something [he] didn't know [he] knew" he confirms Dewey's perceptive remarks on memory in *Art as Experience:* "The old poets traditionally invoked the muse of Memory as something wholly outside themselves—outside their present conscious selves. The invocation is a tribute to the power of what is most deep-lying and therefore the furthest below consciousness, in determination of the present self and of what it has to say" (76). "The Figure a Poem Makes" is perhaps just such an invocation of Memory; that is to say, it is an effort to account for the ways in which the writing of poetry seems to grant the poet a purchase on his deepest individuality and personality, a purchase that he had somehow previously lacked. In Dewey's account, poets traditionally acknowledged the mystery of this experience by alienating "Memory," by locating it *outside* themselves. Frost performs a cognate maneuver when he describes the *self*-realizing capacities, for the poet, of the "harsher discipline[s] *from without.*" As he says in *This Is My Best,* he will "accept from fate"—preeminently an *extrinsic* factor—what actually had always been native and *intrinsic* to himself. And here we find another important intersection with Dewey. I have in mind Dewey's description of "impulsion," the "movement outward and forward of the whole organism" as it (or he or she) acts: "The impulsion . . . meets many things on its outward course that deflect and oppose it. In the process of converting these obstacles and neutral conditions into favoring agencies, the live creature becomes aware of the intent implicit in its impulsion. . . . Blind surge has been changed into a purpose; instinctive tendencies are transformed into contrived undertakings. The attitudes of the self are informed with meaning" (65). We have here a transformation of extrinsic, "alien entanglements" into agencies that actually realize the *intrinsic* will of the self. By means of these extrinsic obstacles we are made conscious of what we did not know we knew of ourselves: "The attitudes of the self are informed with meaning." This is precisely the experience, in Frost's (and Hamlet's) phrase, of discovering the divinity that shapes our ends, rough hew them how we will. It is the experience of discovering the merger of "extrinsic" and "intrinsic" motivations, the merger of the "divinity" of fate and the "divinity" of foresight and intuition.

Only when we have reached an understanding of the covert "divinity" imagined in Frost's poetics are we therefore in a position fully to understand his emphasis on the "harsher discipline from without" as against "inner" form and "*self*-discipline"—his emphasis on "conformity" as against "formity," as he sometimes puts it. The initial and thoroughly dialectical opposition of inner and outer motivation is at last transcended in a unitary perspective. Or as Burke explains in *A Grammar of Motives:*

> The [tragic] act, in being an assertion, has called forth a counter-assertion in the elements that compose its context. And when the agent is enabled to see in terms of this counter-assertion, he has transcended the state that characterized him at the start. In this final state of tragic vision, intrinsic and extrinsic motivations are merged. That is, although purely circumstantial factors participate in his tragic destiny, these are not felt as exclusively external, or scenic; for they bring about a *representative* kind of accident, the kind of accident that belongs with the agent's particular kind of character. (38–39)

In the final or "tragic" merger imagined in Frost's poetics, "self-discipline" and the "harsher discipline from without" become one. In "The Figure a Poem Makes" he explains that a poem "runs a course of lucky events, and ends in a clarification of life" (*CPPP* 777). But these "lucky" events are really "representative" accidents, in Burke's somewhat paradoxical phrase; which is simply to say that they are "somehow" chosen. And the "clarification of life" is actually a revelation of the poet's native insight and will—his "particular kind of character." Frost hereby arrives at a position quite distinct from the one taken by Foucault in "What Is an Author?" although in certain respects, as we have seen, Frost has much in common with him. This circumstance leads Frost at once to affirm an ideal of "authorial presence"—that is, to identify the "author-function" with himself—*and* to raise skeptical questions about the very possibility of such an identification. This complexity is what concerns me in the closing pages of this chapter.

The "machinery of transcendence" whereby "extrinsic" or impersonal motives are assimilated into "intrinsic" or personal ones marks the point at which Frost's poetics might be critically "deconstructed":

it implies a perfect embodiment of intention and desire in the "alien entanglements" of language and poetic form. Or to borrow once again the terms of Frost's poem "Kitty Hawk": in this transcendence, "spirit" is at last perfectly materialized or objectified. In short, Frost's poetics imagines a "final unity" of spirit and matter, as he says in another connection. This may illuminate a difficult passage in "The Constant Symbol": "Form in language is such a disjected lot of old broken pieces it seems almost as non-existent as the spirit till the two embrace in the sky. They are not to be thought of as encountering in rivalry but in creation. No judgement on either alone counts. We see what Whitman's extravagance may have meant when he said the body was the soul" (*CPPP* 790). He is describing the felicity we experience when language seems to lend itself perfectly to our purposes—when freedom (spirit) and fate (material) marry. Poetry holds this promise of marriage for Frost. Consider once again "The Silken Tent," in which he plays out in form and describes in theme the paradoxical experience of freedom-in-bondage. This blending of "answerabilities" is an experience constitutive also of ideal love, as "The Silken Tent" suggests, wherein it is as unintelligible to speak of coercion as of desire: the opposition collapses, fuses. The body *is* the soul. And as for the capitalist "trial by market everything must come to": in Frost's vision of final unity, supply and demand—writer and reader—form perfect complements, as Adam Smith said they providentially would. With such thoughts on his mind as these, Frost writes a little obscurely in a notebook that he kept between 1912 and 1915: "Life is that which can mix oil and water (Emulsion). I can consist of the inconsistent. I can hold in unity the ultimate irreconcilable spirit and matter, good and evil, monism (cohesion) and dualism (reaction), peace and strife. It o'er rules the harsh divorce that parts things natural and divine" (qtd. in Thompson, *Robert Frost: The Early Years* 427).

Above, I alluded to the possibility of deconstructing Frost's poetics—to the possibility of opening once again the "harsh divorce" that parts spirit and matter. But any effort to deconstruct Frost's thinking must first take account of his own preemptive remarks in "Education by Poetry": "Greatest of all attempts to say one thing in terms of another is the philosophical attempt to say matter in terms of spirit, or spirit in terms of matter, to make the final unity. That is the greatest attempt that ever failed. We stop just short there. But it is the height of poetry, the height of all thinking, the height of all poetic thinking, that attempt to say matter in terms of spirit and spirit in terms of matter" (*CPPP* 723–24). We are now in a position to see that two major emphases in Frost's poetics stand opposed: a transcendental aspiration to achieve the "final unity" spoken of here and a recognition of its impossibility. He explains in "Some Definitions by Robert Frost" that a poem "is a reaching-out toward expression; an effort to find fulfillment. A complete poem is one where an emotion has found its thought and the thought has found the words" (*CPPP* 701). But there is a sense in which no poem ever reaches "completion" in these terms, as Frost points out in a letter to Sidney Cox. He is referring to Cox's frustration at being unable adequately to express himself: "That [frustration] rises to heights almost universal in that it voices the complaint of everyone who writes anything, viz., that nothing he writes quite represents his thought or his feeling. It is as hard to fill a vacuum with nothing as it is to fill a poem (for instance) with something. The best one can hope for is an approximation" (Evans 22). In this recognition of the "approximate" nature of expression lies the significance of Frost's insistence in "The Figure a Poem Makes" that a poem is only a "*momentary* stay" against confusion (*CPPP* 777; emphasis mine): confusion, like air into a vacuum, is always rushing in. The consequence, as Derrida acknowledges in "Signature Event Context," is that we may speak only of a "*relative* specificity" of the "presence" of intention and consciousness in language. All is approximation. Bloom's observation in *Agon* about Emerson and Whitman applies equally to Frost: "What the language of Emerson and of Whitman knows then is something about adequacy or inadequacy, something about agon, about the struggle between adverting subject or subjectivity and the mediation that consciousness hopelessly wills language to constitute. In this agon, this struggle between authentic forces, neither the fiction of the subject nor the trope of language is strong enough to win a final victory" (29). Bloom continues with a metaphor quite congenial to Frost's figure of the "greatest attempt that ever failed": "There is [in this agon] only a mutual Great Defeat, but that Defeat itself is the true problematic, the art of poetry and the art of criticism" (29).

Conclusion

> But the comfort is
> In the covenant
> We may get control
> If not of the whole
> Of at least some part
> Where not too immense,
> So by craft or art
> We can give the part
> Wholeness in a sense.
> —Robert Frost, "Kitty Hawk"

> Drink and be whole again beyond confusion.
> —Robert Frost, "Directive"

IN THE ACCOUNT GIVEN in Frost's poetics, writing marks a kind of fall, on the part of the writer, into contingency—into "commitments" and "answerabilities" that severely limit his freedom of movement. It is a lapse from transcendence into immanence, as the existentialists say. The forms of language and poetry never perfectly realize the vague sense of possibility that a poet brings to the act of writing: "Nothing he writes," as Frost puts it, "quite represents his thought or feeling" (Evans 22). Meaning is as much generated as expressed when a poet writes, and this process—to which the poet, at times, can feel merely incidental or catalytic—may be taken as a model for human action in general. We are always losing our "august temper," to borrow Frost's phrase in "The Constant Symbol." We never quite know what we are up to until we have been intemperately carried away by our own actions. Frost writes in "The Figure a Poem Makes": "Like a piece of ice on a hot stove the poem must ride on its own melting. A poem may be worked over once it is in being, but may not be worried into being. Its most precious quality will remain its having run itself and carried away the poet with it. Read it a hundred times: it will forever keep its freshness as a metal keeps its fragrance. It can never lose its sense of a meaning that once unfolded by surprise as it went" (*CPPP* 778).

In chapter 3 I spoke of the "transcendence" imagined in Frost's poetics. I find in this promise of transcendence a gesture, on his part, toward overcoming the writer's fall into contingency, a fall that necessarily becomes, to some extent, a fall out of agency and authority. It is a gesture toward mastering contingency itself, as "The Trial by Existence" suggests: "Life has for us on the wrack / Nothing but what we somehow chose" (*CPPP* 30). Frost achieves this transcendence, at least in thought, by re-imagining agency as a force developed *out* of writing and action rather than as a force expressed *through* them: meaning and purpose are "unfolded by surprise" as the poet writes, or more generally as anyone acts. This suggests that the experience of "agency" and "authority" we usually have, in which our motives and success *seem* transparent and available to us before we act, is in fact rather inconsequential. Or if not exactly "inconsequential," these "available," premeditative motives are in any event not motives upon which a theory of authorship might be grounded. To ask a poet what he "means" in this limited sense is an impertinence. Frost shows us how true "authorial" agency lies much deeper, beneath the awareness even of the poet. And the partly mysterious encounter of authority and contingency on the stage of writing promises, in his poetics, to place the poet in touch with these deeper possibilities of agency. It is a powerful mythology of the self and of authorship because it holds out the possibility of a release from constriction, a new birth of the poet's "highest liveliness escaping from a succession of dead selves," as Frost says in his notebook. The poet is constantly born anew into a sense of individuality and integrity.

Describing the "rudimentary psychology" of what he calls the "religious man," Nietzsche explains that when such a man "experiences the conditions of power, the imputation is [always] that he is not their cause, that he is not responsible for them: they come without being willed, consequently we are not their author: the will that is not free," Nietzsche concludes, "needs an external will" (*The Will to Power* 86). It is perhaps useful to think of post-structuralist critiques of "authority" as "religious" in the sense Nietzsche gives the term here, paradoxical though that may seem. Post-structuralist philosophy and literary theory are, it is true, inimical to such apparently metaphysical concepts as an "external will," at least as a "religious man" might conceive of "external will." But insofar as the motives of language, of literary tradition, and of society may be said to be "external" to the will of the writing subject—that is to say, insofar as language itself, conceived of as a complex of "transindividual" codes, may be said to "speak" us rather than us, it—to this extent, in any case, post-structuralist theories of "authority" regard the poet as a kind of *medium* for the poem rather than as its *real* and only point of origin. All of her authority is *apparent.* And with this, we are pretty well back to Plato's *Ion*—at least for the sake of argument. By contrast, Frost's poetics is a wily—and, let us say, "impious"—effort to recover, in the name of the poet, the agency that is so easily and so often located elsewhere, whether by a mystical theory of "divine" inspiration or by a post-structuralist one of *distributed subjectivity.* One happy consequence of Frost's accounts of authority is indeed that they help us see what these two other theories may have in common as accounts of motivation: "piety" in both cases—to extend Nietzsche's religious metaphor—is a matter of *subjecting* the self to some will "external" to it. Frost's poetics is an alternative effort to redescribe *external* will as in fact *internal* to the subject—an effort to redescribe "the harsher discipline from without" as another (although occult) feature of what he calls *self-discipline.*

Later in the passage quoted above from *The Will to Power* Nietzsche goes on to suggest that "man has not dared to credit himself with his strong and surprising impulses—he has conceived them as 'passive,' as 'suffered,' as things imposed upon him: religion is the product of a doubt concerning the unity of the person, an *altération* of the personality" (86). And so is post-structuralist literary theory, in its own way: the self is always elsewhere. It may help us by way of summing up Frost's project to suggest that he impiously *dares* to credit himself with "authority," with his most "strong and surprising impulses," and that he does so in the face of precisely the "religious doubts" about the "unity" of the self that Nietzsche speaks of here. The writing of poetry, Frost has the audacity to suggest, actually *unifies* the self, actually overcomes the very *altération* or "othering" of personality that always, to some extent, undermines a poet's convictions of integrity and authority. The self of the poet certainly "alters" as he writes, but this "alteration" *becomes* the self—it does not oppose it. Frost tentatively makes the "divinity" shaping his end *his own;* whereas post-structuralist theory secularizes and distributes this "divinity," Frost *personalizes* it. That is why his poetics can never really be assimilated to post-structuralism, much less to *divine* theories of authority such as one encounters in the

Ion. It is as if Frost experimentally submits his own "impersonalist" account of authorship—as I have described it in chapter 3—to a rigorous, Nietzschean critique. We have to arrive at some such formula if we are to appreciate the subtlety of his enterprise in poetry, which has both "pious" and "impious" features—both self-effacing and self-aggrandizing features.

The autonomy and the immense responsibility of the self in Frost's philosophy must strike some readers as regrettable, even as a bit cruel. He seems to say, in such works as "The Trial by Existence": "You built your own world, now live in it—for better and for worse. Life holds nothing for you but what you choose." To put it very broadly—as a friend once suggested to me—this is a way of blaming the victim. Indeed it is, when directed outward toward others rather than inward toward the self. In this respect Frost's thinking is quite consistent with free-market capitalist individualism. Here, too, as in his eulogy on "materialism" in "Kitty Hawk," he follows Emerson's lead in "Wealth." This helps explain Frost's hostility to the New Deal in *A Further Range* (1936), a book that would save the autonomy of the individual even at the expense of accepting a good deal of general purpose misery. Of course, Frost might reply to a critic of his position: "But Roosevelt saved us all from a certain amount of misery at the expense of the autonomy of the individual—the other way." He always wanted to say—as he once did in a depression-era speech given at Amherst College—that we should endeavor to preserve and protect what he preferred to call the "privilege" to meet "emergencies" and even to fail (quoted in Thompson, *Years of Triumph* 417). If that sounds harsh, as it often must, we should bear in mind that Frost, as the foregoing chapters suggest, had the good taste not to except himself from the privilege to fail: he tolerated and even courted hardship because without it he lacked the "privilege" also to succeed—the privilege to *perform,* as he liked to say. That is why, time and again, his poetics recurs to the need for obstacles, resistances, and constraints—to those "harsher discipline[s] from without" within which only can we come to feel the truer "disciplines" of the self: he who knows not both of these disciplines knows neither. The poet needs his immanence and contingency if he is to get his transcendence. Frost's view is therefore essentially tragic, not comic, which is simply another way of saying that the divinity shaping his end, as I already indicated, is always finally personal and individual (as in *King Lear* or *Macbeth*), never social or providential (as in *The Tempest* and many of the comedies). We begin to see just how tightly integrated Frost's thinking is: his Jeffersonian-libertarian response to the New Deal, his "tragic" definition of poetic form, his Emersonian mythology of self—all of these things are intricately intertwined.

Mastery of contingency in Frost's thinking, then, ultimately means mastery of Fate. To this I would add, following Simone de Beauvoir, that it means in some sense "mastery" also of Woman and of Nature. His thinking is patriarchal. Returning to "The Birthplace"—discussed in chapter 1—we can now see that Frost's poetics imagines, if only as a kind of fiction, a narrative in which the father-poet masters Nature, which in "The Birthplace" unmistakably arrives under the sign of femininity—a narrative whereby he fantastically escapes, as de Beauvoir might say, the Fates of the body and of the womb. In other words, we are now in a position to understand better the ambivalence of Frost's attitude toward the Natural and also toward Woman and to understand as well the extent to which, in his accounts, the labor of poetry is specifically masculine.

De Beauvoir argues in *The Second Sex* that through Nature man attempts to achieve his "transcendence": Nature is the thing upon which he exercises his will to order the world after the pattern of his desire. But Nature is also *immanence*—the *matter* that condemns man in the end to finitude. For this reason she wears, for him, a "double visage": man "exploits her, but she crushes him; he is born of her and dies in her; she is the source of his being and the realm that he subjugates to his will" (144). "The Earth Mother," de Beauvoir says by way of summary, "engulfs the bones of her children" (147). This is the prospect that "The Birthplace" considers, as we have already seen, for which reason it may profitably be read alongside Emerson's poem of the Earth-Mother, "Hamatreya." Emerson begins with a muster of local farmers:

> Minott, Lee, Willard, Hosmer, Meriam, Flint
> Possessed the land which rendered to their toil
> Hay, corn, roots, hemp, flax, apples, wool, and wood.
> Each of these landlords walked amidst his farm,
> Saying, ''Tis mine, my children's, and my name's.'
> (Oxford Authors edition 506–7)

The men named are the white patriarchs who first laid claim to the land around Concord, its prominent early landlords and farmers. They tilled the soil, "subjugating" it to their "will," and in that way saw themselves *realized* and perpetuated in the land (or so they believed anyway): "''Tis mine, my children's, and my name's.'" In this presumption they are very like the founding father described in Frost's poem "The Birthplace":

> Here further up the mountain slope
> Than there was ever any hope,
> My father built, enclosed a spring,
> Strung chains of wall round everything,
> Subdued the growth of earth to grass,
> And brought our various lives to pass.

Landlords and patriarchs may imagine that they master the Earth. Each may declare, as Emerson has one declare, that the very waters of the land "know me, as does my dog," which is of course to say that the waters know him as *master.* But in the end, what the landlords would master instead masters them. As Frost himself concedes, there was never really "any hope." Emerson makes the inevitable reply to the pretensions of all founding fathers:

> Where are these men? Asleep beneath their grounds;
> And strangers, fond as they, their furrows plough.
> Earth laughs in flowers, to see her boastful boys
> Earth-proud, proud of the earth which is not theirs;
> Who steer the plough, but cannot steer their feet
> Clear of the grave.

The land these men would make fertile by "steer[ing] the plough" at last becomes the ground of their own dissolution. What is more, they are "cuckolded" by succeeding generations of men, each of which believes it has its way with the Earth, each in turn "fondly"—that is to say, *foolishly*—believing that *their* names are the only ones impressed on these fields. But the Earth knows better. She "laughs in flowers" and engulfs the bones of her children. Emerson has her sing sublimely and unanswerably in "Hamatreya": "How am I theirs, / If they cannot hold me / But I hold them?" The end of these men is their beginning, a circuit that occasions fear for the few who permit themselves to acknowledge its operation. They are quite literally *chastened,* as is Emerson himself at the end of "Hamatreya":

> When I heard the Earth-song
> I was no longer brave;
> My avarice cooled
> Like lust in the chill of the grave.
> (Oxford Authors edition 508)

The analogy to "lust" is perfectly apt: the will to master the Earth by plow and seed—the will to reduce her to order, bounding her with fences and "chains of wall"—is always, in these stories of the patriarchs, residually erotic. After all, that is the meaning of those metaphors of *husbandry:* plowing the furrow, "putting in the seed," "subduing" the earth, and so forth. The Earth seduces the farmer until at last he sees in her not only the object of his desire but also his point of origin and his destiny: to him the fields are at once mother, lover, and grave. The Earth-Mother's laughter in "Hamatreya" suggests the flirtatious, unsettling "smile" that Frost, with due apprehension, finds on the land in "The Birthplace":

> The mountain seemed to like the stir,
> And made of us a little while—
> With always something in her smile.
> Today she wouldn't know our name.
> (*CPPP* 243)

It is as de Beauvoir writes in an apposite (though somewhat more gothic) passage in *The Second Sex:* "The Woman-Mother has a face of shadows: she is the chaos whence all have come and whither all must one day return" (147). She will not remain "subdued," nor reined in by "chains of wall." She won't bear any man's name for long. To the man who receives it, her ambivalent "smile" is therefore the mark of his finitude and contingency, which is why, in Emerson and in Frost, it chastens as well as charms.

But for Frost, to know finitude and contingency is to know also the urge to transcend these things: they are *provocations* to his at times imperial will. And in Frost that urge is both the masculine work of poetry and the poetry of masculine work. A good example of this aspect of his thinking is found in the section of "Kitty Hawk," his late philosophical poem, called "The Holiness of Wholeness." As de Beauvoir might say, this section offers up a "phallic" dream of unity, integrity, mastery, and self-sufficiency—something like the grand fiction of "wholeness" and mastery with which Emerson's farmers in "Hamatreya" deceive themselves: " 'Tis . . . *my* name's." Here, Frost is addressing not only the "pilots" of that first feeble aircraft at Kitty Hawk, whose efforts he takes as the *type* of man's effort to slip the bonds of Earth. He is also addressing "pilots" more generally, a category that extends to include such pioneers and farmers as "The Birthplace" concerns, and also, as we shall see, the figure of the poet himself.

> Pilot, though at best your
> Flight is but a gesture,
> And your rise and swoop,
> But a loop the loop,

Lands on someone hard
In his own backyard
From no brighter heaven
Than a bolt of levin,
I don't say retard.
Keep on elevating.
(*CPPP* 451)

The real meaning of the work imagined here lies in the struggle, not the result: that is what this "gesture" to sustain elevation signifies. Whatever else you may say, *do not* say "retard." At this point it is hard to resist quoting James Brown, a singer everyone has heard to much the same effect: "Stay on the scene, like a sex machine." I do not at all mean to trivialize "Kitty Hawk" by thus setting it to music. I mean only to suggest that this eulogy on transcendence and "elevation" is not without its sexual component, not without, that is to say, a certain *swagger*—as Frost was no doubt aware. Earlier in the poem he writes, in a figure at once sexual and agricultural:

Spirit enters flesh
And for what it's worth
Charges into earth
In birth after birth.
(447)

This is the master trope of "Kitty Hawk" and it binds together several things: "God's own descent into flesh," as when he conceived a son (446); the Wright brothers' great experiment, which is an epitome of what Frost suggestively calls

the science zest
To materialize
By on-*penetration*
Into earth and skies;
(447; my emphasis)

and indeed the entire (masculine) project to "master Nature" (449). Of course, we might object that the Wright brothers' flight was but the "vain hop" of a "grasshopper" (450). That would be a cruel joke at the expense of man's pretensions toward sustained elevation, and Frost admonishes any skeptics:

Don't discount our powers;
We have made a pass
At the infinite,

> Made it, as it were,
> Rationally ours.
>
> (450)

The latent metaphor is the metaphor of sexual conquest: "making a pass." And that sexually possessive (and imperial) phrase "rationally *ours*" has a little something in it of the arrogance of Emerson's farmers in "Hamatreya": "'Tis mine, my children's, and my name's.'" The claim may be impertinent, but it is precisely the "derring-do" of such impertinence that Frost asks us to admire (447). That is where the swagger comes in.[1]

Again taking up the theme of man's limitation, Frost continues in the section of the poem called "The Holiness of Wholeness":

> But while meditating
> What we can't or can
> Let's keep starring man
> In the royal role.
> It will not be his
> Ever to create
> One least germ or coal.
> Those two things we can't.
> But the comfort is
> In the covenant
> We may get control
> If not of the whole
> Of at least some part
> Where not too immense,
> So by craft or art
> We can give the part
> Wholeness in a sense.
>
> (452)

To write these lines is to acknowledge that the "creative" work of men can never really *matter*—whether we think of the work of Emerson's Concord landlords, of the patriarch in "The Birthplace," or of those pilots at Kitty Hawk who heroically (if nonetheless imperfectly) tried to get it up and keep it up. It will never be their lot "to create / One least germ or coal": no matter, no life, no real and permanent transcendence. But—the poem argues—that limitation is nevertheless beside the point. What the "creative" work of these men instead brings about and signifies is some reduction, however temporary and partial, of the cosmos to order. They cannot make "matter," but they can make matter signify: "We may get control / If not of the whole / Of at least some part," Frost suggests: "We can give the part / Wholeness in a sense."

Here is the promising fiction of integrity and autonomy: the "holiness of wholeness." And it is what drives the patriarch in "The Birthplace" "further up the mountain slope / Than there was ever any hope." The passage on the "holiness of wholeness" perfectly expresses what de Beauvoir—in metaphors quite congenial to the aeronautical ones Frost uses throughout "Kitty Hawk"—calls man's aspiration "to the sky, to the light, to the sunny summits, to the pure and crystalline frigidity of the blue sky" (147). The passage concerns, that is, man's unrealizable but nonetheless "heroic" aspiration to escape both gravity and the grave. And it soon emerges in "Kitty Hawk" that the matter of Earth, whose embrace we can never for long elude, is like the matter of language itself, which is only partly and momentarily susceptible to the orders that any particular man would impose on it. The (masculine) poet never entirely achieves escape velocity, never entirely owns what he says, though his "elevation" may at times appear magnificent. "Nothing can go up / But it must come down," Frost says earlier in "Kitty Hawk": "Earth is still our fate" (449). And he continues in "The Holiness of Wholeness" section:

> The becoming fear
> That becomes us best
> Is lest habit ridden
> In our kitchen midden
> Of our dump of earning
> And our dump of learning
> We come nowhere near
> Getting thought expressed.
> (452)

The metaphor of the "kitchen midden" immediately calls to mind Wallace Stevens's often-cited figure of the "dump" in "The Man on the Dump": both refer to the accumulation of tropes, forms, conventions, and images that threaten—as if with "*something* in their smile"—to draw the "habit ridden" poet back down into the immanence of the already-said. They threaten to reduce his agency and personality merely to a quotation: in a word, they would deny him "authority," consigning him instead to borrowed clothes—the "habits" of another. From farmer, then, to pilot, to poet—the nearly impossible effort is in each case the same: to master contingency, to reduce to order something that really *matters,* whether on the land with a plow, as in "The Birthplace," "Putting in the Seed," and "Hamatreya"; in the sky with wings, as in "Kitty Hawk"; or on the page in a poem that achieves, as Frost puts it in "The Figure a Poem Makes," its "momentary stay against confusion" and thus may stand as the "constant symbol" of all these larger undertakings. Man "aspires to the sky," de Beauvoir says. But "under his feet there is a moist, warm, and darkening gulf ready to draw him down" (147). And this "darkening gulf" involves also, as Frost seems to acknowledge, the gravity of the already-said: the grave of the "kitchen midden" of "our dump of learning," a realm of impersonality from which all poetry emerges, and into which, at last, it returns, when the Father-poet comes—as almost inevitably he must—"nowhere near / Getting" his "thought expressed." There can be, at last, no truly "immortal" authority. Frost says, with Shakespeare's Coriolanus: "I'll . . . stand / As if a man were author of himself / And knew no other kin" (5.3.35–36). But he says it with the ironic awareness that no such splendid autonomy is possible. The curtain always comes down on nobility in the fifth act. Nothing gold can stay.[2]

Surely, then, there is great audacity in Frost's suggestion that "life has for us on the wrack / Nothing but what we somehow [choose]," which, in the smaller realm of poetics, amounts to the claim that the casualties and felicities suffered in writing are in fact willed, even if by some as yet unrealized agency of the self. It is a poet's assertion of mastery over his materials and over contingency itself. Frost writes in a 1938 letter to R. P. T. Coffin: "The poet's material is words that for all we may say and feel against them are more manageable than men. Get a few words alone in a study and with plenty of time on your hands you can make them say anything you please" (*Selected Letters* 465). This is perhaps *the* (masculine) supreme fiction of poetic power. More specifically, it is a gesture toward a poetics of pure "formity" in which the opposition of "formity" to "conformity" disappears and in which, as Frost puts it in "Some Definitions," "an emotion has found its thought and the thought has found the words" (*CPPP* 701). No residue remains; all frustration is resolved. Or to adopt the terms Frost uses in the 1934 letter to his daughter Lesley: the "subject" perfectly finds its "form."

Burke succinctly defines "transcendence" in *Attitudes toward History:* "When approached from a certain point of view, A and B are 'opposites.' We mean by 'transcendence' the adoption of another point of view from which they cease to be opposites" (336). Simply put, Frost's poetics (like all great tragedy) provides a point of view from which "formity" and "conformity" cease to be opposites. His greatest "usurpation" may well have been to beat the poets of "pure formity" at their own game, and the doctrine of Inner Form, as he derisively called it, is considerably less ambitious than his own dialectical poetics, in which outer and inner form merge. For him, poetry is not an expression of personality; it is its veritable *incarnation*—the advent of a more powerful self "escaping from a succession of dead selves." Frost's providential "baby giant" comes of age.

The final unity of conformity and formity—its inevitable failure notwithstanding—no doubt appealed to Frost for such personal reasons as I have suggested in chapters 1 and 2. That unity vindicates the determining choices of his career: the decision to "conform" as well as to perform and the decision to accept the conditions of "the trial by market everything must come to." I have also shown in chapter 2 how he defends a poetics of "conformity" on the grounds of health and sanity and on the grounds simply that it is a necessary means to "correspondence" and "fellowship." But he is prepared to go much further in this defense. His poetics is really *not* one of conformity; the countless ties that keep an "intelligible," "conformist" poet in bondage to his audience are really no bonds at all. Frost "somehow chose" and thereby determined the constraints within which he worked; the "second answerability" to his constituents is but an effect of his first answerability to the highest in himself. In visionary fashion, Frost's poetics achieves a resolution of his own "problem of vocation," as I describe it in chapter 1. The final merger of "*self*-discipline" with "the harsher discipline from without" finds its complement in a merger of the poet's "inner" desire with the rigid prescriptions, of which Frost speaks in the introduction to *King Jasper,* as to how his personality ought to unfold in order to remain "charming and bearable" (*CPPP* 746). That is to say, Frost's poetics finally allows him (and us) to redescribe those rigid prescriptions in such a way that they are, strictly speaking, neither "rigid" nor "prescribed." The opposition of "desire" to "constraint," or of native "disposition" to alien "prescription," simply collapses: the "ordeal" of Robert Frost, and the "trial by market" itself, are resolved.

To put the matter more succinctly: In Frost's poetics, *self*-realization exists in no simple opposition to social obligation and social "contract," as it does, for example, in the aesthetic theories of H. L. Mencken, Van Wyck Brooks, and Ezra Pound. In Frost's view, obligations, "answerabilities," and the "harsher discipline from without" all work with, not against, the poet in realizing his desire and personal will. Frost's view therefore precisely opposes Brooks's in such passages as the following from "The Literary Life": "At its very headwaters, as we see, this modern literature of ours has failed to flow clear: the creative impulse in these men [Mark Twain, Henry Adams, William Dean Howells, and others], richly endowed as they were, was checked and compromised by too many other impulses, social and commercial" (191). Frost proposes to show how "creative impulse[s]" and "impulses, social and commercial" are not opponents, but in fact one and the same—at least ideally.

In playing both sides of the "formity"/"conformity" issue Frost's poetics provides a perfect example of what Kenneth Burke calls the "heads I win, tails you lose" device: "whereby, if things turn out one way, your system accounts for them—and if they turn out the opposite way, your system also accounts for them." But in fairness to Frost I should include here Burke's sensible concession: "When we first came upon this formula, we thought we had found a way of discrediting an argument. . . . But as we grew older, we began to ask ourselves whether there is any other possible way of thinking. And we now absolutely doubt there is" (*Attitudes* 260). The ambivalence, the subtle circumspection, and the occasional irony of Frost's remarks about his poetics and about his own problem of vocation suggest (to my mind anyway) that he had reached the same humane and quite intriguing conclusion.

Harold Bloom's observations in *Agon* on Freud's concept of "defense" and the "poetic will" allow us to cast the defensive, "heads I win, tails you lose" emphasis in Frost's poetics in the proper light: "A person tropes in order to tell many-colored rather than white lies to himself. The same person utilizes the fantasies or mechanisms of defense in order to ward off unpleasant truths concerning dangers from within, so that he only sees what Freud called an imperfect and travestied picture of the id. Troping and defending may be much the same process" (119).

Only one such danger from within need be suggested here. Once again it is a danger associated with the poetic vocation. During the 1930s and early 1940s Frost suffered enough misfortune to bring anyone to despair. There were the deaths of his daughter Marjorie and of his wife Elinor; his son Carol's suicide; the mental deterioration of his daughter Irma, whom he finally had to commit to psychiatric care; and the temporary estrangement of his daughter Lesley. Lesley apparently accused Frost of driving his wife to an early death and also of hampering his children's development in his overpowering drive for literary success. The accusation was probably as much Frost's as Lesley's, since in certain moods he was given to blaming his calling as a poet—a selfish calling, it seemed to him—for much of his family's grief. He wrote to Louis Untermeyer in November 1938, referring to the anxious depression he had endured after Elinor died in March of the same year: "I was thrust out into the desolateness of wondering about my past whether it had not been too cruel to those I had dragged with me and almost to cry out to heaven for a word of reassurance that was not given me in time" (*Selected Letters* 484). And he wrote to his daughter Lesley in the year following Elinor's death (the bracketed note is the editor's): "My, my what sorrow runs through all she wrote to you children. No wonder something of it overcasts my poetry if read aright. . . . I wish I hadnt this woeful suspicion that toward the end she came to resent something in the life I had given her. [Four lines deleted.] It seems to me now that she was cumulatively laying up against me the unsuccesses of the children I had given her" (*Family Letters* 209–10). The life he had "given" her was perhaps most importantly his career in poetry, which, after about 1912, fairly dominated his concerns. Frost writes in a September 1930 letter to Untermeyer: "One sickness and another in the family kept us till I could have cried out with the romantics that no artist should have a family. I could have, if the idea hadn't been so stale and unoriginal" (*Frost to Untermeyer* 204). The remark "no artist should have a family" is meant ironically. But the "outer humor" of the letter may occlude an "inner seriousness," to borrow once again Frost's terms in the introduction to *King Jasper.* Reading this 1930 letter I am reminded of a "vocational" meditation of Emerson's in "Wealth." It is certainly "romantic" in the sense given that term in Frost's letter: "Art is a jealous mistress, and, if a man have a genius for painting, poetry, music, architecture, or philosophy, he makes a bad husband, and an ill provider, and should be wise in season, and not fetter himself with duties which will embitter his days, and spoil him for his proper work" (*Essays* 1004).

Lawrance Thompson describes an encounter between Frost and his eldest daughter that occurred shortly after Elinor died and reflects some of the familial bitterness that seems to have attended Frost's career in poetry. The account is based on conversations with both Frost and Lesley Frost:

> Lesley, almost overcome by her own grief immediately after the cremation [of Elinor's body], unintentionally revealed a habit of vindictiveness she had acquired from her father. When he asked if he could make his home with her during the remainder of his life, she bluntly said no. Then she burst into an almost hysterical accusation which further

> amazed him: she said she had seen him cause so much injury to the lives of his own children—particularly to Irma, Carol, and Marjorie—that she would not permit him to come into her home, where he might also injure the lives of her two daughters. Her rage increased as she went on to insist, through her tears, that she could not forgive him for his having ruined her mother's life. It was his fault, she said, that her mother was dead, for it was his own selfishness which had forced her mother to climb those stairs to the upper quarters, repeatedly. Lesley had pleaded that she and her children should live up there, so that her mother wouldn't need to climb. But her father hadn't wanted to hear the children's feet over his head, and that was typical of his selfishness, Lesley cried. Then she hurt him most by concluding that he was the kind of artist who never should have married, or at least never should have had a family. (*Years of Triumph* 495–96)

Lesley probably meant that her father's irritation at the children's noisy feet overhead, presumably because they disturbed his work, was emblematic of the selfish demands of his vocation: "He was the kind of artist who never should have . . . had a family." In any event, the letters quoted above suggest that Frost's self-reproach could be intense: he did not usually require an antagonist. So it was perhaps inevitable that Frost should develop in his poetics, as a kind of countermythology, a vision of self-redemption and regeneration: poetry was among Frost's profoundest pleasures. But it also became associated, in what we know of his family history, with much pain and resentment.

This ambivalence may shed some light on "Directive," a strange and unsettling *ars poetica.* To my ear, the last few lines of the poem sound a little stilted for Frost, uncharacteristically solemn and pious in tone. For this reason, and despite their remarkable gravity, these lines may ironically suggest a certain loss of balance—a certain effort of compensation. I quote the last third of "Directive" for its images of a desolated house, which take on added resonance in connection with Lesley's accusations. In the foregoing lines the speaker has directed us "back out of all this now too much for us" toward a "house that is no more a house / Upon a farm that is no more a farm / And in a town that is no more a town." Whereupon he says:

> And if you're lost enough to find yourself
> By now, pull in your ladder road behind you
> And put a sign up CLOSED to all but me.
> Then make yourself at home. The only field
> Now left's no bigger than a harness gall.
> First there's the children's house of make believe,
> Some shattered dishes underneath a pine,

The playthings in the playhouse of the children.
Weep for what little things could make them glad.
Then for the house that is no more a house,
But only a belilaced cellar hole,
Now slowly closing like a dent in dough.
This was no playhouse but a house in earnest.
Your destination and your destiny's
A brook that was the water of the house,
Cold as a spring as yet so near its source,
Too lofty and original to rage.
(We know the valley streams that when aroused
Will leave their tatters hung on barb and thorn.)
I have kept hidden in the instep arch
Of an old cedar at the waterside
A broken drinking goblet like the Grail
Under a spell so the wrong ones can't find it,
So can't get saved, as Saint Mark says they mustn't.
(I stole the goblet from the children's playhouse.)
Here are your waters and your watering place.
Drink and be whole again beyond confusion.
(*CPPP* 341–42)

The poem is alive with echoes of other passages in Frost's work. A brief overview of these will help us make our way into "Directive." We notice first that Frost often cited St. Mark's proscription, adapted from Mark 4:11–12, in explanation of the difficulty and obscurity of poetry. Hyde Cox apparently first brought this passage to Frost's attention. When Cox read it to him in the early 1940s, Frost immediately applied its argument to poetry. Cox remembered the occasion sometime later: Frost "pointed out that it is the same as for poetry; only those who approach it in the right way can understand it. And not everyone can understand no matter what they do because it just isn't in them" (qtd. in Thompson, *The Later Years* 406). Moreover, the last line of "Directive" plainly echoes "The Figure a Poem Makes"—which prefaced all of Frost's volumes of collected poems after 1939—with its famous definition of a poem as "a momentary stay against confusion." And from its opening image of "graveyard marble sculpture" to its view of a "cellar hole" closing "like a dent in dough," "Directive" as a whole may be said to remember the early dramatic poem "Home Burial": the burial of a "home" is quite literally what it is about. Of course, images of desolate houses and abandoned cellar holes recur throughout Frost's work, in such poems as "The Ghost House," "The Generations of Men," "The Black Cottage," "A Fountain, a Bottle, a Donkey's Ears, and Some Books," "The Need of Being Versed in Country Things," and many others. When we consider, more generally, that "Directive" describes a place where human impositions on the landscape are gradually being reclaimed by natural forces, connections to still more poems become evident.

With its broken drinking goblet, "Directive" probably looks back more specifically to "The Times Table," a poem first collected in *West-Running Brook.* It begins: "More than halfway up the pass / Was a spring with a broken drinking glass." "The Times Table" describes a farmer who has devised a remarkably efficient and cruel means to crush, or at least to contain, the extravagant aspirations of his wife, a figure whom he implicitly compares to his old mare by administering the same proverb to each. It as if the horse and his wife reside in the same bin in his imagination:

> And whether the farmer drank or not
> His mare was sure to observe the spot
> By cramping the wheel on a water bar,
> Turning her forehead with a star,
> And straining her ribs with a monster sigh;
> To which the farmer would make reply,
> "A sigh for every so many breath,
> And for every so many a sigh a death.
> That's what I always tell my wife
> Is the multiplication table of life."
> The saying may be ever so true;
> But it's just the kind of thing that you
> Nor I nor nobody else may say,
> Unless our purpose is doing harm,
> And then I know of no better way
> To close a road, abandon a farm,
> Reduce the births of the human race,
> And bring back nature in people's place.
> (*CPPP* 241)

In imagining what this farmer's wife's existence might be like, I think of the darker representations of the circumscribed lives of country wives in Frost's work: "Home Burial," "A Servant to Servants," "The Hill Wife," "The Fear," "The Housekeeper," and "The Witch of Coös," to name a few. In all of these poems, as other readers have argued, the home has become for the women an environment more oppressive than sheltering. Under such conditions, these women, denied all healthy and manageable expressions of extravagant impulses, are compelled into the final extravagance of flight—or even of madness (another kind of flight). Nothing of this sort is brought into "The Times Table" directly. But its matter-of-fact speaker forthrightly sets out the costs of the farmer's way of thinking. Attitudes toward "extravagance" such as this farmer takes are patently destructive and confining: "I know of no better way / To close a road, abandon a farm." By way of contrast, the idea that extravagance properly indulged can become a force for renewal is the point of "The Investment," which succeeds "The Times Table" in *West Running Brook:* it seems critically to answer the rather grim farmer in "The Times Table."

In any case, the vision with which "The Times Table" ends is just such a vision as has, perhaps, been realized in "Directive": it concerns a farmer whose overbearing energy promises to lay waste a home, or to bury it, at a not inconsiderable emotional cost to his wife. I am suggesting that, for Frost, "Directive" may harbor a similar story. The complication is that the extravagant "springs" of desire, which Frost associated with poetry itself, are, in the sequence in which "The Times Table" appears, unmistakably also forces for renewal—as I have pointed out in connection with "The Investment." "Directive" may involve a similar consideration. Specifically, it presents a way of re-imagining poetry as a form of renewal and salvation: "Drink and be whole again beyond confusion," Frost says—despite the darker possibilities that the calling of poetry apparently mustered in his life. Such poems suggest what a life of poetry can be *ideally,* not what a particular life of poetry—Frost's life, for example—may have actually been or become. The qualifying idea that poetry and the "singing" of it might *bring about* misfortune and grief is set out with disarming clarity in "The Wind and the Rain," which dates from the period in which Frost was mourning Elinor's death. The poem first appeared in *A Witness Tree* (1942), a book plainly concerned at some level with the familial ordeals Frost suffered in the 1930s and early 1940s. In this poem, an older man recalls a moment from his by-gone youth:

> That far-off day the leaves in flight
> Were letting in the colder light.
> A season-ending wind there blew
> That, as it did the forest strew,
> I leaned on with a singing trust
> And let it drive me deathward too.
> With breaking step I stabbed the dust,
> Yet did not much to shorten stride.
> I sang of death—but had I known
> The many deaths one must have died
> Before he came to meet his own!
> Oh, should a child be left unwarned
> That any song in which he mourned

Would be as if he prophesied?
It were unworthy of the tongue
To let the half of life alone
And play the good without the ill.
And yet 'twould seem that what is sung
In happy sadness by the young,
Fate has no choice but to fulfill.
(*CPPP* 306)

In speaking of the songs of his youth, the speaker of these lines seems recognizably to be a poet. (The poem preceding "The Wind and the Rain" in *A Witness Tree*, "Carpe Diem," addresses poetry and poetic convention quite directly.) The songs this poet sings are largely melancholy—such songs as we find, for example, in Frost's own youthful book *A Boy's Will* (1913). And as William Pritchard shrewdly suggests, the biographical context of "The Wind and the Rain" is actually quite clearly marked. Of the passage just quoted, Pritchard writes: "There is no more naked an exclamation or unanswerable question to be found in Frost's poetry, while its personal reference seems unmistakable. 'Song,' the act of poetry, is seen as an indulgence, an unwitting prophecy of one's fate that Frost superstitiously suggests—although the lines don't go so far as to say—somehow incurs that fate" (233). In reading *A Witness Tree* with an eye to these themes, we should also consider the story told in "The Discovery of the Madeiras" for the bearing it may have, for Frost, on his courtship of and long marriage to Elinor White. The poem is a parable about a sailor who persuades a woman to be his mate only to wonder, forever after, whether she accepted him out of desire or merely out of submission:

The most he asked her eyes to grant
Was that in what she does not want
A woman wants to be overruled.
Or was the instinct in him fooled?
(*CPPP* 313)

"The Discovery of the Madeiras" essays one way to think about Frost's peculiarly fierce and importunate courtship of Elinor White and also about the possibility that she may never have forgiven him for "the life" he had ultimately "given her," as he puts it in the letter to his daughter Lesley.[3]

But to return once again to "Directive": I have been suggesting that, to Frost, the vocation of poetry at times seemed something of an indulgence, even a selfish and potentially destructive indulgence, and that because of this Frost sought ways in his writings about poetry, in both verse and prose, to develop a vision of poetry as a force for personal renewal and redemption, even of salvation, as he implies in the last lines of "Directive." My main point should by now be clear: "Directive" takes inventory both of Frost's methods and of his works. In short, *poetry* has been the "water" of this "house that is no more a house," and "Directive" is a kind of parable of the literary vocation. Reuben Brower makes much the same point in his 1963 study of Frost: "The speaker and reader [of "Directive"] arrive at salvation not through embracing a doctrine or through argument as in *A Masque of Mercy,* but through poetry. In comparison with the *Masque,* 'Directive' offers a more complete poetic experience of recovered wholeness, so that questions of what we shall believe or reject are not raised, at least for the duration of the poem. It is the *poem* that saves the poet and his readers" (240). I am arguing further that the *vocation* of poetry—not simply poetry—is an important concern in the poem, and here we must acknowledge that "Directive" probably has a specifically biographical frame of reference for Frost. Given Lesley's accusations about the damage his vocation caused their family—or their "house"—it is not going too far to say that in "Directive" Frost returns to the scene of the crime, so to speak, and that he has come here to ask, in light of the patently "liturgical" qualities of the poem, to be shriven. This may help explain the unstable mixture of tones in a poem that moves between elegy, affirmation, confession, and reproach. I offer the suggestion only as a partial account of Frost's motives in what is a very complicated work. But I find corroboration for my view in Brower's observation about the poem. In it Frost returns, he says, "to the beginning of his life and his poetry, but it is a return after having taken one road rather than another, a journey 'into his own' quite different from that of his early lyric, a contrast that adds an unintended irony to 'Only more sure of all I thought was true.' There was more to be 'thought' and 'known' than the speaker of *A Boy's Will* could imagine." And Brower continues: "The later journey back to a 'ghost house' is less charmingly melancholy, and Sorrow is a less consoling companion than in 'My November Guest'; she has now become a presence more deeply and more painfully affecting. By weeping for 'a house in earnest' the poet recovers a wholeness quite unlike the untried integrity of the youth of *A Boy's Will*" (239–40).

Above I quoted Harold Bloom's observation in *Agon* that "Troping and defending may be much the same process." Frost's poetics and poetry were "defensive" in this sense at least: for Frost, the poet's vocation was emotionally dangerous, but it brought also a mechanism, troping, with which to understand and manage those dangers. To my mind this affirms the justice of Bloom's provocative remark, though it should be remembered that there is nothing at all pejorative in my use, or in Bloom's, of the term "defense." The "sanitary" quality of poetry derives from its power, as we have seen in chapter 3, to restore to the poet a sense of integrity and agency, a sense often damaged when, in disgrace with fortune and men's eyes, he follows out his necessarily contingent and fallen career. Poetry has very much to do, then, with what in "Kitty Hawk" Frost calls "the holiness of wholeness." He expresses the same idea more gracefully at the end of "Directive." After marshalling considerable evidence of the decay and reduction to disorder of this "house that is no more a house," he says, echoing his best-known definition of the value of poetry: "Drink and be whole again beyond confusion." This is preeminently Frost's "trope" of writing, as Bloom would say. And if my speculations about "Directive" are correct, it is also his "defense"—his "apologia."

And at last, the conflict between Frost's merger of inner and outer form, and his recognition that this merger will inevitably fail, is hardly a flaw: it is the natural expression of his dialectical imagination. One finds the same inconsistency in Emerson's work, which comprehends equally the ascendance into "the heaven of truth" of "The Poet" and the interminable self-enclosures of "Circles." This dualism frames the oscillation anyone must feel between dispositions of power and dispositions of servitude and constraint. Frost catches the ambivalence perfectly in the remark reported by his friend Sidney Cox: "I recall the relaxed irony in Frost's voice when I divulged in 1924 that I was learning to accept the inevitable. 'If you could tell what *is* inevitable,' he said." Out of fidelity to this uncertainty Frost never reduces the dualism to a unity. "I want to be good," he explains to his daughter in 1934, "but that is not enough the state says I have got to be good." These two facts will always, and never quite, be identical. It might have been his answer to Foucault.

NOTES

Introduction

1. Frost's spelling and punctuation are often unconventional in his letters. I have let these idiosyncrasies stand, supplying clarification only where this seems absolutely necessary.

2. A fair amount of work has recently been done in these areas. I am particularly indebted, here, to Frank Lentricchia's study *A Modernist Quartet,* which brings to conclusion arguments he has been making since the publication of *Ariel and the Police* in 1988.

3. For discussion of Dickinson's politics, see Erkkila, *The Wicked Sisters,* 44–54. I should also add that I am aware of the irony in this connection of the gendered word "manhood" as Emerson uses it in "Self-Reliance." It is perhaps no coincidence that many of Dickinson's most powerful personae are, as a number of readers have argued, rather more masculine than feminine—an indication of how femininity had for so long been gendered "powerless." See particularly Dickinson's "I can wade Grief," with its striking phallic identifications.

Chapter 1: The Ordeal of Robert Frost

1. I owe much of my understanding of Bourne's and Brooks's arguments against pragmatism to David Bromwich's essay "Literary Radicalism in America" in his *A Choice of Inheritance.*

2. See Robert Bone's discussion of *Cane* in *The Negro Novel in America,* 80–89.

3. The connection between Thurber and Eliot has been noticed before. Eliot praised Thurber in remarks quoted in *Time* magazine in 1951: "[Thurber's] is a form of humor which is also a way of saying something serious. There is criticism of life at the bottom of it. It is serious and even somber. Unlike so much of humor, it is not merely a criticism of manners—that is,

of the superficial aspects of society at a given moment—but something more profound" (qtd. in Bernstein 361n). Thurber's biographer, Burton Bernstein, reports that Thurber considered Eliot's praise "the best estimate of his work ever" (361n). In December 1943 *Poetry* published an article by Peter DeVries, who then edited *Poetry,* titled "James Thurber: The Comic Prufrock." Thurber loved the essay and thanked DeVries for his remarks in a letter, reporting that he regretted not having met Eliot the last time he was in Europe. (Thurber eventually met Eliot in London in 1955.) The correspondence with DeVries led to Thurber's speaking at a benefit dinner for *Poetry* in April 1944 (Bernstein 361).

4. Humphrey Carpenter's biography of Pound gives us reason to suspect that the phallic personae of *Lustra* were in fact a series of masks: "In his poetry [Pound] liked to give the impression of casual virility, with allusions to the 'dance of the phallus.' The month before his marriage [to Dorothy Shakespeare] he published a poem entitled 'Coitus,' which begins: 'The gilded phaloi of the crocuses are thrusting at the spring air.' But it seems doubtful that sexuality played any part in his marriage. When a psychiatrist questioned him about this at St. Elizabeth's in 1946 he showed 'considerable reluctance' to discuss it, and became 'evasive.' When pressed for details he would only say: 'You may state that my sexual and marital adjustments were perfectly compatible'" (240–41).

5. See also Frank Lentricchia's discussion of this letter in *Modernist Quartet,* 90–91.

6. The imagery of the letter derives from Matt. 18:5–6.

7. An April 30, 1927, letter from Frost's friend John Bartlett to Gorham Munson throws additional light on these years. Munson was working on a short critical biography of Frost and asked Bartlett, who had been a student of Frost's at Pinkerton Academy in Derry, for his memories. Bartlett replied, in part: "I have a notion that, as regards his poetry, probably the most valuable years of his life were these on the Derry farm. I believe these were the years when the man Frost was made. You can put them down, though, as hard years. He hadn't 'made a go' of the farm venture. His farm neighbors, some of them, judged him wholly by farming, and they didn't approve. He had hay fever every summer. It was the child-bearing period of the family, with the measure of sickness and strain which always comes then. He had neither intellectual fellowship nor church fellowship, to any extent. Literary work had brought him little recognition. Measured by the things men measure by, Frost hadn't 'got anywhere in particular.' His problem of personal adaptation to the world of affairs in which he was placed was actually steadily progressing toward solution, but in ways the world could not see. In his social contacts, he found during these years a good deal to embarrass and sometimes to humiliate him. The way he ordered his life and conducted his affairs did not evoke either confidence or respect in the community, and for a long period Frost bore, consciously we may be sure, the cross of social disapproval" (Bartlett, Letter to Gorham Munson). It is possible that some of this account was shaped by Frost's own conversations with Bartlett. But Bartlett was an independent observer as

well as a native to the kind of community he describes. His impressions have considerable authority.

8. For an interesting discussion of gender in "The Code," "The Grindstone," "A Hundred Collars," and other poems, see Dawes.

9. In his testimony before the Senate Subcommittee on Education in 1960, Frost told this anecdote: "The other day I met a young Greek poetess. I wonder where she is. She talked to me as if she thought I would not see her again. She said, 'I fear for your country.' And I said, 'What are you afraid of?' And she said, 'The sort of thing people are talking about, fear that there's not enough feeling for anything but business and Hollywood and all that kind of thing.' And I said, 'I don't believe you know us enough. It's too superficial. There's more to us than that.' But she was very grave about it, charmingly grave. And she was nice to me, made me an exception; how did I manage in an ungrateful country like this? I have never talked that way myself. Even when I was out [of the country in 1912–15] I never talked that way. I always held my peace about it. If things do not go right for me between me and my Government, as last night when I did not get a chance to talk to Congress, you know, if they do not go right, I blame myself. I am not a drawing card" (U.S. Senate 17–18).

10. The inaccuracy of Pound's remarks lies in the fact that Frost was never actually "disinherited," though he seems to have given Pound to understand that he had been. However, as his remarks to Louis Mertins and others confirm, he did feel that his grandfather disdained his aspiration to become a poet.

11. I am grateful to Mark Scott for bringing the phrase from Browning to my attention. He has traced out a number of echoes of Browning in Frost's poems and letters, several of them dating from this period. Further evidence of Frost's intimate knowledge of Browning's poetry is found in Lawrance Thompson's "Notes on Conversations with Robert Frost," held now at the University of Virginia Library. In the entry for August 3, 1959, Thompson writes: "Frost went on from there to talk about Browning, and to make his point that what he liked particularly about Browning's poetry was his power of catching tones of voice in his lines. He quoted several—I would say he knows hundreds of lines of Browning by heart—and it was all very good."

12. The first edition published in America consisted of sheets printed by David Nutt and shipped to Henry Holt and Company to be bound under their imprint. "Good Hours" did not appear in this edition. It was published in the first edition set completely from new type in America by Henry Holt.

13. I draw the details of Gingrich's speech and lectures from Remnick "Lost in Space."

14. In *Secular Vocations* Bruce Robbins offers an interesting account of T. S. Eliot's fortunes in the academy in the 1940s and 1950s, which has some bearing on the present discussion: "Eliot's success in the academy did not depend only on a formulation of apocalyptic pessimism that happened to strike the right chord in the disillusioned post-war generation; it was a useful means of letting society know what it needed (culture) and who could provide it (those who could make sense of the footnotes to *The Waste Land*).

For would-be professionals of the first half of the century, struggling to displace the gentleman-scholar's tasteful, unhurried, independently funded appreciation of the finer things, Eliot's despair was enabling and invigorating. It declared in effect that their more rigorous and earnest professional activities were urgently required. If the society of the present is fallen and degenerate, then it hungers, however unknowingly, for acquaintance with values, ideals, and achievements that by definition are not accessible within it—except to a corps of experts specialized in retrieving such knowledge from the culture of the past" (17).

15. A more recent discussion of the situation of the academic intellectual in contemporary American culture may be found in *Academe* 82.4 (July–Aug. 1996), a special issue entitled "Professors and Public Perception: Why Is Society's Scrutiny So Tough?" *Academe* is published by the American Association of University Professors.

Chapter 2: Robert Frost and the "Fear of Man"

1. Pound wrote to Harriet Monroe in November 1917: "I wonder if you have seen H.L. Mencken's *Book of Prefaces*, especially the last essay in it. I think *Poetry*, with its intense, its almost oppressively respectable reputation for respectability, is in a good position to take up this matter of interference with the mails. (Not re war and pacifism, for I believe it is legal for a government to do almost anything in war time. That is, anything short of military law itself may be regarded as a palliative or substitute for military law.) But re the pre-war and coming post-war interference with the mails by Comstock's committee of blackguards, something certainly OUGHT to be done. And as *Poetry* has never printed anything that could bring the blush to the cheek of a deaf nun I think the magazine is in an excellent position to act" (*Selected Letters* 125–26).

2. See Cowley, "The Case against Mr. Frost," and Arvin, "A Further Shrinking" (the latter is a review of Frost's 1936 volume *A Further Range*).

3. The letter, previously unpublished, is held now at Dartmouth College Library.

4. See Mencken's survey of the relevant legal codes in *A Book of Prefaces*, 264–65. One federal judge absurdly ruled that any book was obscene "which is unbecoming, immodest" (264).

5. Statements such as those made in "Pan with Us" were common at the time. In "The Comedian as the Letter C," Wallace Stevens writes of Crispin, who has just arrived in the New World:

> He perceived
> That coolness for his heat came suddenly,
> And only, in the fables that he scrawled
> With his own quill, in its indigenous dew,
> Of an aesthetic tough, diverse, untamed,
> Incredible to prudes, the mint of dirt,
> Green barbarism turning paradigm.
> (31)

6. In a recent biography of Frost, Jeffrey Meyers provides a partial catalog of allusions in Frost's poetry to earlier British poets. See 357–68.

7. When, in disgrace with Fortune and men's eyes,
I all alone beweep my outcast state,
And trouble deaf heaven with my bootless cries,
And look upon myself, and curse my fate,
Wishing me like to one more rich in hope,
Featured like him, like him with friends possest,
Desiring this man's art and that man's scope,
With what I most enjoy contented least;
Yet in these thoughts myself almost despising—
Haply I think on thee: and then my state,
Like to the Lark at break of day arising
From sullen earth, sings hymns at Heaven's gate;
For thy sweet love rememb'red such wealth brings
That then I scorn to change my state with Kings.
(15)

8. I wonder whether Frost incidentally puns on Shakespeare's own puns in the sonnet "Whoever hath her wish, thou hast thy *Will*" (number 135) and its partner (number 136). The echo may sound dimly in the distance since Frost is, after all, talking about sonnets in general and Shakespeare's sonnets in particular; that is to say, in "The Constant Symbol" he is talking about the entanglements of the will and of Will(iam). At any rate there is no entanglement of "will" in a sonnet or any other sort of poem to compare with what we find in sonnets 135 and 136.

9. See "Kulturbolshewismus and Mr. Van Wyck Brooks," collected in Macdonald's *Memoirs of a Revolutionist.* The article originally appeared in *Partisan Review* in 1941. It is important to point out here that in the 1941 speech Brooks illustrated just how completely he had renounced the countercultural polemics of his youthful cultural criticism, in which he vigorously supported positions that in 1941 he denounced. Macdonald effectively quotes a few passages from Brooks's early work *Letters and Leadership* to make the transformation clear.

10. For an interesting investigation of how Pound's theory of literary patronage was conducive to an aristocratic aesthetics, see Wolfe.

11. The column is actually unsigned, as are many of the columns in *The Freeman.* My attributions of authorship to Nock here and later in this chapter are based on G. Thomas Tanselle's "Unsigned and Initialed Contributions to *The Freeman.*"

12. See also Frost's poem "The Cow in Apple Time," which nicely complements the theme of "Mending Wall": "Something inspires the only cow of late / To make no more of a wall than an open gate, / And to think no more of wall-builders than fools" (*CPPP* 120). The "something" is in this case the intoxication of autumn—the cow is drunk with overripe apples—which matches the intoxication of spring affecting the speaker in "Mending Wall."

13. See Poirier, *The Work of Knowing,* 87–172, passim.

14. See Erkkila's discussion of Dickinson's politics in *Wicked Sisters.*

15. Here we find an interesting analogy to T. S. Eliot, who very much distrusted what he called "the Inner Voice," a strongly egoistic voice that speaks of lust, madness, and violent self-assertion. Eliot and Frost alike felt a need to hold in check this inner impulse, which is at times associated with creative energy. I have been tracing out in Frost's work a dialectic of "*self*-discipline" and the "harsher discipline from without," of "formity" and "conformity," of vagrancy and control. Ronald Bush traces a similar dialectic in Eliot in his book *T. S. Eliot:* "In the major poems . . . Eliot's power is a result not of feeling and intellect working hand-in-glove but of powerful emotion held in powerful check. So constructed, the poems mime the central configuration of their author's psyche. Consider this epistolary remark, which for the casual reader of Eliot might seem exaggerated, but which represents one of the most telling confessions Eliot ever made. Writing at Easter 1928 to his religious confidant William Force Stead, Eliot told Stead that he needed the most severe kind of discipline. It was, according to Eliot, a question of compensation. Nothing, he said, could be too ascetic, too violent, for his needs. The discipline that Eliot sought in his life, and felt he achieved only sporadically, permeates his work, where his success was more frequent, though never complete. If we forget this tension between what may be variously seen as impulse and discipline or sympathy and judgment, if we forget what may be generalized as the conflict between the 'inside' and 'outside' perspectives of Eliot's work, then we lose touch with what makes it most valuable and most characteristic" (xi-xii). I discuss this connection between Eliot's thought and Frost's in chapter 3.

16. Richard Poirier writes of "A Prayer in Spring," "Rose Pogonias," and "Putting in the Seed": "Implicit in all three poems is the proposition that sexual love can make us aware that we participate in the larger creative processes of nature, and that poetry 'keeps' or preserves that awareness in metaphors" (*Robert Frost* 206).

Chapter 3: Believing in Robert Frost

1. In chapter 2 I draw an analogy between Frost and Freud; there is, I think, another such analogy to be drawn here. Alongside of Frost's remarks in the manuscript draft of "The Constant Symbol," consider this passage from *Civilization and Its Discontents:* "Just as a planet revolves around a central body as well as rotating on its own axis, so the human individual takes his part in the course of development of mankind at the same time as he pursues his own path in life" (768). It is a figure of the blending of Frost's "two answerabilities."

2. Allen Tate (citing Cleanth Brooks) notices a similar effect in the fourth stanza: "The external pattern reflects perfectly what we are told; instead of the third unrhymed line, as in the other three stanzas, there is . . . one rhyme: deep-keep-sleep-sleep. As one falls asleep it takes too much effort to find a rhyme; so sleep echoes sleep. We may see here what Mr. Cleanth

Brooks formerly saw as a paradox: the poet falls asleep as he tells us that he will not" (67).

3. See Arnold, "The Scholar-Gipsy," line 147.

4. Frost quotes from Catullus, poem sixty-five. The lines in question read, as translated by F. W. Cornish: "I am worn out with constant grief, Hortalus, and sorrow calls me away, apart from the learned Maids, nor can the thoughts of my heart [*mens animi*] utter the sweet births of the Muses, tossed as it is with such waves of trouble."

5. In this regard Frost affirms the skeptical responses to Barthes's, Foucault's, and Derrida's positions that have been registered in various quarters. For example, see Colin MacCabe's contention in "The Revenge of the Author": "If there was great importance in emphasizing the potential polysemy of any text, its potential for infinitization, and if there was fundamental significance in analyzing the transindividual codes from which any text was composed, it is still the case that texts are continuously determined in their meanings. The question is how we are to understand those determinations without producing, on the one hand, an author autonomously producing meanings in a sphere anterior to their specific articulation and, on the other, an audience imposing whatever meaning it chooses on a text" (40–41). This is essentially the problem Frost addresses in his homelier way in the Kenyon College remarks. See also Dasenbrock, "Taking It Personally: Reading Derrida's Responses." An engaging survey of Derrida's efforts to monitor the meanings ascribed to his defense of Paul de Man leads Dasenbrock to the following conclusion: "Writing inevitably involves a loss of authorial control, a symbolic death of the author. But the actions of the older Derrida remind us that being an author means to fight against that loss of control, to fight to stay alive. A theory of writing that brackets the intentional states of the author—leaving aside the intentions, hopes, desires, fears, and anxieties of authors simply because intentions have no perfect theft-proof lock on textual meaning—leads to an extraordinarily impoverished because depersonalized view of the scene of writing" (276). This view is close to Frost's. He too recognizes that writing involves a "loss of authorial control," though, as will presently become evident, his interest is finally more seriously engaged by the author's "fight against that loss of control," as Dasenbrock puts it. Frost's remarks in the Kenyon College speech also have obvious affiliations with Stanley Fish's arguments in *Is There a Text in This Class?* And in that connection, see as well Dasenbrock's skeptical response to Fish (and to Barbara Herrnstein Smith), "Do We Write the Text We Read?"

6. Frost echoes the following passage of Emerson's poem, which concerns Michelangelo:

> The hand that rounded Peter's dome,
> And groined the aisles of Christian Rome,
> Wrought in a sad sincerity;
> Himself from God he could not free;

He builded better than he knew;—
The conscious stone to beauty grew.
(Oxford Authors edition 496)

Frost's allusion to the poem is shrewd and consequential. The implication in "The Problem" is that the "author" of the dome of St. Peter's or any work of art is but an instrument for a divine superagent that works through him; in that sense, Michelangelo "builded better than he knew." Emerson regards art as a kind of second nature: the same transcendent creative force that "built" the Andes "builds," through the instrument of human "art," the dome of St. Peter. As will become clear later in this chapter, Frost transforms this idea, ascribing ultimate authority not to a divine agent but to a deeply *personal,* albeit initially occult, agent. To be precise, he ascribes authority to a hidden component of the artist's self that is discovered in the act of composition.

7. In his biography of Frost, Jeffrey Meyers makes much the same point about the connection between Eliot's and Frost's ideas. See Meyers 69–70.

8. Emerson seems to have this Calvinist economy in mind in "Wealth": "The world is full of fops who never did anything, and who have persuaded beauties and men of genius to wear their fop livery, and these will deliver the fop opinion, that it is not respectable to be seen earning a living; that it is much more respectable to spend without earning; and *this doctrine of the snake* will come also from the *elect sons of light;* for wise men are not wise at all hours, and will speak five times from their taste or their humor, to once from their reason" (*Essays* 992; my emphasis). Here the rhetoric of good business and the rhetoric of Calvinism are perfectly wedded.

9. Lawrance Thompson describes the genesis of the poem in *Robert Frost: The Early Years,* 120–21.

Conclusion

1. I should add that "Kitty Hawk" is very much a cold war poem: not for nothing do I refer to its "imperial" swagger. At one point Frost writes of the American leap into flight in the twentieth century (perhaps strategically ignoring Sputnik):

And the radio
Cried, "The Leap—The Leap!"
It belonged to US,
Not our friends the Russ,
To have run the event
To its full extent
And have won the crown,
Or let's say the cup.
(*CPPP* 448)

Here and elsewhere in "Kitty Hawk" Frost forthrightly chooses the West. It is perfectly fitting that the poem should be collected in *In the Clearing* (1962), which contains also Frost's dedicatory poem "For John F. Kennedy

His Inauguration" (*CPPP* 435–37). Indeed, *In the Clearing* is a book marked throughout by cold war culture and politics. I have in mind especially its fascination with the newly militarized science of physics and its several poems on the meaning of American nationality, which was, of course, consolidating itself along new lines in those days. In addition to "Kitty Hawk" and the poem for Kennedy, see, on American nationality, "A Cabin in the Clearing," "America Is Hard to See," and "Our Doom to Bloom," which latter poem takes as its ironic epigraph this line from Robinson Jeffers: "Shine, perishing republic."

2. In the foregoing paragraphs, I am particularly indebted to Katherine Kearns's arguments in her fascinating book *Robert Frost and a Poetics of Appetite*.

3. Alternatively, Jeffrey Meyers reads "The Discovery of the Madeiras" in connection with Frost's relationship to Kathleen Morrison. See Meyers, 266–68.

WORKS CITED

Arnold, Matthew. "The Scholar-Gipsy." *Poetry and Criticism of Matthew Arnold.* Ed. A. Dwight Culler. Boston: Houghton Mifflin, 1961. 147–52.

Arvin, Newton. "A Further Shrinking." *Partisan Review* 3.5 (June 1936): 27–28.

Barthes, Roland. "The Death of the Author." *Image-Music-Text.* Trans. Stephen Heath. New York: Hill and Wang, 1977. 142–48.

Bartlett, John. Letter to Gorham Munson. April 30, 1927. Unpublished typescript. University of Virginia Library, Charlottesville.

Bercovitch, Sacvan. *The Office of "The Scarlet Letter."* Cambridge: Harvard University Press, 1991.

Bernstein, Burton. *Thurber: A Biography.* New York: Dodd Mead, 1975.

Bernstein, Richard. *Dictatorship of Virtue.* New York: Random House, 1994.

Bérubé, Michael. *Public Access: Literary Theory and American Cultural Politics.* New York: Verso, 1994.

Blackmur, R. P. *The Lion and the Honeycomb.* New York: Harcourt, Brace, and World, 1955.

Bloom, Harold. *Agon.* New York: Oxford University Press, 1982.

Bode, Carl. *Mencken.* Carbondale: Southern Illinois University Press, 1959.

Bone, Robert. *The Negro Novel in America.* New Haven: Yale University Press, 1965.

Bourne, Randolph. "Twilight of Idols." *The World of Randolph Bourne* 191–206.

———. *The World of Randolph Bourne.* Ed. Lillian Schlissel. New York: E. P. Dutton, 1965.

Bromwich, David. *A Choice of Inheritance.* Cambridge, Mass.: Harvard University Press, 1989.

———. *Politics by Other Means: Higher Education and Group Thinking.* New Haven: Yale University Press, 1992.

Brooks, Van Wyck. "America's Coming of Age." Brooks, *America's Coming of Age* 1–90.

———. *America's Coming of Age; Letters and Leadership; The Literary Life in America.* Garden City: Doubleday and Company, 1958.

———. "The Culture of Industrialism." Brooks, *America's Coming of Age* 103–17.

———. "The Literary Life in America." Stearns 179–97.

———. *The Ordeal of Mark Twain.* New York: E. P. Dutton, 1970.

———. *Van Wyck Brooks: The Early Years, a Selection from His Works, 1908–1921.* Ed. Claire Sprague. New York: Harper and Row, 1968.

———. *The Wine of the Puritans.* Brooks, *Van Wyck Brooks: The Early Years* 1–60.

Brower, Reuben. *The Poetry of Robert Frost.* New York: Oxford University Press, 1963.

Browning, Robert. "Fra Lippo Lippi." *The Norton Anthology of English Literature.* 4th ed. Ed. M. H. Abrams, E. Talbot Donaldson, Hallett Smith, Robert M. Adams, Samuel Holt Monk, Lawrence Lipking, George H. Ford, and David Daiches. New York: W. W. Norton, 1979. 1261–69.

Burke, Kenneth. *Attitudes toward History.* 3d ed. Berkeley: University of California Press, 1984.

———. *Counter-Statement.* 3d ed. Berkeley: University of California Press, 1968.

———. *A Grammar of Motives.* New York: Prentice-Hall, 1945.

———. "I, Eye, Ay—Concerning Emerson's Early Essay on 'Nature' and the Machinery of Transcendence." Burke, *Language as Symbolic Action* 186–200.

———. *Language as Symbolic Action.* Berkeley: University of California Press, 1966.

———. *Permanence and Change.* 3d ed. University of California Press, 1984.

———. *The Philosophy of Literary Form.* 2d ed. Baton Rouge: Louisiana State University Press, 1967.

———. *A Rhetoric of Motives.* Berkeley: University of California Press, 1969.

———, and Malcolm Cowley. *The Selected Correspondence of Kenneth Burke and Malcolm Cowley.* Ed. Paul Jay. New York: Viking, 1988.

Burnshaw, Stanley. *Robert Frost Himself.* New York: George Braziller, 1986.

Bush, Ronald. *T. S. Eliot: A Study in Character and Style.* New York: Oxford University Press, 1984.

Carpenter, Humphrey. *A Serious Character: The Life of Ezra Pound.* New York: Delta, 1988.

Catullus. Poem sixty-five. *Catullus, Tibullus, and Pervigilium Veneris.* Trans. F. W. Cornish. Loeb Classical Library. Cambridge: Harvard University Press, 1912. 127.

Charvat, William. *The Profession of Authorship in America, 1800–1870.* Ed. Matthew J. Bruccoli. Columbus: Ohio State University Press, 1968.

Ciardi, John. "Robert Frost: The Way to the Poem." *Saturday Review of Literature* 41 (Apr. 12, 1958): 13–15, 65.

Comstock, Anthony. *Traps for the Young.* Cambridge: Belknap Press of Harvard University Press, 1967.

Cook, Reginald. *Robert Frost: A Living Voice.* Amherst: University of Massachusetts Press, 1974.
Cowley, Malcolm. "The Case against Mr. Frost." J. Cox 36–45.
———. *The Dream of the Golden Mountains.* New York: Penguin, 1981.
———. *Exile's Return.* 2d ed. New York: Viking Press, 1951.
Cox, James, ed. *Robert Frost: A Collection of Critical Essays.* Englewood Cliffs, N.J.: Prentice-Hall, 1962.
Cox, Sidney. *A Swinger of Birches: A Portrait of Robert Frost.* New York: New York University Press, 1957.
Crane, Joan St. C. *Robert Frost: A Descriptive Catalogue of Books and Manuscripts in the Clifton Waller Barrett Library, University of Virginia.* Charlottesville: University Press of Virginia, 1974.
Culler, Jonathan. *On Deconstruction.* Ithaca: Cornell University Press, 1982.
Curren, Erik D. "No Openings at This Time: Job Market Collapse and Graduate Education." *Profession 94* (1994): 57–61.
Dasenbrock, Reed Way. "Do We Write the Text We Read?" *Literary Theory after Davidson.* Ed. Reed Way Dasenbrock. University Park: Pennsylvania State University Press, 1993. 18–36.
———. "Taking It Personally: Reading Derrida's Responses." *College English* 56.3 (Mar. 1994): 261–79.
Dawes, James R. "Masculinity and Transgression in Robert Frost." *American Literature* 65 (June 1993): 297–312.
de Beauvoir, Simone. *The Second Sex.* New York: Vintage, 1989.
Delbanco, Andrew. "Contract with Academia." *New Yorker* Mar. 27, 1995: 7–8.
Derrida, Jacques. *Limited Inc.* Evanston: Northwestern University Press, 1988.
———. "Signature Event Context." Derrida, *Limited Inc* 1–24.
DeVries, Peter. "James Thurber: The Comic Prufrock." *Poetry* 63.3 (Dec. 1943): 150–58.
Dewey, John. *Art as Experience.* Ed. Jo Ann Boydston, et al. Carbondale: Southern Illinois University Press, 1987.
Dickinson, Emily. *The Complete Poems of Emily Dickinson.* Ed. Thomas H. Johnson. Boston: Little Brown, 1960.
Donne, John. "The Ecstasy." *Norton Anthology of English Literature.* Vol. 1. 4th ed. Ed. M. H. Abrams, E. Talbot Donaldson, Hallett Smith, Robert M. Adams, Samuel Holt Monk, Lawrence Lipking, George H. Ford, and David Daiches. New York: W. W. Norton, 1979. 1070–72.
Dupee, F. W. "The Americanism of Van Wyck Brooks." *Literary Opinion in America.* Vol. 2. Ed. Morton D. Zabel. New York: Harper and Row, 1962. 561–72.
Eagleton, Terry. *Ideology: An Introduction.* New York: Verso, 1991.
Eliot, T. S. *Selected Essays.* New York: Harcourt, Brace, Jovanovich, 1950.
———. "The Three Voices of Poetry." *On Poetry and Poets.* New York: Farrar, Straus, and Cudahy, 1957. 96–112.
Emerson, Ralph Waldo. *Emerson in His Journals.* Ed. Joel Porte. Cambridge, Mass.: Harvard University Press, 1982.

———. *Essays and Lectures.* Ed. Joel Porte. New York: Library of America, 1983.

———. *Ralph Waldo Emerson.* Ed. Richard Poirier. Oxford Authors series. New York: Oxford University Press, 1990.

Erkkila, Betsy. *The Wicked Sisters: Women Poets, Literary History, and Discord.* New York: Oxford University Press, 1992.

Evans, William R. *Robert Frost and Sidney Cox.* Hanover, N.H.: University Press of New England, 1981.

Fish, Stanley. *Is There a Text in This Class?* Cambridge, Mass.: Harvard University Press, 1980.

Foucault, Michel. "What Is an Author?" *Textual Strategies.* Ed. Josué Harari. Ithaca: Cornell University Press, 1979. 141–60.

Francis, Robert. *Frost: A Time to Talk.* Amherst: University of Massachusetts Press, 1972.

Freud, Sigmund. *Civilization and Its Discontents. The Freud Reader.* Ed. Peter Gay. New York: W. W. Norton, 1989.

Frost, Robert. "Before the Beginning and after the End of a Poem." *The Carrell* 6 (1965): 6–8.

———. *Collected Poems, Prose, and Plays.* Ed. Richard Poirier and Mark Richardson. New York: Library of America, 1995.

———. "The Constant Symbol." 1946. Unpublished manuscript draft. Robert Frost Collection (#6261). Clifton Waller Barrett Library. Special Collections Department. University of Virginia Library, Charlottesville.

———. *Interviews with Robert Frost.* Ed. Edward Connery Lathem. New York: Holt, Rinehart, and Winston, 1966.

———. Lecture delivered in Boulder, Colarado. 1935. Unpublished typescript. Robert Frost Collection (#6261). Clifton Waller Barrett Library. Special Collections Department. University of Virginia Library, Charlottesville.

———. Lecture delivered at Kenyon College. 1950. Unpublished typescript. Amherst College Library, Amherst.

———. *The Letters of Robert Frost to Louis Untermeyer.* Ed. Louis Untermeyer. New York: Holt, Rinehart, and Winston, 1963.

———. Letter to Van Wyck Brooks. Sept. 1921. Unpublished manuscript. Dartmouth College Library, Hanover.

———. *Prose Jottings: Selections from His Notebooks.* Ed. Edward Connery Lathem and Hyde Cox. Lunenburg, Vt.: Northeast-Kingdom, 1982.

———. "The Return of the Pilgrims." *The Pilgrim Spirit.* By George P. Barker. Boston: Marshall Jones Company, 1921. 134–36.

———. *The Selected Letters of Robert Frost.* Ed. Lawrance Thompson. New York: Holt, Rinehart, and Winston, 1964.

———, and Elinor White Frost. *The Family Letters of Robert and Elinor Frost.* Ed. Arnold Grade. Albany: State University of New York Press, 1972.

Gold, Mike. "Proletarian Realism." *Mike Gold: A Literary Anthology.* Ed. Michael Folsom. New York: International Publishers, 1972. 203–8.

Hawthorne, Nathaniel. *The Life of Franklin Pierce.* Boston: Ticknor, Reed, Fields, 1852.

———. *The Scarlet Letter. Novels.* Ed. Millicent Bell. New York: Library of America, 1983.

———. "The Custom-House." *Novels.* Ed. Millicent Bell. New York: Library of America, 1983. 121–56.

Hoopes, James. *Van Wyck Brooks.* Amherst: University of Massachusetts Press, 1977.

Howells, William Dean. *Literature and Life.* New York: Harper and Brothers, 1902.

———. "The Man of Letters as a Man of Business." Howells, *Literature and Life* 1–35.

Hulme, T. E. *Further Speculations.* Ed. Sam Hynes. Minneapolis: University of Minnesota Press, 1955.

James, Henry. *Hawthorne. Henry James: Literary Criticism.* Vol. 1. Ed. Leon Edel. New York: Library of America, 1984.

James, William. *Pragmatism. William James: Writings, 1902–1910.* Ed. Bruce Kuklick. New York: Library of America, 1987.

Jarrell, Randall. *Poetry and the Age.* London: Faber and Faber, 1973.

Kearns, Katherine. *Robert Frost and a Poetics of Appetite.* New York: Cambridge University Press, 1994.

Kenner, Hugh. *The Invisible Poet: T. S. Eliot.* New York: Harcourt, Brace, and World, 1959.

———. *The Pound Era.* Berkeley: University of California Press, 1971.

Kimball, Roger. *Tenured Radicals.* New York: Harper and Row, 1990.

Lasch, Christopher. "The Revolt of the Elites: Have They Canceled Their Allegiance to America?" *Harper's* Nov. 1994: 39–49.

Lentricchia, Frank. *Ariel and the Police.* Madison: University of Wisconsin Press, 1988.

———. *Criticism and Social Change.* Chicago: University of Chicago Press, 1983.

———. *A Modernist Quartet.* New York: Cambridge University Press, 1994.

———. "Resentments of Robert Frost." *Out of Bounds: Male Writers and Gender(ed) Criticism.* Ed. Laura Claridge and Elizabeth Langland. Amherst: University of Massachusetts Press, 1990. 268–89.

———. *Robert Frost: Modern Poetics and the Landscapes of Self.* Durham: Duke University Press, 1975.

Levine, George. "The Real Trouble." *Profession 93* (1993): 43–45.

Lewis, Sinclair. *Main Street.* New York: Signet, 1980.

MacCabe, Colin. "The Revenge of the Author." *Subject to History.* Ed. David Simpson. Ithaca: Cornell University Press, 1991. 34–46.

Macdonald, Dwight. *Against the American Grain.* New York: Random House, 1962.

———. "Kulturbolshewismus and Mr. Van Wyck Brooks." Macdonald, *Memoirs of a Revolutionist* 203–14.

———. *Memoirs of a Revolutionist.* New York: Meridian Books, 1958.

———. *The Root Is Man.* New York: Autonomedia, 1995.

Mattheissen, F. O. *The Achievement of T. S. Eliot.* 3d ed. New York: Oxford University Press, 1958.

Mencken, H. L. *A Book of Prefaces.* New York: Alfred Knopf, 1920.
———. *H. L. Mencken's Smart Set Criticism.* Ed. William H. Nolte. Ithaca: Cornell University Press, 1968.
———. *My Life as Author and Editor.* New York: Vintage Books, 1992.
———. *A Mencken Chrestomathy.* New York: Vintage Books, 1982.
———. *The Philosophy of Friedrich Nietzsche.* Boston: Luce and Company, 1908.
———. *Prejudices: First Series.* New York: Alfred Knopf, 1919.
———. *Prejudices: Third Series.* New York: Alfred Knopf, 1922.
———. *Prejudices: Sixth Series.* New York: Alfred Knopf, 1927.
———. "Puritanism as a Literary Force." *A Book of Prefaces.* 197–283.
Mertins, Louis. *Robert Frost: Life and Talks-Walking.* Norman: University of Omaha Press, 1965.
Meyers, Jeffrey. *Robert Frost.* Boston: Houghton Mifflin, 1996.
Morrison, Kathleen. *Robert Frost: A Pictorial Chronicle.* New York: Holt, Rinehart, and Winston, 1974.
Mumford, Lewis. *The Golden Day.* New York: Boni and Liveright, 1926.
Munson, Gorham. *Robert Frost.* New York: George H. Doran, 1927.
Nelson, Cary. *Repression and Recovery: Modern American Poetry and Cultural Memory.* Madison: University of Wisconsin Press, 1989.
Newdick, Robert. *Newdick's Season of Frost: An Interrupted Biography of Robert Frost.* Ed. William A. Sutton. Albany: State University of New York Press, 1976.
Nietzsche, Friedrich. "On Truth and Lies in an Extra-Moral Sense." *The Portable Nietzsche.* Trans. and ed. Walter Kaufmann. New York: Viking, 1969. 42–46.
———. *The Will to Power.* Ed. Walter Kaufmann. Trans. Walter Kaufmann and R. J. Hollingdale. New York: Vintage, 1968.
[Nock, Albert Jay]. "The Reviewer's Notebook." *The Freeman* 6.131 (Sept. 13, 1922): 22–23.
———. Unsigned column. *The Freeman* 16 (Sept. 1922): 22.
Olson, Charles. *Selected Writings.* Ed. Robert Creeley. New York: New Directions, 1966.
Paglia, Camille. *Sex, Art, and American Culture.* New York: Vintage, 1992.
———. *Tramps and Vamps.* New York: Vintage, 1994.
Parini, Jay. "Robert Frost." *The Columbia History of American Poetry.* New York: Columbia University Press, 1994.
Poirier, Richard. *The Performing Self.* New York: Oxford University Press, 1971.
———. *Poetry and Pragmatism.* Cambridge: Harvard University Press, 1992.
———. *The Renewal of Literature: Emersonian Reflections.* New York: Random House, 1987.
———. *Robert Frost: The Work of Knowing.* New York: Oxford University Press, 1977.
———. *A World Elsewhere: The Place of Style in American Literature.* New York: Oxford University Press, 1966.

Pound, Ezra. *The Letters of Ezra Pound.* Ed. D. D. Paige. New York: Harcourt, Brace, and Company, 1950.
———. *Literary Essays of Ezra Pound.* Ed. T. S. Eliot. New York: New Directions, 1968.
———. *Pavannes and Divagations.* London: Peter Owen, 1960.
———. *Personae: The Shorter Poems of Ezra Pound.* Rev. ed. New York: New Directions, 1990.
———. *Selected Prose, 1909–1965.* Ed. William Cookson. New York: New Directions, 1973.
Pritchard, William. *Robert Frost: A Literary Life Reconsidered.* 2d ed. Amherst: University of Massachusetts Press, 1993.
Read, Herbert. *Form in Modern Poetry.* London: Vision Press, 1948.
Reid, Louis Raymond. "The Small Town." Stearns, *Civilization in the United States* 285–96.
Remnick, David. "Lost in Space." *New Yorker* Dec. 5, 1994: 79–87.
Richardson, Mark. "Collected Prose of Robert Frost: A New Critical Edition; Together with 'The Ordeal of Robert Frost, A Study of Biography and Style in His Poetics.'" Diss. Rutgers University, 1993.
Robbins, Bruce. *Secular Vocations: Intellectuals, Professionalism, Culture.* New York: Verso, 1993.
Roosevelt, Theodore. *The Strenuous Life.* St. Clair Shores, Mich.: Scholarly Press, 1970.
Rorty, Richard. *Contingency, Irony, and Solidarity.* Cambridge: Cambridge University Press, 1989.
———. "Demonizing the Academy." *Harper's* Jan. 1995: 13–17.
———. *Objectivity, Relativism, and Truth.* New York: Cambridge University Press, 1991.
Ross, Andrew. *No Respect: Intellectuals and Popular Culture.* New York: Routledge, 1989.
Rotella, Guy. *Reading and Writing Nature.* Boston: Northeastern University Press, 1991.
Rotundo, E. Anthony. *American Manhood: Transformations in Masculinity from the Revolution to the Modern Era.* New York: Basic Books, 1993.
Sabin, Margery. "The Fate of the Frost Speaker." *Raritan* 2 (Fall 1982): 128–39.
Santayana, George. *Interpretations of Poetry and Religion.* Cambridge: MIT Press, 1989.
Searle, John. "The Storm over the University." *New York Review of Books* Dec. 6, 1990: 34–40.
Sell, Roger D. "Robert Frost: Two Unpublished Plays, *In an Art Factory* and *The Guardeen,* with an Introduction." *Massachusetts Review* 26 (Summer–Autumn 1985): 265–340.
Shakespeare, William. *Coriolanus.* Ed. Tucker Brooke. New Haven: Yale University Press, 1957.
———. *Hamlet.* Ed. Tucker Brooke and Jack Randall Crawford. New Haven: Yale University Press, 1954.

———. *Shakespeare's Sonnets.* Ed. Edward Bliss Reed. New Haven: Yale University Press, 1956.
———. *A Winter's Tale.* Ed. Tucker Brooke and Jack Crawford. New Haven: Yale University Press, 1954.
Spacks, Patricia Meyer. "President's Column: Enlargements of Interest." *MLA Newsletter* 26.4 (Winter 1993): 3.
Stearns, Harold E., ed. *Civilization in the United States.* New York: Harcourt, Brace, and Company, 1922.
Stevens, Wallace. *Collected Poems.* New York: Alfred Knopf, 1965.
Tallmer, Jerry. "Frost: The Crux of Life Is Deepening Commitments." *The Dartmouth* 105.33 (May 22, 1946): 3.
Tanner, Tony. *Jane Austen.* Cambridge: Harvard University Press, 1986.
Tanselle, G. Thomas. "Unsigned and Initialed Contributions to *The Freeman.*" *Studies in Bibliography* 17 (1964): 153–75.
Tate, Allen. "Inner Weather: Frost as a Metaphysical Poet." *Robert Frost: Lectures on the Centennial of His Birth.* Washington: Library of Congress, 1975.
Thompson, Lawrance. "Notes on Conversations with Robert Frost." 1939–63. Unpublished typescript. Thompson-Frost Collection (#10042). Clifton Waller Barrett Library. Special Collections Department. University of Virginia Library, Charlottesville.
———. *Robert Frost: The Early Years.* New York: Holt, Rinehart, and Winston, 1966.
———. *Robert Frost: The Years of Triumph.* New York: Holt, Rinehart, and Winston, 1970.
———, and R. H. Winnick. *Robert Frost: The Later Years.* New York: Holt, Rinehart, and Winston, 1976.
Tocqueville, Alexis de. *Democracy in America.* Ed. J. P. Mayer. Trans. George Lawrence. New York: Harper and Row, 1988.
Toomer, Jean. *Cane.* Ed. Darwin Turner. New York: W. W. Norton, 1988.
Trilling, Lionel. "A Speech on Robert Frost: A Cultural Episode." J. Cox 151–58.
Twain, Mark. "Corn Pone Opinions." *Mark Twain: Collected Tales, Sketches, Speeches, and Essays.* Ed. Louis J. Budd. New York: Library of America, 1993. 507–11.
Untermeyer, Louis. *The New Era in American Poetry.* New York: Henry Holt, 1919.
U.S. Senate. Committee on Labor Public Welfare. Subcommittee on Education of the Committee. *Providing for a National Academy of Culture: Hearing before the Subcommittee on Education of the Committee on Labor Public Welfare, United States Senate.* Washington, D.C.: GPO, 1960.
Wagner, Linda W., ed. *Robert Frost: The Critical Reception.* New York: Burt Franklin and Company, 1977.
Walsh, John Evangelist. *Into My Own: The English Years of Robert Frost.* New York: Grove Press, 1988.
West, James L. W. *The American Author and the Literary Marketplace since 1900.* Philadelphia: University of Pennsylvania Press, 1988.

Wolfe, Cary. "Ezra Pound and the Politics of Patronage." *American Literature* 63 (Mar. 1991): 26–42.
Wreszin, Michael. *A Rebel in Defense of Tradition: The Life and Politics of Dwight Macdonald.* New York: Basic Books, 1994.

INDEX

MARK RICHARDSON is the coeditor with Richard Poirier of *Robert Frost: Collected Poems, Prose, and Plays* and is an assistant professor of English at Western Michigan University